COACHING

What really works

COACHING

What really works

JENNY ROGERS

Los Angeles | London | New Delhi
Singapore | Washington DC | Melbourne

Los Angeles | London | New Delhi
Singapore | Washington DC | Melbourne

SAGE Publications Ltd
1 Oliver's Yard
55 City Road
London EC1Y 1SP

SAGE Publications Inc.
2455 Teller Road
Thousand Oaks, California 91320

SAGE Publications India Pvt Ltd
B 1/I 1 Mohan Cooperative Industrial Area
Mathura Road
New Delhi 110 044

SAGE Publications Asia-Pacific Pte Ltd
3 Church Street
#10-04 Samsung Hub
Singapore 049483

Editor: Susannah Trefgarne
Assistant editor: Ruth Lilly
Production editor: Manmeet Kaur Tura
Copyeditor: Sharon Cawood
Proofreader: Clare Weaver
Indexer: Cathryn Pritchard
Marketing manager: Dilhara Attygalle
Cover design: Naomi Robinson
Typeset by: KnowledgeWorks Global Ltd.
Printed in the UK

Library of Congress Control Number: 2020947334

British Library Cataloguing in Publication data

A catalogue record for this book is available from the
British Library

ISBN 978-1-5297-4473-6
ISBN 978-1-5297-4472-9 (pbk)

At SAGE we take sustainability seriously. Most of our products are printed in the UK using FSC papers
and boards. When we print overseas we ensure sustainable papers are used as measured by the PREPS
grading system. We undertake an annual audit to monitor our sustainability.

Contents

About the Author

Jenny Rogers was an early entrant to the world of coaching, beginning when she ran the BBC's management development department after earlier careers in teaching, television production and publishing. She left the BBC to start her own coaching company and has been a coach ever since, specialising in the world of senior executives. As well as working with her own coaching clients, she trains and supervises other coaches.

Her books range from a 4th edition of *Coaching Skills: The Definitive Guide to Being a Coach*, a book used around the world as the 'Bible' on how to be a coach, to her four best-selling books on the psychometric instruments, the MBTI and the FIRO-B. She has also written books about how to start a coaching business, how to navigate career crises and how to get through a job interview successfully.

Jenny was married for many years to the former BBC Editor and journalist Alan Rogers. He died in 2010. She lives in central London and is close to her two sons and three grandchildren. She is a keen cook, cat lover, filmgoer and walker.

Acknowledgements

The origins of this book go back a long way. About twenty years ago, when I had already been a coach for ten years, I read Irvin Yalom's *Love's Executioner*, and later, *The Gift of Therapy*, a book of reflections on his many years of psychotherapeutic practice. By that stage in my coaching career I had concluded that the boundaries between coaching and therapy were nothing like the concrete walls that so many of us early adopters of coaching were inclined to claim. Dr Yalom's books had a radical impact on me. It was the first time that I had read any practitioner who wrote candidly, generously, and with humour and humility, about his own feelings towards clients, about his outright failures as well as his modestly-described successes. I had read many other writers who emphasised the importance of the practitioner-client relationship, and of listening without judgement. I had never seen it put so plainly that this was easily the most important predictor of success, and that furthermore, the topic needed to be brought from the shadows into the actual conversations with clients. I acknowledge the profundity of my debt to him here.

I had always understood that early life shapes who we become as adults, but my own development as a coach took a leap forward when I realised the significance of Julia Vaughan Smith's ideas on trauma. Julia is a longstanding friend and colleague but it has been a revelation to benefit from her many years of work with Professor Franz Ruppert on the pervasive and largely ignored impact of childhood trauma on all of us. Julia is an inspiring teacher and her book *Coaching and Trauma* has enabled me – and hundreds of other coaches – to understand and implement safe ways of using these vital concepts in our coaching work. I have called on these ideas throughout this book, though any misinterpretations are my own responsibility.

At the practical level, there are some wonderful people who have helped the book on its way. They include: Jane Cook, Monika Lee, Jaime Marshall, Sue Morrison, Joe Treasure and Leni Wildflower. I have hugely valued their nudges, encouragements, ideas, suggestions, feedback and patient re-reading.

Working with other coaches has been a constant source of ideas. I am lucky to act as supervisor to talented fellow professionals, many of them people who have come to coaching from a wide range of earlier careers. Confidentiality prevents me from naming them but I hope they will know who they are. Training beginner coaches is another fast track to discovering what really counts in coaching. Working alongside Jane Booth and her team at the Guildhall School of Music and Drama and with Joanna Harrison at the English Institute of Sport has been a privilege here. Like every other coach, I owe gratitude to my clients for their willingness to trust me, sometimes with exceptionally taxing issues. It is easy to forget that the client can often have as much impact on the coach as the coach has on the client: it's always a two-way process.

I thank Susannah Trefgarne of Sage Publishing for being such an insightful, warm and steadying guide throughout the commissioning process.

As ever, I thank my loyal PA Angie Adams, my inner circle of close friends and my dear family for their unfailing support.

Jenny Rogers

Introduction

The scene is a coaching room in London, or maybe it's Los Angeles, Johannesburg, Berlin, Mumbai or Sydney. There is a moment of anticipation, a sense of trembling on the edge of something important. The coach has just asked a question and the client pauses, leans back, looks down. There is profound silence. Then the client bursts out, 'Wow!' or some such exclamation, indicating that a great revelation has just struck them. It's one of those light bulb moments that every coach prizes, without thinking for a moment of the light bulb joke where the question is, 'How many coaches does it take to change a light bulb?' The answer is, 'Only one, but the light bulb must want to change'. But that is an irreverent thought and the coach won't allow themselves to entertain it during a moment of such solemnity and significance. The client has achieved insight; their life will be immeasurably improved and the coach can take enormous satisfaction in knowing that they have made a difference.

Except that this is not how it happens, wonderful dream though it is. Coaching is not a courtroom drama where an inspired last-minute chase for evidence by the defence attorney produces a dramatic turning point. The coach is not the handsome prince who wakes the sleeping princess with a kiss. The coach is not the maverick cop who solves the murder mystery through eccentric genius, despite having a drink problem and being despised by her boss.

There is another seductive narrative often dangled in front of beginner coaches. We might call this the Tools 'n' Techniques approach but, like the myth of 'insight', it has its roots in magic. Here, there is a charismatic performer with twinkling eyes and an impressive mop of hair. He descends in a direct line from 19th-century evangelists. He demonstrates that with some simple visualising, a few powerful questions and a little light trance, problems will go away, never to return. Phobias, anxiety, depression, stammering, blushing, lack of confidence: all can be banished through his special brand of positive thinking. He sells his ideas through licensed associates to people who long for the healing power he claims to possess. Training courses are essentially bundles of techniques. In this approach to coaching, every session needs its 'exercises'. No attention is paid to any underlying psychological causes of the problems. Who needs that when, if you master the techniques and follow the formulas, the client will, like Lazarus in the Bible, pick up their bed and walk?

In my work as a supervisor to other coaches, I see how so many of them have read the tales of triumph in so many books on how to coach; they have listened to conference speeches where senior coaches have modestly boasted about their successes. They have been through training courses where the tutors have shown how simple it all is, as long as you ask the right questions. I readily confess that it's possible, though never meaning less than well, that in my efforts to encourage novices, I have been part of creating this fantasy world myself.

Some of the newer coaches whom I supervise will often describe puzzlement and dismay that coaching in practice is nothing like so easy as they had supposed, and that clients do not seem to have light bulb moments or miracle cures, not even once, let alone in every session. Sometimes they look at me yearningly or with far too much respect, for some sign that with my 30 years of experience, I will be able to offer glimmers of hope that there is a magic ingredient. If only they knew my secrets, they, too, could solve every client's problems.

There is no magic ingredient, but we coaches and sometimes our clients, too, are strongly drawn to the idea that there can and should be inexorable movement towards achievement, an orgasmic moment of relief where what was blurred becomes clear, where what was painful becomes comfortable, where what was obstructed becomes open, where long-buried confusion is swept away. Who would not like to be the person who leads this quest? The trouble is that, as we know from more than a hundred years of research into therapy, 'techniques' and 'exercises' are not what make the difference, and insight alone is never enough. Most often, the insight is entirely the creation of the coach and is meaningless to the client, however brilliant we think we have been in our analysis. The real work of coaching is done outside the coaching sessions when the client begins the task, with trial and error – a lot of error – of integrating new ideas into their daily lives. Here, there are many other players, most of them far more important to the client than their coach is ever likely to be.

It does not help that, at the same time as they hope for miracles, clients are rightly wary and sceptical about how far we will be able to make a difference. We are strangers, so why would they entrust us with what they may feel to be embarrassing and humiliating? That is why, certainly at the beginning of a coaching programme, they typically bring us safely simple questions. These are what a fellow coach once called 'photocopier problems'. An example would be, 'My colleagues keep asking me to explain how to feed paper into the photocopier and it's interrupting my proper work'. The answer to this problem surely has to be, 'Just say no'.

These are proxy issues. They sound respectable but they are not the real problem. However convincing clients are about the agony that the proxy issue is causing, the very fact of the client's presence in your coaching room is proof that, as a tactic, the proxy issue is not working in its intended role as a distractor. If that were all it was, the client would already have implemented the obvious solution. If you enthusiastically accept the proxy issue as something substantial to work on, the client may privately scorn you for your gullibility. If you don't accept it, the client may accuse you of discourtesy, may resist your attempts to probe or may tell you with a scowl that even Dr Freud once allegedly said (though this is another myth), 'Sometimes a cigar is just a cigar'.

Human change is not easy. The more important the need for change, the more slowly it is likely to happen. The more it matters, the more the client will resist. A set of beliefs that has taken several decades to become an intricately knotted barrier to happiness and peace is not going to unravel in a few hours of coaching. This is not extraordinary or weird, it is only right. If we were open to every influence that came our way, we would soon lose our bearings, make disastrous decisions and flounder helplessly. When we slowly replace one belief with another, we need to understand what we will lose and what we will gain. The gain needs to be incontrovertibly more attractive than the loss, if that desirable change is to become permanent.

The client wants their stress to go away or wants an easily identifiable win, for instance that their CV/résumé is a better fit with what their market wants and that they have improved their chances of getting the ideal job. This client will probably need to work at a different level to find out what they want and who they are before they write a convincing CV. The client who cannot refuse to help the persistently clueless colleague at the photocopier already knows the answer to the problem, but this client does not necessarily understand how and why they let it happen. They don't know why they seem to be perpetually at other people's mercy nor how to take the risk of being disliked. The coach's aim is to equip the client with the tools and skills for making reliable decisions in the future. This is the difference between transactional and transformational coaching. Where coaching can go wrong is in the many times that client and coach collude to concentrate on what is simple and obvious because the transactional issues seem so much less difficult.

Despite all these illusions, blocks and barriers, coaching does work. By creating that safe space, by offering people the chance to lower their defences, to explore their problems by seeing them in a different way, we see positive change emerge. People get the jobs they have longed for, they reduce their stress, become more confident leaders, more self-aware in their relationships at work and at home, and they make better choices. Clients achieve this because we work as equals and we ask questions in a way that few others around the client are likely to do. We suspend judgement because we have curiosity rather than demanding to know who is to blame. We keep ourselves out of the way and yet we are fully present. We are prepared to go beyond the simplicities of the presenting issues. We are not afraid to ask about how what is going on in the client's life now links with what has gone on in their past. Unlike some other helping professionals, we have the time and space to see the client as a whole person, not just someone who is an employee, a patient or one half of a troubled relationship. The time element is important. I see much disillusion with coaching from buyers and sellers alike when the coaching is limited to far too few sessions to make a difference. Some coaches are too modest to ask for what they know to be necessary for long-term impact. All of this is why it is demanding to do coaching well and why it takes time to learn how to do it well. If you are relatively new to coaching, be persistent, be forgiving of your stumbles, build your hours and get yourself to as much further training and supervision as you can afford.

Coaching works when we see ourselves as being a coach rather than doing coaching. We are working alongside the client rather than taking refuge in superior knowledge or status. We have humility because we never know what is good for the client and yet we are confident that we can help them: that is the paradox.

Coaching has grown to become a profession of many specialisms. People who were previously content to describe themselves as consultants or advisors have now rebadged themselves as coaches in the belief that this is a more attractive word to use, regardless of whether what they do can be described as coaching. The field encompasses personal coaching ('life' coaching), sports coaching, team coaching, parent coaching and many more. My own work has been in executive and career coaching, where I assume that personal life decisions will always be on the agenda as well as the outcomes that the organisation wants to see happen. In writing this book, I have drawn on my own experience as an executive coach because this is what I know. But my hope is that most of what I describe will be relevant to any coach who is working with clients on change, whatever the context.

What really works in coaching? Whatever the extraordinary achievements of neuroscientists and neuro-psychologists, we cannot map the intricate emotional processes of decision-making. We cannot conduct an ultra-sound or MRI scan to look for psychological lesions. In this book, my aim is to explore the thorny and often exasperating territory of the transformational. In coaching, as in therapy, we are dependent on apparently simple tools: empathy, asking questions, listening, observing, feedback, offering acceptance. How to use those tools in the quest for radical change is my aim in this book.

In giving my book its possibly over-bold title, what I mean is what works *for me* in coaching. It may not work for you. Everything I write here is for you to test and question. Argue your way through it and, if some of it needs more than just arguing in your head, please email me: jenny@jennyrogerscoaching.com

1

Making Sure That You Have a Real Client

There are many ways in which, especially earlier on in a coaching career, you may meet people who are not genuine clients. When you don't have a genuine client, the coaching will be a failure. Here is the secret to making sure that you have a real client. All these questions need to be answered unequivocally with *yes*:

- Is the client a volunteer?
- If someone else has suggested coaching, is the client entering into the coaching relationship willingly?
- Are you satisfied that there is no hidden agenda where coaching is a duplicitous attempt to solve a serious performance problem?
- Can the client describe what they want to achieve from the coaching programme?
- Can the client accept responsibility for their part in any problems they face?
- Are you free from any conflicts of interest where this client is concerned?

Where the answer to all six questions is *yes*, then you will be off to an excellent start. If any of the answers is *no* then think again. If they are *maybe*, then clarify any ambiguities with the potential client before arranging your first meeting. One of the core principles of coaching is that it is about change. The change has to be something that the client wants. It is not enough that the client needs to change, they must actively want it. If people secretly or overtly believe that everything in their life is rosy right now, or that someone else wants them to change but they don't agree that this is necessary, or that all their problems are other people's fault, then they are not a candidate for coaching.

New coaches can fall right into this ambush when they finish the first part of their training. In order to get qualified, virtually all accrediting bodies ask for evidence that you have coached people who are not fellow participants on the course. As a new coach, you are desperate: *who can I ask?* More often than not, you are an inexperienced seller of coaching, possibly because none of your previous roles has included an element where selling is involved. You are still clinging to the idea that 'selling' might be a bit tacky and undignified. Underneath that, you might be unconfident about your worth as a coach and hotly aware of your status as a beginner. You are probably not asking for money, but you are asking for people's time and will have been required to get feedback from the client at the end of the sessions.

The prospect can be so terrifying that you turn to people in your family and friendship circle, or close colleagues at work. Understandable though it is, there is so much wrong with that as a tactic. You will already know far too much about the volunteer client; where you are part of the same family, you will most likely share the same blind spots, or even be part of the problem. Objectivity is impossible. Worse, the volunteer may be offering themselves 'to help'. Wanting to help the coach is not a reason for being a client.

In the role of assessor for coaching qualifications, I have heard countless recorded examples of what follows. The session begins with some pleasantries or gossip and this may go on far too long because the coach is jumpy about stepping into an unfamiliar role with someone who knows them well. In order to overcome this problem, the coach then gives what is, in effect, a slightly clunky-sounding mini-lecture about coaching, and often you can hear the client making uh-huh noises in the background or else apparently disappearing from the conversation completely. There is then some slightly pedantic goal-setting. All too soon, the session begins to form a circular shape. It is going nowhere.

There are two reasons to explain what is happening and either or both may be present. The first is that the 'problem' the client brings is one that is safely trivial or has already been solved. The second is that the coach is wise enough to know that because they value the relationship, they cannot and should not challenge a close friend, colleague or family member. When asked for feedback, the client gives faint praise because they don't want to be nasty. This does not fool the coach: they are aware that something went horribly wrong. They may even conclude that they have been bamboozled about the power of coaching or that they are a failure as a coach. The lesson here is: friends, close colleagues and family should be a coaching-free zone because no one inside it can be a genuine client.

When people go on management development programmes, it is common to offer participants some follow-up coaching. This is sensible because the nickname for such courses is 'sheep dip', an accurate if cynical label. The sheep get dipped and are clean for a fleeting moment and then the muddy field claims them once again. In the same way, the good intentions of a course can quickly get forgotten. The dominant culture sucks people back into their familiar patterns. It is rare for this offer of coaching to be generous. Often, it is as little as three one-hour sessions, there is no choice of coach and it would be unusual for sponsors to make it clear that the offer of coaching is optional.

One coach described his experience of working in a uniformed organisation where the post-course coaching was described as 'non-mandatory'. 'Unfortunately', he said, 'people didn't hear the word *non*, they just heard *mandatory*'. In this strictly hierarchical organisation where rank mattered and people were used to obeying orders, the assumption was that not to take up the offer could be career suicide, so virtually every participant did. What was the result? First, there were the many people who inexplicably 'forgot' their sessions or arrived late. Second, there were the endless sessions where, when asked for their goals for the session, the client looked bemused, sulky or politely disengaged. When this happens, a coach can get desperate: 'I'm being paid for this! I must be seen to be adding value!' This leads to inventing goals for the client or drawing some 'helpful' four-box matrix models of leadership to add to the many that the client had already encountered on their course. It is possible that some of these people could have been helped by coaching, but by being subtly ordered, as they believed, to attend the sessions, their motivation had been undermined.

When you encounter this, don't struggle on. Say to the client, 'Coaching is about change. I'm here for you to discuss anything that's happening in your life that you feel needs attention. I'm at your service.' Then wait. This may be enough for the client to name a topic they want to work on. If they still, in effect, shrug and say everything is fine, unlikely though this probably is, then suggest, courteously and firmly, that you end the session. The word will soon get out that this has happened and may discourage others from pretend attendance. Following up: contact the course sponsors immediately to ask them to consider changing how they describe the offer of coaching.

The great majority of larger organisations have embraced coaching for at least some of their executives because they have seen repeatedly that it is a worthwhile investment. Sometimes what happens is that they confuse coaching with performance management. A senior employee is failing at work in the eyes of their boss. Instead of tackling it by giving the person feedback, discussing it, waiting to see if there is improvement and then deciding what to do, the organisation outsources the problem to a coach.

Disastrous consequences follow. The coach rarely knows enough about the background. The client is confused about what is going on, may deny that there is a problem, spending the session complaining about their boss – and, for all you know, the boss may indeed be the issue, not the person you have in the room. The coach feels immense pressure to force the client to improve. I see many experienced and highly paid executive coaches entangled in this web of impossible expectations. Never take on this kind of assignment unless you are certain that the organisation has already tried all the standard performance management approaches. Then ensure that you have discussed your role, making it clear that you are not responsible for the client's performance. At the point where you are negotiating with the organisation and the potential client, check whether they are willing to investigate causes and effects and that they have the patience and budget to wait while you and the client do this.

In some organisations, coaching is routinely offered to every member of the senior executive team. Being able to brag casually about 'my coach' comes to be a badge of honour because coaching at this level is bought at a premium price. Some people regard their coaches as a portable asset. They build a continuation of the relationship into their negotiations for a new job. This can mean that an executive who does not have a coach feels under pressure to acquire one, regardless of whether they want coaching. Again, this is a recipe for failure. A client who says, in effect, that the coaching is free so why not try it, or that it might be 'interesting' or that they vaguely suppose you could be useful as a 'sounding board', may not be serious about it. If so, the inevitable result is sessions with no energy. The coach emerges exhausted because they have been doing all the work.

The answer to all these common problems is to make it a rule to have a so-called 'chemistry' conversation before anything else happens. This is quite apart from any meetings you have as a three-way or four-way conversation once you are embarked on the coaching programme (Chapter 3). In this conversation, you make it clear that you are choosing the client as much as they are choosing you. Ask what has triggered the thought that coaching might be a good idea and what challenges the potential client faces.

Where the answer is that someone else has proposed it, acknowledge the positive intention behind this suggestion but follow up with, 'But what do *you* think?' The reply here is critical. If the client is saying they want to work with you solely in order to please someone else then it is unlikely that the coaching could be successful. This is what can happen, for instance, with young graduates who are experiencing what has been called 'failure to launch'. They are back at home, still uncertain of their career path. Their parents are frantic with worry and sometimes with resentment – they don't want this adult child back at home. But until the young adult earns enough to be self-sufficient, they are stuck with each other. The coaching would be funded by the parents but the actual client is the young person. If they seem not to care whether they get a job or not, then refuse the assignment.

The million-dollar question in this exploratory conversation is, 'What do you want to achieve from any coaching that you undertake?' An alternative, equally powerful one is, 'If this coaching were successful, what would have changed for you?' Some people will give you vague and generalised answers such as, 'I want to know what to do with the rest of my life' or ' I want to sort out my relationship with my boss'. These are acceptable because you can work with the client on refining them, turning them into something more specific. When the client can't answer the question at all, then now is not the time to take them on because motivation to change is the bedrock. You can certainly sharpen a client's motivation through the way you coach them but you can't create it if there is nothing there in the first place.

This is different from but linked to the question of *coachability*. The client may be eager to start the coaching but may have a multitude of problems.

This was the case, for instance, when I was approached by an HR contact to ask if I would take on an executive who had just had devastating feedback on a 360-degree questionnaire showing how much his team disliked him. She told me that he was struggling to master the technicalities of his job and that if he could not demonstrate rapid improvement, he was likely to be fired. 'He's desperate to work with you', she said, and I believed her. In this man's situation I, too, would probably be reaching out blindly to any source of help. However, the organisation was only willing to pay for four sessions, far too little in these circumstances, nor was it willing to find him a mentor who could help with the specialist aspects of his role. I declined the assignment with relief, without ever speaking to the potential client.

Sometimes, the chemistry conversation will reveal that the client has plenty of motivation – you have an affable chat – but it is clear that what the client needs is not what you can offer. A colleague recently gave me a good example of this when she described being approached about coaching someone who was returning to work after a maternity leave which had included a serious postnatal depression. My colleague was also a working mother, much the same age as the prospective client. She had herself recently recovered from a recurring depressive illness and felt that she was not in the right place to coach someone whose mental state, she judged, might still be fragile. 'I revealed this to the client', she said, 'explaining that I was not turning down the chance to coach her because of her illness but because of mine, and I enthusiastically recommended another coach.' The client was grateful for her candour, took up the contact and a successful set of coaching sessions was duly held. Another example is when what the client needs is specialist advice, not coaching.

Because coaching has become popular and does not have any of the still-lingering sense of shame that can be associated with needing psychotherapy, you may sometimes be approached by people with serious mental health problems. Others may launch into describing complex family and relationship difficulties. In that initial discussion, you will hear some of the anguish associated with this. There will be an intensity and complexity to it which could alert you to the probability that this is psychotherapeutic and not coaching territory. If this is the case, say so sincerely and directly, telling the client that what they need is not a good fit with your own set of skills and interests, and wishing them luck with finding what they need elsewhere.

Listen to your instincts here. If something feels wrong, it probably is.

2

Drawing Those Boundaries

Once upon a time, long ago, there were seven tribes. Their names were Coach, Mentor, Trainer, Consultant, Psychologist, Counsellor and Therapist. These tribes had to live in separate enclosures because, if they were to meet and cross each other's boundaries, immense harm would be caused. Intermarriage was discouraged. Each tribe, but especially the Coaching tribe, spent much time and energy patrolling their boundaries, apologising to each other if they carelessly stepped over the line, promising to be more vigilant in future.

Well, I exaggerate a bit, but not much. Fortunately, when I first began to work as an internally based coach at the BBC, I had never heard of these 'rules', just as I had never heard the word 'coach' used the way we use it now. My clients were as unaware of these boundaries as I was. Although allegedly coming with questions about their work, many would mention worries about their marriage and children, their health and their future career. Tears, anger and vividly expressed frustration were not at all uncommon. Sometimes people would ask for specific structured help on a skill such as negotiating, or for advice about a factual matter on which I had known expertise. What I was supposed to have done was to say, 'OK, I'll take my coaching hat off now and put on my [some other] hat.' Good job I had no idea about this as I might have been crazily snatching invisible hats off and on throughout the sessions. When I began to read some of the early writers on coaching, I was amazed to see it suggested that emotion had no place in executive coaching, and that if clients started getting upset or wanted to talk about their personal lives, you were supposed to say, kindly but sternly, that this was not what coaching was about, and to suggest that they needed therapy or relationship counselling.

Partly this was to do with coaching as an immature profession trying to establish itself as different, and partly to get away from what some coaches perceived to be the slightly dubious reputation that some types of therapy had. Sometimes, my suspicion is that these writers themselves had problems with emotional intimacy and took it for granted that others would share their fears. In addition, there was the idea that you only needed therapy if there was something secretly and terribly wrong with your mental health. Because of this apparent stigma, if it looked to clients as if you were dabbling in therapy, it was alleged that they would glare at you suspiciously and tell you to keep off. There was at least a little truth in this. Only a few years ago, a client asked me if coaching was 'therapy in disguise', and the way she asked the question suggested that she did not want the answer to be 'yes'. At the same time, therapists and counsellors were jumpy about coaches who appeared to be encroaching – untrained, clumsy and ignorant – on their territory.

There was an understandable but exaggerated fear among coaches of something called 'doing harm'. Most probably the only harm an amateur therapist-coach could do would be to appall clients with their incompetence after which the client would wisely vanish. Senior executive clients usually have a healthy sense of agency, they are used to hiring consultants and suppliers of all sorts and are unlikely to be impressed by someone obviously out of their depth. If you stick to non-directive coaching questions and avoid interpretation, you may not do much obvious good for someone who is distressed, but you are unlikely to do harm either.

Boundaries have relaxed since those early days of coaching. Many of the professional associations for psychologists, therapists, trainers and counsellors now have coaching 'chapters', along with routes to qualification as a coach. Training for coaches has improved, embracing the importance of in-depth psychological understanding, with many universities providing advanced degrees in coaching along with initial training and accreditation. Coaching has acknowledged the profundity of its debt to psychotherapy. Therapists have seen that there is much to be learned from the world of coaching, for instance in its greater emphasis on goal-setting and its focus on solutions. There is now a whole cadre of people who have dual training as coaches and as therapists and who are happy to toggle between the two. While there are still some coaches who describe their work as 'performance coaching', it is far more widely accepted that you are always dealing with the whole person, though how any individual coach will interpret that will vary widely.

None of this diminishes the importance of knowing what your professional boundaries are as a coach.

In the very first conversation you have with a client, so probably during the 'chemistry' session, ask what the client's ideas are about coaching. Now that it has become a familiar route to learning in organisations, most people will readily answer that it is a private forum for exploration of their goals for change, that they do not expect to encounter advice-giving but that they do expect something they will often call 'wisdom'. It is worth asking what they mean by this. The answer is usually about working with someone who has seen similar issues many times, who is unshockable and, where executive coaching is concerned, understands the often bizarre nature of organisational life. When people come for more specialist kinds of coaching, they rightly expect the coach to have access to reliable, up-to-date information and advice. It is far from the case that coaching is always 'non-directive'. Where there is any kind of mismatch between what the client wants and what you offer, this is the time to explore it, sometimes agreeing to take the relationship no further.

Boundaries in some professions are more about protecting the professional than the client. In medicine, for instance, many doctors ask to be addressed as Dr [Surname] while sometimes, without asking, addressing the patient by their first name or as an anonymous 'you'. As a patient myself, I find this objectionable and usually say what I want to be called. My late husband, who had far too many doctors in his life, insisted on addressing them all by their first name, regardless of their eminence. A GP friend explained to me that she chooses formal forms of address for herself and for all her adult patients: 'I have to give life-changing news to people on a daily basis and it feels better for me if I stay inside my doctor identity rather than revealing too much about myself.' When I have first met clients from countries with more formal cultures, they have sometimes wanted to endow me with fancy titles, so I have been greeted as Dr Rogers and Professor Rogers by people who have expected that I will use their own formal title. I have always said immediately that I am no kind of doctor or professor, so I say, 'Please call me Jenny. And what name may I use for you?'

You will decide what boundaries you want to create around access to you between sessions. Increasingly, I offer clients a whole package which stretches over a stated period of time where the client can have whatever sessions they want in whatever form they want (face to face, phone, Skype, Zoom, email) during the period of the engagement. It may seem as if this invites abuse, though in practice it rarely has. Clients are respectful of my time. If they contact me out of hours, I know it is an emergency. With other types of contract, where the client books and pays in advance for a set number of sessions of agreed length, I again encourage contact as this keeps the momentum going, often necessary when there are long pauses between sessions. In my confirmatory email to the client after we have agreed to work together, I usually describe what this might look like, for instance saying something along the lines of 'it may be useful to have brief 5–10-minute phone calls to discuss something urgent which has come up between sessions, or there may be quite a bit that we could do by email.' I realise that many coaches might prefer not to take this line, keeping contact purely inside the face-to-face sessions. If you begin to feel resentful about clients intruding into your time, then you might consider either raising your fees so that these extras are covered or just deciding to stop offering access at all between sessions.

Last-minute cancellations are a problem for many coaches. Clients who have never had to earn a living by selling their time may struggle to understand why it is so maddening, though most do appreciate that, at the very least, it will be inconvenient. The truth is that each cancelled session creates an opportunity cost as it is unlikely that you will be able to re-sell the slot at short notice. It is easy to state a strict cancellation policy but hard in practice to invoice a client for a session they have not had. Clients cancel for many reasons. Their train may have been chronically delayed to the point where it would have been foolish to get on it. They may have been taken ill with one of those sudden gastric upheavals or respiratory infections which wipe you out for several days. Insisting on invoicing at such times will look self-important and rigid. It is more problematical when a client's colleagues command attendance at what sounds like a routine meeting, but as an outsider it is hard to judge whether this is genuinely a priority or just them not valuing their coaching and the coach's time enough to make the effort. It is worrying when a client cancels repeatedly. Then it is time for a frank discussion.

Lateness may be a problem. Again, there may be many perfectly reasonable explanations. I once had a client who arrived for a two-hour session an hour and thirty minutes late with what seemed like a flimsy excuse. She had the half hour that was left and I did not offer to add extra time to her next session. She was on time for every subsequent session. Clients who are repeatedly late with you may be late for every other meeting in their lives and they may bring their chronic lateness to you as part of their agenda. But this is not a reason for extending their sessions. Often, my own schedule is tight and I will want time to write up my notes, have a break, prepare for the next client or just go for a much needed walk along the canal towpath right next to my building. I can't do a good job if any of this is rushed.

Just as is the case in some forms of therapy, there are coaches who like to end a session with 'homework' for the client. Sometimes I do this, for instance I might ask a career coaching client to draft something which is their 'brand statement' or maybe a new version of their CV, based on the work we have taken several hours to discuss. Clients rarely renege on this kind of commitment because they see how quickly it can advance their agenda. What works less well is the little tasks and experiments which often seem to come from the coach's wish to demonstrate to themselves and others that progress is being made, rather than coming from the client. When this is the scenario, the client is unlikely to do the homework and then the coach will feel that some boundary has been breached. But has it? We are not teachers who will punish pupils for failing to complete an assignment. We only have the moral authority that is based on trust and respect. This is fragile, easily destroyed by a move which can look heavy-handed and out of proportion to the offence.

As in other professional relationships, there are two kinds of contract in play. There is the actual legally binding contract. You may want to send clients some version of this as a formal set of terms and conditions. In my early days as a coach, I paid a lawyer to draw something up for me along these lines but it is many years since I have sent it to a client; it just seems far too pretentious when a simple email confirming dates, times and fees will do the same job. I know coaches who believe that the formal document is a necessary safeguard and perhaps they are right.

Running alongside this stated agreement, there is a psychological contract which is much harder to define. Its essence is the dual nature of the obligations. The coach promises high levels of expert listening and questioning, fulfilling any commitments about follow-ups to sessions, never cancelling for trivial reasons and pledging to protect the client's confidentiality. The client's role is to bring the agenda, to be honest and to be ready to surrender much of their normal defensiveness in the interests of learning.

There are certain kinds of client behaviour which are rare but nonetheless suggest that some of these boundaries have been breached. Where a large proportion of your practice is made up of clients paying for themselves, it will help to set clear limits in writing about the latitude you allow for payment. It is time-consuming to pursue bad debts and risky to carry on coaching with a client who has bills outstanding over a long period. In the sessions themselves, you do not have to tolerate rude behaviour. A coach described a client who complained loudly about her fees even though it was his organisation that was paying the bill. The client told her that 'this coaching thing is a waste of time' and met many of her questions with the scornful phrase, 'what kind of a silly question is that?' After putting up with two such conversations, the coach called the client, explaining firmly and courteously that she was not prepared to continue and that she would leave it to him to explain her decision to the organisation.

In the late 1990s, I was running the coaching company that I had founded and we often won contracts which involved offering short coaching programmes to large numbers of people, most of them staff who had just been given the bad news that they were to lose their job. It was inevitable that there were some disturbed and puzzling characters among their number. I think here of the woman who claimed that she had been sexually abused by every one of her many bosses. There was a man whose horrifying tales of life as a refugee were transparently untrue, and a woman who compulsively pulled out her hair during the first session. Coaching was not the right path for any of these people and telling them so had to be done mercifully and directly.

Trust on both sides is of the essence. This is easily said but what do you do if you discover half way through an apparently smooth programme that a client has told a grossly damaging lie about you? Or that a client who has told you how much they value their sessions has been telling colleagues that coaching is a confidence trick and that you are the trickster? The answer is obvious. You double-check that your information is accurate, you confront the client and you end the relationship. These are rare, unpleasant events and it is clear what to do.

The more ambiguous territory is about confidentiality, especially about what happens when there are three parties in the relationship – part of the subject of the next chapter.

3

Negotiating the Confidentiality Maze

It would be common in the first session for the coach to make a little speech about confidentiality, pointing out that 'it's not a blank cheque'. When we do this, we are rarely specific, perhaps praying that we never have to work out what it could mean when it is not a blank cheque. Mostly, this works well because the hopeful assurances are never tested. In practice, every coach needs to know what their personal boundaries are.

It starts with accepting that coaching confidentiality is not protected by law so you could be asked to provide notes, for instance to an employment tribunal. If you refuse, your notes could be subpoenaed. This possibility loomed for a coach whom I was supervising when her client was suing her former employer for wrongful dismissal. She asked for the coach's notes to support one aspect of her case. The case was settled out of court so the threat never became real, but it might have done.

A coach told me in a supervision session that her client had boasted of an undiscovered fraud in his previous job. Because of the way it had been described, she was uncertain whether the client was joking or serious and what his own role, if any, had been. By telling me, she was then implicating me in this dangerous secret even though she had not divulged the client's name. We agreed that she would question the client on his 'joke'. She did and he told her that she had misheard him. He claimed that he had talked about how easy it would have been to have committed the fraud because of the organisation's laxity, not that he had done so. This left us both uneasy. She told the client that she expected him to raise it with the organisation in question and he airily pooh-poohed the need for it. She then said, using a subsequent email to underline the seriousness of the matter, that she would inform the organisation of this potential breach of their accounting procedures and of the source of her information. The client was furious and left the session angrily, saying that he would not return. She carried out her promise. As far as she and I were aware, no further action was taken so perhaps it was just a little empty bragging after all.

It is often far from straightforward to assess what confidentiality might mean in any situation where there is potentially danger to the client or someone else, or where the law might have been broken. For instance, if a client seemingly casually tells you, 'I have often thought of jumping off a high building', is this a suicide threat that must be taken so seriously that it needs to be shared with someone else? Is it enough to explore it with the client so that you understand how far they have actually made plans to take their own life? Part of the answer is never to leave the ambiguity loose in the session. Ask for more information so that you are clear what the client means or intends. Express your reservations and dilemmas openly, rather than leaving it until it might be too late. The first line of defence is always to coach the client around making the disclosure themselves, rather than going straight to action yourself. 'Duty of care' is an imprecise concept, even in medicine, but I still find it useful to ask in any dilemma of this sort, 'What is my duty of care in this situation? To whom do I owe this duty? What needs to happen if safeguarding is an issue here?'

The more senior the client, the more important it might be that they know they can trust you with commercial and sometimes with national secrets. To work with senior civil servants, I had to go through the high-level security screening known as Developed Vetting and mostly this works well: they know that they can talk frankly and this is a welcome additional guarantee to the promise of confidentiality. They will want and need to tell a coach about dilemmas that will make no sense unless you know who and what is involved. This came home to me vividly when a client in government was explaining a complex problem. He had been sent in to another department as a trouble-shooter. It was in all ways a sensitive matter with high stakes. He referred throughout to the main character in the saga as 'they' and shrouded the whole tale with such a thick fog that it was impossible to discern what his actual dilemma was. Despite the obfuscation, it suddenly dawned on me who he meant and that he had felt the heavy disguise to be necessary because he knew that the 'difficult' senior person at the centre of the story had been one of my clients. But then my own dilemma was, *Do I tell him that I have guessed?* I did, but without naming the person involved. So, although he knew that I knew who he was talking about, neither of us was able to be straightforward. This felt extremely peculiar and in the end unnecessary, but I felt I had to respect his own reluctance.

It may seem easy to keep client names confidential unless they have given you specific permission to disclose that they are a client. A coach told me that she had thought her partner understood what this commitment to confidentiality meant and had briefly mentioned that she was coaching a colleague in his organisation. At a meeting that he and this client both attended, the husband said, by way of nonchalantly making conversation, 'Oh, I hear you're working with my wife'. The client was incensed, assuming this meant that the wife was gossiping with her husband, though this was not the case. But that was the end of the coaching. It is easy to assume that you have permission to make one of those common email introductions, identifying one half of the pair as your client. Always ask first, not just if you can give the person's address but if you can say how you know them.

It is sensible to assume that you should always double-check whether you can say that someone is your client, even if you think you already have such permission. A long-standing client, an only son who had been estranged from his homophobic parents for many years, was devastated by the sudden death of his partner. He asked me if I would be what he called 'my stand-in parent' at the funeral. I was touched and said yes immediately, but I still asked how I should describe my relationship with him at the event. His reply was to say that I was 'a friend' and to be imprecise about how we knew each other. Another client asked me to his wedding. I was prepared to be similarly vague, only to discover that seemingly all his guests, including his childhood friends, parents and siblings, already knew that I was his coach, some of them even claiming to know what we had discussed in our sessions. I just acknowledged these statements inscrutably, without confirming or denying them.

In her memorable BBC *Panorama* interview, the late Princess Diana famously said, 'There were three of us in this marriage so it was a bit crowded.' She was describing her humiliation over her husband's long-standing relationship with Camilla Parker Bowles. Three is an uncomfortable number in any relationship as there is always someone who is left out. In executive coaching, there are three parties: the coach, the client and the organisation. The left-out party is usually the organisation. The complication is that the organisation is the one paying the bill, so it is understandable that it can be uneasy about the nature of its investment.

To guard against this, it is good practice to facilitate a meeting where you first meet the sponsor, ideally the line manager, for a 20-minute frank and confidential discussion about what the sponsor wants to see as a result of the coaching. Then you are joined by the client where you encourage the sponsor to be equally frank about what they have just said to you, without you revealing anything from the conversation that you have just had. The client gets the opportunity to seek clarification, including some possibly indignant questions about why some or all of this has never been said to them before, as the chances are that it has not.

At this meeting, you discuss what confidentiality means, usually that the client can say what they like about the coaching but that you cannot. Where you meet some surprise or resistance from the sponsor, explain that the client cannot be as open as they need to be if they know that you will be feeding back information to their boss. You can have no reliable way of seeing what changes the client is making at work as you only hear their account during the coaching. Instead, discuss how the sponsor can get an idea of how the coaching is going direct from the client, including how they might agree to give him or her on-the-spot feedback since they see the client at work and you do not. Challenge any aims that you know are unachievable in the timeframe suggested or that are too vague. Be clear at this meeting that you cannot be responsible for whether or not the client achieves whatever changes the boss wants to see made; this is the client's job, not yours.

Demands for information usually come from the boss's lack of understanding of how important it is for the client to be unguarded with their coach. Where the client has any suspicion that you will be reporting back to their boss, they are most unlikely to be frank with you. One coach had to explain this patiently to a boss who asked if he could join every fourth coaching conversation in a programme that was being carried out via Zoom during the 2020 Covid pandemic. The boss was surprised, saying that his only intention was to be 'helpful'.

Where it gets more complicated is that some organisations demand what they often call 'public goals'. They are more likely to do this when there has been no three-way meeting. This can happen for a variety of reasons, including complex matrix arrangements where it is unclear who the actual boss is. I have had clients who have adamantly refused to name 'public goals' or who have said openly, rightly recognising that this is a box-ticking exercise, that they will invent some 'goals'– and have.

Coaches vary in their willingness to report on the low-level factual signs of progress, for instance whether the client is attending sessions and if so how many they have had, saying that this, again, is up to the client, as the coach is not their keeper.

Ideally, it should always be the client who triggers the sessions. It can often happen that an organisation will contract a coach to deliver six sessions over a six-month period but the client has not taken up their full entitlement. The coach emails the client, politely reminding them that they have sessions in the bank and that the coach is ready and willing to arrange them. Sometimes there is silence and there is no way of knowing what the silence means. Now what is the coach to do? One coach who prided himself on his professionalism felt disabling unease when this happened: 'If I do nothing, I feel I am letting it slide and letting the sponsor down. If I email the sponsor or HR person without copying the client in, it feels as if I'm ratting on them. If I do the email but copy the client in, it may feel as if I am criticising or harassing them.' The solution here is probably to do a friendly but factual email to both, noting how many sessions the client has had and saying that they are sure X (the client) will take up the others when they are ready.

Organisations can be impatient for progress. Sometimes they are less than frank with both coach and client at the outset of a coaching programme. They are often expecting too much too soon. This is especially true in high-tech companies that pride themselves on their ability to innovate and move quickly. The HR person contacts the coach: 'We're a bit disappointed that we haven't seen more change in X. He/she needs to step up to the plate.

If something doesn't happen soon we will have to part with them'. The coach is aghast. No one said anything about this at the outset of the programme. The coach has carried out 360-degree feedback for the client (Chapter 20), revealing how much learning the client has to do and how far they are from doing it. The coach has been paid over the odds for their work because this is a very senior person, so they are feeling guilty, pressured and perhaps that they have failed. They realise that change on the scale that is needed is likely to be slow, despite the massive efforts that the client is making. What is the coach to do? Can they tip off the client on what has been said in confidence? Can they share the output of the highly confidential 360 with the HR person so that they understand the demanding nature of the task facing the client? Can they ask for more time and budget? Probably the answer to all these questions is no. Nor can you un-remember what you have been told; it will sit awkwardly with you, an unwelcome burden. The best you can do may be to encourage the HR person to be honest with your client, at the same time as you encourage the client to check up with both the HR person and the sponsor about their impressions of progress, giving one or both the chance to be more straightforward.

Sometimes, despite the lack of candour all round, it is possible to realise that the client entirely lacks any political nous and is failing to see that their future with the organisation is limited. They will tell you that they believe it to be humiliating or immoral to broaden their networks beyond a narrow professional sphere. They may even say that they 'hate politicking', a sure sign that they do not understand it or why it is important. They are not reading the signs of their impending doom, even though these may be obvious to everyone else. All you can do here is to challenge their belief that organisational awareness of this sort is unimportant, without for a moment implying that you know or guess what is in store for them.

Prevention is always the best policy but it is easy to be wise after the event. At the initial three-way meeting or in the separate conversations with boss and HR professional, a key question is to ask, 'What is at risk for this client if they don't make the changes you have suggested?', or even more bluntly, 'Are they at risk of being fired?'

It is difficult to coach people who are members of the same team and impossible to coach people who are in a line management–direct report relationship because it is inevitable that the relationship with the other person will need to be on the coaching agenda. Dodging the forbidden topic then gets to be like that episode in the classic 1970s BBC sitcom, *Fawlty Towers*, where the preposterously angry and resentful Little Englander, Basil Fawlty, has to receive a German guest at his hotel and knows that he has to remember, 'Don't mention the war!' Naturally the war intrudes into every exchange. I was once in the situation of coaching two people who found each other obnoxious. I had taken both on as clients in this large organisation under the incorrect impression that they were in different teams and only discovered my mistake when both coaching programmes were well under way. Since they avoided each other whenever possible, the chances were low that they would find out through idle chatter that they had the same coach. But I lived in dread that if either had raised the direct question of how to deal with the other person, I would have needed to explain to one or both what the situation was. I knew that either could then have said, 'But why didn't you say?' Would a lame discussion of coaching ethics have satisfied them? I think that probably it would not.

4
Listening for the Client's Boundaries

I am in a puzzlingly darkened room, even though it is a bright June afternoon outside. There is some kind of plinkety-plonk music in the background, sounding vaguely Tibetan. The acupuncturist leans forward, oozing sympathy; she's my new best friend. She takes my wrist, telling me that she needs to feel my pulse. I submit to this, wondering why it's necessary.

'Is there a lot of anxiety in your life?' she asks softly, engaging me with intense eye contact.

'Not really.'

She persists. 'Your pulse is quite fast, so I did wonder…'

'It's probably fast because I'm in a strange place and wondering what's going to happen as I've never had acupuncture before.'

'Tell me what's going on in your life right now.'

The coach-trainer in me is exasperated by this vague question which seems to have nothing to do with why I am seeking acupuncture, but I quell my unbecoming wish to give her the kind of feedback I would have offered to a trainee coach and say blandly, 'It's just going on as usual.'

'Are all your relationships in good order, for instance?'

'Ummm. Yes.'

Perhaps this acupuncturist was a qualified therapist but, if that had been the case, I would have expected her to tell me. Or perhaps she might have explained that, in the school of acupuncture to which she belongs, they take the view that body and mind are so intimately connected that it is essential to ask the client questions which might make such connections clear. I am familiar with these ideas; I draw on them myself, but I have not come for therapy or for mystical Eastern wisdom. I am there because I have some troubling pain in my right knee and a friend who believes she had good results from acupuncture has recommended that I try it.

Later, having stuck innumerable fine needles into my leg (it didn't hurt, just as she had promised) she tiptoes out of the room for 10 minutes after saying, 'I'm just covering you with a nice soft blanket. I want you to relax and perhaps you could visualise your knee getting better...'

I could not wait to escape from that room, with its clinging odour of aroma-therapy oils and its unwished-for atmosphere of holy hush. The acupuncturist had not appeared to notice my resistance to talking about my personal life, or, if she did, had discounted it. The acupuncture did not alleviate my knee pain, perhaps because, given my attitude, any placebo effect was unlikely. Possibly my particular joint problem was not one that lent itself to acupuncture. Six months later, I was having the knee surgery which would produce a radical improvement.

I have heard versions of this story from coaching clients and from the other side too – from some of the coaches whom I supervise. The core of it is failing to listen and to contract properly with the client.

This is what happened with a client who was seeking a new coach after deciding that she no longer wanted to work with the old one. I asked what had gone wrong, since this is always vital information and usually a clear warning about how to avoid repeating the other coach's alleged mistakes. The client's reply was that her company had engaged a coach to work with her on how to make the transition from the role of technical expert to her first role as a boss. The coach had done what virtually all of us do in the first session and had used some version of the 'Wheel of Life'. This is the familiar eight-wedge pie chart which divides your life into Work, Health, Money, Friendships and Family, Partner, Personal Development, Leisure and Physical Environment. It asks you to rate your satisfaction with each of these areas on a 1–10 scale. Its purpose is to position any work issues within the wider context of the client's life and offers a painless way for clients to disclose anything which could affect the coaching.

This client had readily enough described the relationship with her husband as 'in terminal decline' and had revealed the difficulties of finding enough money to pay for the care of a severely disabled daughter. At the same time, she had firmly told the coach that she did not wish to discuss either of these matters because there was more than enough to cover where the work issues were concerned.

'The coach wouldn't leave it alone', said the client. 'She insisted on three-hour sessions, all of them in her own home with, by the way, far too much domestic clutter visible. She told me that we needed to take at least half our time looking at what she called "that personal stuff". When I protested, she told me I was "in denial" and that for my own mental health we should work on them.'

The client found this coach intrusive. She felt that the coach was an unqualified dabbler in therapy. She did not want to discuss what she called 'intractable problems at home' with this coach. Perhaps she was not ready to discuss them at all because their intractability felt overwhelming. Perhaps she might have been willing to do so with a different coach. Perhaps she had already discussed them with an actual therapist. It was not for me to say which of these explanations, or any of the many alternatives that occurred to me, was the 'real' one. The fact was that the client had clearly signalled 'no' and the coach had ignored her. The client had then ended the coaching programme.

I daresay that if I had been the supervisor of this coach I would have heard a different story. It would probably have centred around the puzzling refusal of the client to acknowledge that work and home are indivisible because it is the same person who goes to work and comes home again at the end of the day, that work problems are bound to affect home life and vice versa. She might have described herself as 'offering challenge', saying that all coaches have to be willing to do this even when it is uncomfortable. I make these points repeatedly to the coaches I train. In practice, the principle needs to be tempered by two things: first, our own confidence, competence and experience; and second, the willingness of the client to explore this territory and to do so with you.

The way clients show their reluctance varies enormously. Some will tell you outright that the topic is forbidden. Some will tell you that they might want to discuss it later when the relationship of trust between you is more firmly rooted and when they have more of a sense of how you work. This means that they do not yet feel comfortable enough with you to make themselves yet more vulnerable. Some will give subtler signs of refusal and these are the ones that we can easily miss. The client may, for instance, change colour slightly, may look away, fidget, fold their arms, hunker down in their chair, hesitate or ask for a break.

The true answer to such problems is to minimise the risk of them happening in the first place. Before you meet for the first session, make how you work as plain as you can. Describe it clearly on your website because virtually all potential clients will scrutinise you here first. By this, I don't mean the feeble coaching jargon that so many of us write, where we talk about 'working in partnership' and 'releasing your inner resources'. If you take a whole-life approach, say so – and say what this means. If you are one of the extremely rare coaches who is a qualified and experienced therapist or clinician as well as a qualified and experienced executive coach plus having managerial track record yourself, say so. If you blend coaching with mentoring, business advice or consulting, say so. Then say all this again in the chemistry conversation, only this time with some lively anecdotes, scrupulously anonymised to bring it all to life. The client may express reservations at this point, though politeness may prevent them from doing so. They may prefer instead to simply go for another coach. Be willing to explore such reservations and, if necessary, to agree that you are not a good match. It is better for this to happen at the 'chemistry' stage than in the first session.

It is good practice to ask clients to tell you what is going on generally in their lives, whether you use a tool like the Wheel of Life, or just ask them questions which will draw out the same material. If clients don't wish to talk about any of these topics, then just move on. The way I put it to clients is that I am asking them on a 'need to know' basis, rather than as a way of establishing the agenda for our coaching. So, I may need to know from them that an important relationship is deteriorating, that they have a chronic long-term health condition themselves or that their mental health is precarious. I follow the questions which have drawn out this material with something like this, depending on what they have said:

What do you need from me on this topic?

Or

How far should this form part of what we work on?

Clients vary in how they reply. Some will say the minimum that they believe is required for courtesy. Many will make it clear that they do want us to consider personal and family issues.

While writing this chapter, I worked with three clients who brought their typical work issues to the session: a difficult relationship with their boss; managing a complex new project where the outcomes remained sketchy; and how to make a scattered global group of individuals feel like one team when remote working was the only way of connecting. But each also brought personal life problems. There was an adult son with drug and alcohol addiction and still living at home; there was planning a wedding where who to invite was becoming the focus of family battles; and there was what to do about a husband whose bi-polar condition was becoming even more concerning. I was relaxed about working on these issues because, to all intents and purposes, they are about listening to the client without judgement, encouraging them to set aside preconceived ideas, looking at their influencing skills, reviewing their listening skills and knowing when they may need to find additional help. In other words, these were no different from the work issues in the kinds of questions they raise and the sorts of intervention a coach might make. None of these conversations involved more than general familiarity with addiction, family therapy or bi-polar illness, but all included the invitation to explore how to get specialist help on these same topics.

No client has ever brought me a wish to work on their own addictions, sexual issues, or asked me to be, in effect, a couples' therapist. If they did, and it's probably not chance that in 30 years of practice this has never happened, I would have to say that I was not the right person to consult but that I could probably help identify a fellow professional who was.

5

Staying Within Your Areas of Competence

I am standing anxiously beside a hospital bed, yet again. The patient is my husband, Alan, and he is there because he has had a serious accident in his wheel-
chair. His shoulder is broken. A doctor in green scrubs is sitting beside him.

'My name's Simon and I'm one of the Senior Registrars for orthopaedics and
I'm in charge of your care, Alan.'

Alan grins. Despite his pain, ever sociable, he holds out a big paw to be shaken.

An unhurried examination follows, with Simon listening carefully, talking as he
goes and asking some more questions.

He straightens up and then sits down where Alan can see him easily. We all
know that Alan is a complex case. He has so much wrong with him, so many
previous surgeries, one of which was a repair to a broken neck, and this makes
it hazardous to intubate him.

'Alan, I'm unsure what to do here. Shoulders are tricky. Sometimes it's better
to do nothing than to intervene. And there are risks for you with surgery, as we
know.'

There is a thoughtful pause, and Simon glances at me to show I'm part of the
conversation, then, 'I think I need to consult my senior here. I'll be back soon.'

This incident sticks in my mind because it is such a perfect example of a highly qualified professional knowing when he was unsure about what to do and needing to refer. A Senior Registrar in the UK is an experienced clinician, just an ace away from finishing a 15-year training, but this doctor still recognised the limits of his knowledge when it came to making such a difficult decision. He treated us as equals, involved us fully in the discussion. When he returned with the senior colleague, her opinion was that 'do nothing' was the best of several unattractive options.

There are lessons for us as coaches in how outstanding medical professionals handle these dilemmas. They are relaxed when they know they are on sure ground. They make their thinking visible to the patient. They are confident enough to say when they are uncertain because they have high levels of self-awareness. When they realise they are out of their depth, they ask for help from a colleague who knows more. Discussing this with a doctor client who IS that senior person in an unusual speciality where she has no colleagues of equal standing, she told me how often she finds herself feeling intolerably isolated, so perhaps even in medicine it's not all perfect.

This issue is usually discussed in coaching circles as if it is entirely about the borderline between coaching and therapy, but it is much wider than that. It applies to any situation where what the client presents may be beyond what you feel you can deal with. A pleasant client came to me with a brief about becoming a more effective leader after a puzzling failure to achieve promotion. He was working in a senior IT role for the British group of a Swiss-owned company. Most of our agenda was straightforward but there was one part that was not. This man spoke at about 250 words a minute, roughly twice the speed recommended for ease of understanding. He had just been given some intensely critical feedback by his boss after a disastrous presentation in Geneva where there were many non-native English speakers present. They had complained that he was incomprehensible. I, too, found him difficult to follow and had frequently asked him to slow down in our sessions. I had already raised the question of whether his rushed manner of speaking, something I assumed that he would have been doing at interview, was part of the answer to why he was repeatedly failing to get jobs, despite having been shortlisted. He had shrugged this off with a joke, saying that he had always spoken fast and that in his view this was merely a sign of how rapidly his brain worked. Now he had to take the comments seriously. I have worked successfully with many clients who have had this problem but this time I realised that I was stumped. I could see that there was much more to it than just his rapid-fire speech. Perhaps part of it was the cadences of the Geordie accent he had retained from growing up in the north-east of England? What was it, exactly? I had no idea. I referred him to a trusted voice coach who quickly made an intricate diagnosis which involved breath, diaphragm, tongue, palate as well as consonants, accent and speed. It was hard work for this client, but once he realised what was at stake he was a diligent pupil and in just a few weeks he had made significant progress.

In other professions, after achieving basic qualification you have a period of supervised learning. So, for instance, newly registered nurses have *preceptorship* which can involve logging procedures that are new to them and that must be carried out under the eye of a more experienced nurse. Teachers become NQTs – newly qualified teachers – where they have a reduced timetable, their lessons are regularly observed, they are assigned a mentor and formally assessed. Being 'out of your depth' is accepted as part of the process of making the transition from theory to practice, from beginner to probationer and from NQT to fully experienced professional. We have nothing like this in coaching, other than working with a supervisor (Chapter 29), so no wonder it is so common to worry about being overwhelmed, or sometimes, even worse, not to realise that you have been overwhelmed.

How do you know when you are out of your depth? You might find yourself going on thinking and worrying about a client long after the session is over, or even dreaming about them. During the session itself, you might have had that feeling that is often described as 'gut instinct'. The label is accurate as this is the response of our autonomic nervous system to any situation where we feel threatened. You may notice a change in breathing and an increased pulse, a dry mouth, a prickling all over your body, or your hands might feel cold. At a cognitive level, your thoughts are likely to be racing and might include:

I'm confused.

I don't know what's going on; the conversation seems to be going round and round in circles without getting anywhere.

I'm not sure what to do now; nothing I've tried seems to have had much impact.

I'm hearing things that are frightening me and I don't want to listen.

I feel on the back foot.

What I want to do feels like it would be wrong; I'm not sure what the right thing is.

I don't want to be here.

A coach described it to me like this: 'I felt a sudden adrenaline rush which made me tingle all over with heat. My stomach felt in turmoil. I wanted to run.' The occasion was the last five minutes of a session where, as the client stood up to leave, he suddenly announced that he had fallen in love with her and moved forward to touch her. She said, 'I felt in danger. I was seeing him at home. No one else knew he was there. I had to get him out of my flat.' Somehow the coach stumbled to her door, opened it and the client left. Afterwards, as many women do, she wrongly blamed herself for failing to see that the client had misinterpreted her friendliness as flirting. There had been signs that something was amiss, for instance the intensity of his gaze, and the fact that he had brought a gift to the session. The incident did lead to this coach deciding that she needed to review her assumptions about personal safety and to make changes in who had access to her calendar.

The easiest area to tackle is the one that involves technical knowledge, such as the voice and speech area I described above. When you have come to coaching from another discipline such as the law, teaching, HR or medicine, you may feel that you are on firm ground when a client raises an issue that has some bearing here, but are you?

One coach who was still in theory a practising lawyer gave me an example of how alluring this can be when a client proposed the immediate dismissal of an under-performing team member. The coach said, 'My own area had been intellectual property and the last time I handled a case involving employment law was 20 years ago. I was sorely tempted to pose as the wise lawyer as part of being the wise coach. Just in time I remembered to say "My impression is that what you've described would not fall into the category of gross misconduct and that you would be in danger of being taken to a tribunal for unfair dismissal if this is what you do. But I'm not up to date on this. Check it out with your in-house lawyers first."'

It is sensible to have a range of trusted contacts, for instance personal finance specialists, lawyers, psychotherapists, and style and image consultants. These will be people on whom you get regular feedback, while recognising that it is the client's choice about whether to take up your recommendation.

A coaching programme may be swinging along nicely when you have asked what seems like an innocent, bland question and this has provoked a wave of tears from the client. I have heard many coaches describe their great unease when this happens: 'I felt desperately sorry. I didn't know what to do', 'Had I made it happen?' The sensation of being out of your depth here is caused by assuming that you have somehow caused it and then have to make it right for the client. The answer here is that less is more. All you have to do is to listen. Being heard is enough. Most clients will not need or want you to be a parent coach, relationship counsellor, addiction specialist or mental health expert, but they may want you to understand that they have these issues in their lives. If in doubt, ask, 'What do you need from me here?' The kinds of answers clients have given me in these circumstances have included, 'I want you to know this is what's going on because it's affecting my ability to do my job' or 'I need to tell someone because it's on my mind.' Often, people will say, 'I'm not sure what to do about this problem.' Being unsure about a problem is not the same as asking you to work with them on solving it, though getting some coaching on whether or how to find specialist help may be what the client wants.

Where it can go wrong is any mismatch between what the client is prepared to work on and what the coach wants to do. So, a client can bring what appears to be a transactional issue such as, 'How do I get this meeting to work better?' The coach tries to help with immediate practical suggestions, only to be countered with, 'I've tried that' or 'yes, but...' Here, the coach has missed the underlying issue, which is the client's overwhelming need to avoid upsetting people. This means that he allows members of the meeting to ramble on, unchallenged. Or the opposite may happen – the coach eagerly treats an entirely transactional issue as if it has some enormous underlying significance and tries to ask 'profound' questions which merely annoy the client.

When coaches discuss this area, they will often speak of 'intuition'. Intuition is not the mysterious process it can seem to be. It is based on many years of internalised knowledge and experience, a build-up of awareness that tells you that something is wrong – or right. It is about making a rapid judgement. In a coaching situation, it may mean that intuition has alerted you to the probability that there is more than appears on the surface. One client promised me that she was in a fit state to make her way home after two hours of distress where she had told me about her coming redundancy. This assurance was belied by the tic around her left eye, her blank expression and the worrying slackness of her body. I ordered, paid for and then walked her to a taxi to take her home, despite her protests. Then there was the client who told me that an internal investigation had failed to clear him of a sexual misdemeanour but that he was innocent. He could not look at me while saying this and squirmed in his chair. This behaviour might have had many other explanations, but I felt sure that he was equivocating. Much later, he admitted that he had been 'too ashamed and embarrassed' to tell me the truth. Intuition is wrong as often as it is right. It may arise out of prejudice and confirmatory bias, that is, looking for evidence that a wrong conclusion is the right one because it fits with your existing opinions. Take a moment to reflect on what is going on for you if this happens: what is the actual evidence? How far does it back up your intuitive conclusions?

The more brief and transactional the coaching you do, the less likely you are to be troubled by any of the problems I have described here. An inexperienced coach may even meet these issues but not recognise them, and equally may not understand the connection between something unacknowledged that happened during the coaching and the fact that a client never reappears. But if you are prepared to work at depth and over a longer period of time, it is inevitable that you will encounter situations which tax you. Stay alert to those small signs during a coaching session that something is different or needs attention, even if you are uncertain what it is. Raise it with the client: 'I notice that you seem less cheerful today than usual...' or 'Something seems to have changed in our conversation during the last five minutes. I'm not sure what – how has it been for you?' Where you are puzzled, express it. Where the client is willing to divulge whatever it is, ask them what they need from you. If what they want is not what you can give, then say so: 'I'm more than willing to hear your story, but I'm not an expert on [whatever the issue is].'

Self-awareness is the key: *What happened here? What does this say about me? What do I need to learn from it? What do I need to look out for in the future?* As ever, take these questions to supervision because another perspective will be vital.

6

Breaking the Boundaries

Sometimes you have to break all the sensible rules about boundaries. It may be that you have reliable information that the client clearly needs and there is little point in retreating into what will then seem like the uneasy security of coaching questions. Sometimes the client is too distressed to respond with resilience; they need something else. Sometimes the client will tell you straight that what they need is not coaching because there is a watershed in their lives and what they need is different – and they need it from you. If the client thinks this is right and you think it is right, then it probably is.

Each of these situations is unique and I will describe one such here as an example of the unexpected and exceptional.

It was already obvious that this was not going to be a conventional coaching engagement.

'I'm worried about Anne-Marie.'

It was Lester, himself a trained coach, from a well-known gallery-museum. He was talking about one of his team members:

'She's not living with her husband but he still seems to be around and I'm concerned that he may be getting violent, and I don't think she's coping. I've suggested counselling but she's asked if she can talk to you.'

This was how I found myself in a small room somewhere around the back of this prestigious institution. Unlike the splendid public areas, the room was grubby, badly lit and cold. It was cluttered, making it difficult to find somewhere to sit.

Anne-Marie had separated from her husband but he was still in her life. He had a key to her flat and went into it when she was at work, giving flimsy excuses about needing to retrieve some forgotten possession or to collect a toy, if it was one of his days for picking up their 3-year-old son from nursery. The immediate cause for concern was that he was talking about taking their son 'home' to Bangladesh, his country of origin. Without consent, he had removed the boy's passport on one of his many unannounced visits to her flat. Anne-Marie lived in fear of her husband. When he lost his temper, he would seize her by her neck or hair, telling her that he needed to teach her a lesson because she had defied him. Later, when he apologised, he claimed that his violence was her fault, caused by her 'provocative' actions.

This husband's behaviour was a classic example of coercive control, a crime in the UK since 2015. When they met, he had groomed her with carefully chosen gifts and flattery. This progressed to telling her that her friends and family did not appreciate her, or interpreting their actions as hostile. He steadily separated her from them. He criticised her clothing and her accent. He accused her of 'forgetting' important details he claimed to have told her, implying that her memory and mental health were deteriorating. On one occasion, she could not find their son's money box and he told her she had imagined that the boy had ever possessed such a thing. This lie was only exposed when their son innocently babbled a story about 'Daddy taking my money box home'. He could not accept that the relationship was over. After one of his explosive outbursts, he would apologise, buy more gifts, wine and flowers, saying that his life would be over if she did not agree to return to him.

Anne-Marie had got as far as a legal separation but I wondered aloud about what had prevented her taking it to divorce. Her reply was equivocal and she quietly said something about wanting their son to stay in touch with his Bangladeshi heritage through contact with his father. She was fearful about his coded but unsubtle threats of suicide: 'What if he did it? It would be my fault.' The immediate cause for concern and the reason that Lester had raised the question of help was that Anne-Marie was describing intolerable stress, she was on heavy medication for anxiety and sleeping badly. She had lost about 20 pounds in weight over a short period of time. I asked what had changed in her husband's behaviour:

> 'He's coming round more often. He's sending me dozens of texts a day, some of them with threats, he's still got my son's passport. He's telling me I must come back to him or he'll do what he calls dying of humiliation.'

I asked what contact Anne-Marie had had with the police. She gave me a vague reply. She showed me a letter from her solicitor, urging her to trigger the divorce proceedings that had already been discussed between them several times.

It is often inexplicable to onlookers that the target of coercive control does not fight back – or just leave. The moment you look closely at one of these relationships, the reasons become obvious. The abuser does not choose people with a healthy degree of 'agency' but goes with unerring instinct for people whose sense of self is clotted by doubt, even though this is often masked by the appearance of confidence. Anne-Marie told me that her family background had been one of tragedy. Before she was born, a sibling died as a result of a hit-and-run accident in a car driven by her mother. The driver of the other car was caught and sent to prison. Anne-Marie's mother had spent many months in hospital and both parents were overwhelmed by grief and anger. She was the 'replacement' child who could never be good enough.

The targeted person is often afraid to leave, fearing more violence from the perpetrator, or harm to their children. Most sinister of all, by the time it gets to crisis point, people like Anne-Marie can have lost whatever confidence they had. They more than half-believe the perpetrator's accusation that it is all their fault, that they have brought it upon themselves. Anne-Marie's career as a promising young curator was stalling because of her inability to demonstrate enough assertiveness. As Lester described it, 'Anne-Marie is far too ready to apologise. She apologises for things that are nothing to do with her own behaviour.'

Before the session, I took the precaution of discussing this case with my supervisor. She strongly questioned the wisdom of accepting the invitation, anticipating that, as ever, when people are contemplating difficult and necessary change, their resistance to it rises. She raised the possibility that this couple were in a dance of co-dependency, or a *folie à deux*, as she put it. She emphasised the need to avoid two extremes: either of getting lured into the role of rescuer, seeing my client as pathetic and powerless, or of being so horrified by the client's pain that I became judgemental, steely and harsh.

At the start of our session, I wondered aloud with Anne-Marie about why she had asked to see me when she had spurned other offers of help:

> 'You won't remember me', she said, 'but I was one of the group in that workshop on being a manager-coach that you ran for the gallery a few years back. I thought you might be someone who could help me get myself out of this. You seemed sort of kind but tough.'

> 'Mmmm. Kindness and toughness ... So what do you need from me in this conversation today?'

There was a brief pause:

> 'I want to talk through the whole thing. I want to describe what's happened. I know what I need to do but I have no idea how to do it. You can help me do that.' She paused. 'Tell me first how you see what I've said.'

I opened my iPad and found the appalling news story from only a week before which described how a distressed, angry and controlling man kidnapped their two children from his estranged wife, shot them dead and then turned the gun on himself. Silently I handed the iPad to her.

> 'That's what I see and I am very afraid for you.'

Anne-Marie talked. Then she talked some more. It was at least an hour of telling her story.

> I said, 'Let's speak now about what you need to do immediately to protect yourself.'

Anne-Marie did not know that the police have a domestic violence unit which can provide a dedicated phone line and trained advisors. She had not taken simple precautions to enhance her physical safety, for instance by changing locks and making her flat secure in other ways. She had not instructed her solicitor to send a warning letter to her husband, or to trigger an injunction if her husband stalked her, intruded and made threats of violence. She had not changed her phone number, nor taken up her solicitor's suggestions about fast-tracking a divorce. She had not told her parents or friends the whole truth about what was happening in her life. I suggested that she should do all of this. I asked her how the healthy, resourceful part of her would respond to my suggestions and what this healthy, resourceful self would say to the frightened, damaged self that had endured such abuse.

In the last 30 minutes of our conversation, I listened again as she reeled off the list of actions that she would take. I felt sure that she would implement them.

After two hours, it was getting even chillier in the room. We stood up and dusted off our clothes. It was winter and it had darkened outside. We had already agreed that the normal rules of confidentiality could not apply and I suggested that I write an immediate email to Lester, copy to her, with a summary of our conversation. I named the points that I intended to make, including some suggestions about how the gallery could help her. These included providing taxis to and from her son's school and then on to work, then of reviving the idea of counselling or therapy for which they would pay. Anne-Marie nodded. 'That's right, it's fine to make all those points. I will be grateful if you do that and I will email him too.' As soon as I got back to my desk, I sent this email and wrote up my notes, making them a great deal more detailed than is my usual practice.

Anne-Marie's divorce happened speedily. The police gave her a liaison officer. She changed her name. Her husband returned to Bangladesh, disappeared and never paid a penny as a contribution to bringing up their son. The gallery promoted her and recently I saw her credit on the programme of a major exhibition there. We stayed in email touch for a while but we only ever had that single session.

In thinking later about this conversation, I concluded that Anne-Marie had required someone – not her boss, not her colleagues, not her doctor, not her friends, not her family, not her solicitor, not a counsellor or therapist – to tell her straightforwardly that she had to act swiftly. Her story had to stop being a secret. She needed someone who would let her tell the whole tale and, in effect, give her permission to break away and to broaden out her support network. In briefly commenting on how all those other sources of help had not helped, Anne-Marie said that each had seen her as fragile, they had undermined her with their interruptions and their well-meant pity. 'However upset you are', she said, 'you can see so clearly when people are uncomfortable, and they all were, they wouldn't sit with my unhappiness. They couldn't just listen'.

I was a stranger whom she had met only once and she had attributed kindness with toughness to me as the qualities she needed in an adviser. It was true that I had not remembered her. However, she had cast me carefully for this role and I had played it to order.

Sometimes you have to depart from orthodoxy. This was not a coaching conversation. I'm not sure what it was but it still feels as if the way it happened was the right way.

7

Faking it is Not Making it

Almost every week, my email inbox contains invitations to publicise other people's blogs in exchange for having my own sprayed out to what are allegedly tens of thousands of followers, or to take advantage of unmissable opportunities to train as a coach at bargain rates. Usually these come from the same or similar sources. These are so-called life-coaching companies trying to lure in customers with the promise that, by learning a few techniques, these beginner coaches will infallibly create rapport with other people. By creating rapport, their commercial success will be guaranteed. In more sinister style, they often convey that these techniques have supernatural powers, people will not be able to help themselves: they will be puppets, they will simply have to do what you want.

Top of the list here is a suite of techniques that cluster under the general banner of *mirroring*. If the client crosses their right leg over their left, you do the same. If they scratch their right ear, you scratch yours. The people who teach these courses claim that you can and should copy everything a client does, including their breathing. I have never seen a single convincing example of how this could work. I imagine the following scene:

Client: [looks worried] Are you OK?

Coach: [panting slightly] Yes, I'm OK, why?

Client: You seem to be struggling for breath, I was wondering if you're asthmatic.

Coach: Er … Are you OK? I thought you seem to be breathing a bit fast.

Client: [puzzled] No … I think I'm just breathing normally.

Coach: Ummm…

Please feel free to adapt this script for a cabaret turn at the next coaches'
Christmas party you attend.

We know now from many dozens of studies that warmth and rapport top
the list of what clients say works for them in psychotherapy and it must be
the same in coaching. The idea of mirroring is based on a real enough phenomenon. This is that when we are genuinely in rapport with another person,
we do look like mirror images. It's an unconscious response that results from
curiosity and respect on both sides. This is very different from deliberately setting it up in order to convince a client that we like them. Perhaps those who
run courses promising instant liking have never noticed that the intention to
deceive is obvious. These people seem to me to be the jackdaws of the coaching
world: looking for something bright and glittery without understanding that
what they have picked up may be unconvincing paste, not diamonds.

Anyone who has been the customer of a salesperson taught to seduce customers by using these techniques will instantly recognise the symptoms. Here
is an example. I am in that hallowed temple of white goods, John Lewis and
Partners. My quest is to replace my kitchen's leaking, hopelessly inefficient
fridge-freezer. I have no idea why one model is more than double the price of
another or what features I should be looking for. Such is the competition for a
salesperson's expertise on these subjects that JL has a queuing system. After
15 minutes it's my turn. My salesperson does not look happy. He forces himself to make eye contact and asks me in a sulky and notably lacklustre style
how I am today. He makes it clear he does not want a reply. We drift to the
fridge-freezer section where he languidly points to a few appliances and asks,
again forcing himself to give a pouting smile, what I am looking for. I find
myself matching him all right, but I'm matching sulk for sulk, sigh for sigh,
reluctance for reluctance. No surprise then to find that, although I entered the
shop determined to make and pay for my choice, I left without doing so, feeling irritable and disappointed.

All coaches, even the saintliest, know that we can be guilty of the same
thing. Maybe we do a better job of disguise but we never fool our clients; they
spot it all right. How do they know? Here are some signs: playing with watch,
fingers, hair or phone, foot-tapping, hand-twitching, slouching in the chair,
displaying a tiny frown between the eyes, an air of tiredness, avoiding eye
contact, and giving a pouty smile that does not reach the eyes. Watch any TV
programme with a celebrity host to see further examples of where the chilly
celeb, who has been ordered by the producers to be pleasant to 'civilians',
gives a frosty display of grimacing 'friendliness'. This is about as convincing as
the bad acting of a porn star pretending to have an orgasm.

Congruence and rapport are two-way processes. If the client can't be con-
gruent and warm with us, then it will be extremely hard for us to be congru-
ent and warm with them. We search each other for signs of rapport. All of
us are experts at interpreting what we experience. We judge by eye contact,
handshake, clothing, age, height, vocal tone, accent, facial expression, body
posture, how much space there is between us and then on how unforced all of
this seems. It is amazing how much reliable feedback there is on both sides.

Some people are stiff and shy when meeting others for the first time. It is understandable that they may be anxious about the idea that they should open up to someone they have only just met. They may be fretting about your fee or distracted by what has happened earlier in their day. They may be nervous because they are meeting you on your territory and they don't know quite what is expected of them, wondering if they can trust you. You may misinterpret any of this as hostility and sometimes it might be. Or it can be the other way around and you might be overawed by a client who is older, more senior, more articulate, more gracious. You might be meeting them on their territory where they have the power conferred by being the host. When any of this happens, you will be aware of having to work hard to avoid falling into an unhelpfully wary state. If we cannot be our true selves with clients, they are unlikely to be their true selves with us.

Coaching is about creating rapport and asking good questions. But you can't do this if you are overwhelmed with worry about whether you are competent or about whether coaching 'really works'. Your first task is to work on your ability to listen. None of us can ever get good enough at it. Notice where you distract yourself by doing any of this: thinking that you already 'know' the answer to the client's problems; wanting to share your own experience; yearning for the client to like you; having too many currently unresolved issues of your own; being unable to suspend the urge to criticise; loving to explain, interpret and theorise; feeling that you have to rescue or reform the client. All of these get in the way. They need to be replaced by curiosity, empathy, observation and the wish to understand.

Language is important. It is a myth that non-verbal communication is hundreds of times more important than what is said. If that were true then no one would ever need to learn a foreign language; we could converse with grunts and gestures. Listen for the metaphors and similes that clients use because they will be a reliable guide to the client's preoccupations. The most apparently banal clichés are worth exploring, so when a client says they are 'in a dark place', ask what kind of a dark place it is. One client who used this metaphor startled and moved me by saying, 'it's a submarine where all the lights have failed'. We spent a good 10 minutes discussing the despair that this further metaphor implied. Another client repeatedly used the word *structure* when she was telling me about how she ran her company. We looked at what this meant for her and how she coped with team members whose need for structure was considerably less than her own.

As coaches, we need to be capable of triple observation. We are observing ourselves, we are observing the client and we are observing ourselves observing. When we do this, we may notice that something has happened to the rapport. The coach is leaning forward eagerly but the client is slumped. The client is talking fast, while the coach seems to be drawling. Both parties will be aware of it at some level but the person who needs to take action is the coach – and sometimes this will mean doing some overt matching or making an immediate and obvious change in your own body and speech. The reason for doing it is not to be manipulative but to ask yourself why the mismatching has happened.

Unless we are brilliant actors, we just cannot fake rapport; it is too complex. It may grow slowly, so be patient. It can't be speeded up by inflicting 'techniques' on the client. It is certainly possible to accelerate the process by noticing what is happening and being determined to stay interested, curious, welcoming and understanding. This is very different from *acting* interested, curious, welcoming and understanding. That is the paradox. You can't do it by faking it.

Nervous presenters are often told that they can overcome their terror of speaking to a live audience by faking confidence, for instance standing tall, keeping their heads up and their voices strong. This may work for public speakers. In the case of coaching and how to create rapport, *fake it till you make it* is not good advice.

8
Switching Off Judgement

Looking back at the history of 'talking cures', it is easy to see that Carl Rogers' work and ideas were a mid-20th century turning point. They represented a distinct change from the early days of psychoanalysis where the role of the therapist was diagnosis and interpretation. To do this, you had to be cleverer and more insightful than your patient, seeing yourself as a detective-like figure who interrogated early life for clues and then made your pronouncement. Psychoanalysis became much more than that as it evolved, but there is no getting away from the emphasis it placed on the therapist's judgement.

Rogers' theories about 'unconditional positive regard' from therapist to client have been immensely influential, even though he never seems to have thought of them as an exact prescription for therapist behaviour. I see his ideas as being part of the 'human potential' movement, which began after the Second World War and whose genesis was as much social as philosophical. It could not have happened without the changes produced by two wars, universal suffrage, prosperity, the decline in religious belief, the increasing accessibility of higher education plus the changes in public health produced by clean water, antibiotics, vaccination programmes and the arrival of reliable contraception. Rogers, and other pioneers such as Eric Berne, the developer of Transactional Analysis, stressed the importance of choice. When we acknowledge that we are free to choose, we can avoid the lure of martyrdom and victimhood. As a result, we may make better quality decisions. Carl Rogers saw the role of the therapist as providing the necessary conditions where this could happen, through withholding the judgements which are a familiar and necessary part of everyday life.

Rogers' principles have been criticised, for instance by people who point out that 'unconditional positive regard' is in itself a value that the therapist or coach is imposing on clients, or that it is not enough to produce movement in attitudes and behaviour. But the underlying case for it remains as strong as ever as a starting point for any conversation in which the aim for one human being is to help the other to change. You are accepting, you do not judge. This enables the client to feel heard and, unless that happens, nothing else can happen.

That's the theory and it underpins virtually all coach training programmes. In practice, it can be astonishingly hard to do. The clue is in the word 'unconditional'. As infants and small children, what we invariably experience is that attention, love and acknowledgement are *conditional*. They are conditional on rules set by the adults in our lives; we are too small, too immature and too powerless to be able to put them into any kind of context. The rules themselves will vary hugely: be diligent at school, be physically strong, do exactly what I say, be pretty, dress nicely, honour God, be sporty, put other people's needs before your own – and so endlessly on. What we learn is that we will get love only if we obey these rules. The rules are underpinned by implicit or explicit values. It is taken for granted by those around us that diligence, physical strength, obedience, prettiness, dressing well, being godly, being sporty or putting other people first are by definition good things to be, so we generalise them to encompass our world.

As we mature, if we are lucky, we acquire the independence of thought associated with education, reading, debate and being exposed to people who are different and whose values are different. We gradually come to see that what we learnt in childhood may not be as reliable as it once seemed. There are no universally held values among human beings. Even the apparently sacred bond between mother and child is breached in those agrarian societies where boys, with their greater muscular strength, are more highly valued than girls, and where female foetuses can be aborted or girl infants abandoned and left to die. All of this we may know intellectually, while the underground river of attitudes, absorbed in childhood, may continue to run somewhere in our psyches.

For clients, our offer of unconditional regard is going to be a welcome and unusual relief from the exhausting business of defending yourself. It means that they do not have to be 'interesting', 'articulate', 'clever', 'humble' or to assume any of the many disguises and subterfuges they adopt in their everyday exchanges with colleagues and often with friends and family too. Our attention as coaches is not conditional on any of these things. It is worth pondering the word 'judgement' itself. A judge pronounces, decides on truth. Judgement involves identifying wrongdoing and then punishment. This is not the role of a coach. Where there is a difficulty, it is not our job to ask, 'Whose fault is this?' – the default mode of the world at large.

Our promise of a judgement-free zone extends to the entire cast in the psychodrama that the client brings. The client vividly describes their boss as a bully, but as their coach it is wise to hold back on agreeing. You have far too little data to know where 'truth' lies. By judging the boss, you could raise the suspicion that you will be privately judging the client. Stay neutral. The role is to raise the client's awareness of what is going on, including what part, even if just the smallest one, that the client has played themselves. Sometimes I have met the allegedly tyrannical boss or 'cold' sibling and have found them to be nothing like the description that the client has given me. This is not to criticise the client for their apparently warped view, only that you have heard it through their filter and this often innocently edits out their own part in creating a dysfunctional relationship.

It is inevitable, as you widen and deepen your coaching experience, that you will meet clients whose behaviour or beliefs you find unpleasant or with which you strongly disagree. In my own practice, I have worked with clients who held racist or sexist views. I have met clients whose obsession with accumulating money was overwhelming, and many more whose behaviour with their staff was authoritarian, dismissive and sometimes abusive. I work as a volunteer job interview coach at a charity whose aim is to get unemployed women back into work. Here, I occasionally meet women who have served custodial sentences for extremely serious crimes. It is most unlikely that in the normal run of social contact I would feel affinity with any of these people, yet they appear regularly in my coaching room and it would be unusual not to enjoy working with them.

It is not easy, nor is it in any way 'natural' to be non-judgemental. While we all have the capacity to be non-judgemental, like empathy, it has to be learnt and this learning can be painful.

It starts with self-awareness as so much does in successful coaching. In your coach training, you will most probably have done work on your own taken-for-granteds and 'limiting beliefs'. That's a helpful beginning. But, as you begin to coach beyond the sacred circle of your own colleagues and social contacts, you will find that you seem to like some clients a lot more than others. There will be some where you feel an instant and vivid sense of connection and some where you feel antipathy. Where you feel dislike, the point here is not what this says about the client but what it says about you. The first place to look is at the likelihood of the phenomenon known as *projection* or *splitting*. This means that what we fear might be true, or know to be true about ourselves, is too difficult to face, so we turn dislike for ourselves into dislike for the other person.

The giveaway is the intensity of the feeling; it is out of proportion to what the client has said. We are somehow taking it far too personally. There was a year in my life when my husband needed 24-hour care; we had minimal state help, so money was draining out of our bank accounts faster than we could put it in. I found it uncomfortable to manage my overwhelming feeling of dislike for a client whose problem was that she had a wealthy husband who wanted her to give up her career in order to be a trophy wife who lolled about at home. Poor client. She did not deserve the half-hearted coaching she received from me and she drifted away before I could address my own shaming departure from coaching principles.

Prejudice is inevitable: it is hard-wired into us. We have not evolved from the brains we had when we first emerged as a species 200,000 years ago. Then, in a small group of probably no more than 150 people, when life was short and perilous, it was essential to be able to spot the difference because difference meant a threat to survival. A disabled child, a frail elder, an incomer from elsewhere, someone who held unconventional views – all could mean disaster for the tribe. This is why we all know how to spot the 'Other', whether they have a different skin colour, a different accent, different clothing or different opinions.

In supervision, I explore my own likely prejudices and, when supervising others, encourage them to do the same. There is the coach who has a viscerally negative response to fat clients; the reason is that she has battled obesity all her life. Then there is the person who reminds you uncomfortably of someone in your earlier life, perhaps someone of whom you felt afraid most of the time. This was true for a coach whose aggressive, high-flying banking client evoked memories of her own aggressive father who had also been a senior banker.

Without self-awareness, we are likely to judge others in a generalised way on what we think of as their 'personality', while, when we make the same mistakes, we explain it away as having being caused by the situation. If I am more abrasive than I need to be in a conversation with the person who is late delivering my groceries, I will explain it by saying that it was a one-off and that I had an unusually pressing set of commitments that day; whereas if I see someone else behave the same way, I might describe them as 'rude' and 'thoughtless'.

The client is more than just their behaviour. This is why in hearing clients describe behaviour which crosses some boundary for you, the challenge is not how to condemn it but how to enquire into it. Nor do you need to imply that you approve of it. You are replacing judgement with curiosity and open-mindedness. You are exploring how decisions were made and what their consequences were, or might be. When people make mistakes, it would be rare for them to be solely responsible, so good questions here are, 'Who else was involved?' or 'Talk me through how this happened' or 'What went through your mind in the run-up to this incident?' or 'Let's discuss what's shaped your assumptions here'. Nearly always there will be a long-standing cultural element in the organisation, in the client's social environment or in their personal history which has facilitated whatever has happened.

In coaching, we are mercifully free from the need to diagnose and label. When we label other people, we imply that we know what their motivation is. We can never be certain of our own motivation let alone what motivates other people. Beware of thinking of a client as 'narcissistic', 'sociopathic', 'lacking self-esteem', 'depressive' or 'neurotic'. This is like the bad old days of clinical practice in hospitals where staff would refer to 'The Hernia in bed 2' or 'The post-op Hysterectomy who isn't eating'. These labels objectify people and narrow our view of them; we stop seeing them as unique and they become their label in our eyes. The client may have a history of depressive illness but they amount to more than their depression; it does not define them.

None of this means that you have to like or feel the same way about every client. It is not about being 'soft' or being easily manipulated. You can decline work with people where the values clash seems to make it impossible. Nor does it mean that all behaviours carry the same weight. Some of what clients describe may make you recoil in its extremity. The Christian philosophy is useful here: you condemn the sin while accepting the sinner.

As coaching has grown, it has become an attractive commercial proposition, not for people practising as coaches so much as for people selling the notion that coaching is 'easy' and a lucrative way to earn a living in a new career as a 'life coach'. They offer courses, podcasts, blogs and books. In so many of these companies, some of them very successful, what they are really doing is aiming to teach novice coaches how to replace one set of client beliefs with another. When you look carefully at how this is described, you will see that these alternative beliefs are pre-determined. They are about optimism and self-esteem. The websites are full of slogans such as 'living your best life', 'listening to your inner starlight', 'finding fluidity in joyfulness' or 'nurturing compassion for yourself'. You might say that surely these things are benign; they are what we all want – and that could be true. But it is a false trail in coaching because it starts with the assumption that the coach knows what is best for the client: *living their best life, listening to their inner child*, and so on. The coach, who may be drawn to the work because they have similar issues in their own life, already has the diagnosis and the cure before they have even had their first session with the client. They know what the problems are, they know what the solutions are. Coaches trained in this approach are at severe risk of missing what the client truly wants, engaging in a well-meant programme of ineffectual reassurance about the client's 'unique and wonderful you', probably offering some expensive and pointless 'rescuing' (Chapter 14) and entirely missing the real agenda and the underlying issues. Such coaches are fooling themselves if they believe that they have suspended judgement.

By staying open to hearing more, you may find that what starts off looking like a simple issue of right and wrong, strong or weak, good or bad, turns into something much more nuanced as you learn more about the person, their background and the immediate circumstances that have brought them to you. A client who had serious difficulties with assertiveness displayed the same lack of assertiveness in her early conversations with me. She apologised constantly, for being just a minute or two late, for her coat being 'heavy' as I hung it up, for asking for peppermint instead of regular tea. It would have been easy to have felt just like I already knew her colleagues did – annoyed by this unnecessary deference. Instead, in commenting on it in a neutral way with her, I suggested we should enquire into its biography, saying, 'If this lack of assertiveness were a person, where was it born, how did it develop, what does it do for its owner?' Her reply, which was about growing up with an angry and controlling stepfather, showed me how this client had needed the protective shield of submissiveness to keep this man's worst characteristics at bay. Her answers led to a series of productive discussions about its likely lack of usefulness in the present.

The journey to shedding judgement as a coach can be long and slow, as it has been for me. I grew up in suburban Cardiff where people's family histories, houses, décor, clothing, styles of eating and opinions were seemingly identical. There was a narrow band of behaviour that was acceptable for women:

getting married young, having children young, giving up paid work if you were a mother, being heterosexual, not boasting or showing off, being white, being British, working hard, deferring to men and to anyone in authority, being self-sufficient, being frugal – I could go on – and on. As a social environment, it was saturated in disapproval. From about 15 years old onwards, it felt stifling. But it was still a bracing surprise as a young adult to meet openly gay men when I was sharing a flat with a friend working in the theatre. Then there was a giddying first love affair with a Nigerian fellow student, then another jolt when I realised that a good friend truly loved his wife and yet had been serially unfaithful. Then I met working mothers whose children were not crazy delinquents. Then I slowly realised that nothing terrible would happen if you went against so many of these 'rules' which involved harsh judgements against people who were different.

Today I am proud to call myself a Londoner, a citizen of possibly the most diverse and tolerant place in the world, though of course we have our bigots like any other city. I have come a long way from those Cardiff days. I'm thankful that education gave me the chance to free myself from needing to operate on those tramline opinions that I remember so well from childhood, but as a journey it is still incomplete and always will be.

Coaching is not about being approving or disapproving of who the client is and what they do. It is to identify the choices, overt and unconscious, that they are making and then to explore the consequences.

9

Looking Openly at the Coach–Client Relationship

The longer I work as a coach, the more I see how different a coaching conversation is from so many others.

When you begin as a coach, you will have learnt the importance of keeping yourself out of the way. In all probability, 'It's not about you!' will have been sternly drilled into you during your training. You learn that you don't know, and you never will, what is good for the client. Then it gets interesting. You realise that you can bring yourself back into the conversation. You don't have to be a dull cipher, droning your way through a rigid set of questions. You can begin to be your authentic self. If you are not your authentic self, you will seem colourless and why should a client choose you if this is how you are? They might just as well communicate with a robot on one of those many apps that claim to offer 'coaching' and where the robot 'replies' with comments like, 'Oh gee [your first name], that sounds tricky!' or 'Tell me more about that!'

It begins from the first contact and it goes on from there. A potential client emailed me from an organisation where they were encouraged to 'interview' at least four coaches, so already this looked like a one-sided process. This was emphasised by insisting that the meeting was face to face rather than by the phone or video call that does the same job with far less hassle on both sides. I was warned that security was tight. I had to bring my passport as well as a printed copy of the potential client's email. My bag had to go through a scanner, I had to surrender my phone. The reception staff scowled, I was kept waiting for 30 minutes, the building was grubby, poorly lit and chilly. A uniformed person was my silent escort everywhere.

The potential client seemed like a palpably jumpy man. When he sat down, his feet twitched constantly and he looked somewhere over my shoulder rather than at me. In the first few moments, he combined garbled sentences about his frustration over career issues with disconcerting silences. Deciding that I had nothing to lose, because why would I want to work with anyone in this hostile place, I said, calmly and with a smile, holding eye contact with him, 'This seems like a terrible way to have this conversation. I'm feeling uneasy. It's been more like being marched through a prison than going to a place where you can have a friendly exploratory discussion with a colleague. I'm wondering what it's like for you to work here.' Somehow we limped through another 20 minutes then, abruptly, it was over. I left feeling certain that I would never see him again. To my surprise, he contacted me a few days later to ask if I was willing to work with him, 'despite everything'. I said yes.

It was now just five minutes into our first proper coaching session. I had offered him the choice between meeting at his place of work or coming to me. He chose to come to me.

> I said, 'I never thought we would set this up. You kept that meeting to the minimum and although I invited you to, you didn't ask me a single question about me or how I work, so I assumed you'd already written me off.'
>
> 'I kept it short because as soon as you were so honest about that [expletive deleted] awful building, I felt you were the right coach.'
>
> 'Well, I'm amazed to hear that. I did find your work environment intimidating and never felt that we made a connection. You seemed so uneasy and restless. You barely looked at me and your feet were tapping away throughout our conversation! I tried not to make assumptions but I did wonder if it might be me that you were objecting to. I'm wondering now whether other people get the wrong impression of how you feel about them – something to add to our agenda maybe?'
>
> 'Oh [expletive deleted]! You're not the first person who's said that! I was embarrassed about the way you'd been treated and restless because I was a bit afraid of what you might see and might judge as a result. Can we start again? I want to make that connection.'

I quote this exchange, not in itself unusual for me, only to make the point that there was no doubting its rapidly developing intense candour and humour, including his liberal use of what broadcasters euphemistically call 'strong language'. It led directly to 10 minutes of vigorous discussion of what 'making a connection' would look like, sound like and feel like from either side. I explained my belief in the value of exploring early childhood with its impact on self-image and this deeply private man agreed that he would take the risk of going along with it, including telling me to stop if he felt that I was pressing too hard. We talked about what confidentiality would mean in terms of what he felt able to tell me about being a senior leader in this organisation where national and international secrets were part of its reason for being. Then, as someone who had just blurted out an admission that he was struggling with the strains of parenthood, he asked me if I had children and, if so, how I had found their early years. I was glad to answer that I had found it perpetually exhausting and to explain very frankly why, agreeing that we could add these domestic concerns to our agenda.

I asked him how I had struck him at that initial meeting and whether or not I seemed different at this second meeting. The answer was that I had seemed 'unconventional; a bit scary as well as friendly and funny' and older than he had thought I would be; in fact, probably about the same age as his mother. We discussed how much any of that might matter, especially the mother bit where my comment was that it was hard enough being an actual mother and that I had no wish to be mother to anyone else.

I imagine that some coaches reading this might be horrified. They might consider that I had gone a lot too far in my comments about his workplace, that I should perhaps have been repelled by his 'strong language', that I should never have talked so freely, even if briefly, about my own experience of being the parent of young children, and that I was at risk of getting too soon into territory that was too personal. But, at the time and in retrospect, all of this felt entirely right. This coaching programme zoomed ahead at speed, despite its unpromising beginnings.

When a client makes a disclosure about something they feel is a shameful secret, there are two ways you can respond. You can take what I think of as the clinical view by enquiring into its aetiology: When? How often? How many? Who was involved? What purpose did it serve? Sometimes this can seem like a pointless exercise in fact-seeking. What is far more important is to ask, 'What decided you to tell me this today? How was it doing the telling?' A client who told me that at weekends she, as she put it, 'gave in to' her need for cross-dressing, answered this question by saying that she felt the time had come to talk about it and that I was her chosen listener. Only at this point were we able to discuss what this meant for her future identity and career, a subject that had been on our agenda from the outset. It had felt frustratingly obscure up until this point.

Another client, whom I'll call Bev, renowned in her sector for her alleged 'harshness', gave way to tears many times in her sessions. I asked, 'So you've decided to cry here and I'm seeing the vulnerable Bev – what's made this possible?' The answer was that in the coaching room, the vulnerable Bev was able to be present and accepted. This suggested that the vulnerable Bev would be accepted elsewhere, as she turned out to be.

What works in coaching is to put the relationship between coach and client at the heart of the process, something with which most coaches would doubtless agree without hesitation. But what is a lot less common, and I observe to be rare, is to check frequently with the client on what this means and what needs to happen to sustain the relationship. That means having the courage to discuss it openly, something that goes beyond almost all 'normal' conversations. In daily life, when feelings are under discussion, it is usually either in the heated frenzy of initial infatuation or in the angry days of a dying relationship. By contrast, a client–coach discussion is often notable for its humour, calm and maturity. I customarily start a session by asking what reflections the client has had on our last session. 'What worked for you? What didn't?' This is why two of the most important questions to ask at the end of the session are, 'How has this been for you today?' and 'How are we getting along, you and me?' It is most unlikely that clients will play their part in this without your encouragement, but when you model how to do it, including demonstrating your vulnerability and openness to their feedback, they will mostly join in with enthusiasm.

10

Being Authentic

Authenticity: possibly one of the most bandied-about words in personal development and in coaching. When you enter *coaching authenticity* into a browser, it immediately takes you to a mass of sites where companies boastfully promise that they will show you how to become 'an authentic leader'. Authenticity is the perfect example of a *nominalisation*, an abstract word which is a shapeshifter. It can mean anything you want it to mean. You can't see, touch, buy, commoditise, package or market it. By its essence it is intangible. All the synonyms for authentic are equally ambiguous: *real, natural, genuine, truthful*. No wonder it can seem so difficult to know whether we are being authentic, or just giving a display of authenticity.

This is a hard question to answer because being authentic does not mean treating the world to our every passing thought, nor giving way to our meanest impulses and basest feelings. Our wish to 'be ourselves' is moderated by our overwhelming need for approval and our fear of rejection. The balance of authenticity to inauthenticity is a constant process of dodging, ducking and negotiating, a state of interdependence. Nor is authenticity something you can 'achieve', as in saying to yourself, 'Yes, at last I am authentic'.

You can see this dance at its most extreme in politics where the wishes of the electorate for money, security and the primitive needs associated with identity will trump authenticity in politicians any day. A few years ago, I was approached by a politician who had just been fired from his government by the prime minister of the day: 'Politics has been my life and now I don't know what to do, I think I might need a coach.' Further on in the conversation, there was a candid comment that politics trains you to conceal who you really are:

'You always have to smile, never show self-doubt, be prepared to promise what you know you can't deliver. I'm not sure whether I will be capable of honesty with you, even though I know that I'd have to if I was going to get any value out of it.' I never found out the answer to this intriguing question as, a few days later, I read that this person had been offered a peerage, a low-key way for the sacked, the sick and the senior to continue their political careers.

Authenticity is closely allied to congruence, one of Carl Rogers' (Chapter 8) core conditions for successful therapy. Again, this is easier said than done. In many professions, being incongruent is built in, symbolised by clothing. A police officer client explained to me that, by putting on his uniform, he was doing his job the moment he left home. My physiotherapist wears a white polo shirt with the words *Chartered Physiotherapist* embroidered on to the pocket. Hospital doctors and nurses wear scrubs. Lawyer clients, men and women alike, arrive for their sessions in the black suits and sober shirts that they don for court appearances. When I run events for professionals who work in sport, they virtually always wear their team kit. Clothing can mask the real person. Judges, academics, mayors, military officers and priests display their robes as a way of enhancing their authority and emphasising their separateness. Looked at objectively, these disguises have a ludicrous aspect: a friend who works as a freelance housekeeper to senior professional people told me of her well-disguised amusement at meeting a High Court judge client at the height of the Covid-19 lockdown, when cases were being heard through Zoom. He was wandering through his house in full judges' kit. At their most extreme, ceremonial robes become pure theatre; the people who wear them are playing roles. Then there is the army of service-providers who wear their employer's uniform, another way of blurring individuality.

Even though there is far less formality in work clothing now, it would still be unusual for people to wear exactly the same clothing at work as they do in their leisure time. As coaches, we can give ourselves a lot more freedom. My own only concession is that I never wear jeans or sweat pants for a coaching session, but in all other ways what I wear is the same as my everyday choices. I am relieved that I no longer have any kind of suit in my wardrobe.

These choices are wider for women. It is almost impossible to avoid falling into a clichéd style of dressing, for instance Romantic Lady with ruffles and flower prints, Serious Businesswoman with some echo of male clothing, Drama Queen, Sporting Heroine, Natural Girl – and many more. Three quarters of British women wear makeup, but the question then is, how much and what sort? I ran a colour and style session for a group of young office friends, one of whom was going on holiday the next day. She had just been to a tanning booth and her skin was orangey brown, she was wearing contact lenses which changed the colour of her eyes to bright green, and her hair was a rigidly straightened, dyed white-blonde bob with extensions. Her outfit was what she herself described as 'Barbie-doll clothing'. It was pointless to waste her time with the same process that I was offering her colleagues and I asked her to return on her own after she came back from holiday. She was literally unrecognisable as the same woman, with pale, freckly skin, casually classic clothing and hazel eyes, telling me that her natural hair was what she called 'a wavy dingy ginger'. We spent most of her session talking through her compulsion to conceal the delicate looks that had been so comprehensively hidden under layers of artifice and the exhausting effort involved in maintaining it.

Male clothing customs have their own constraints. Men preparing for a job interview will agonise about whether to wear a tie. 'What if I'm the only one wearing a tie and I look ridiculous while my interviewers are in open-neck shirts?' Recently, I was being shown around a possible new apartment by a young estate agent. He kept running his hand under his collar, repeatedly unbuttoning and then re-buttoning his tightly fitting suit jacket. He caught my glance and said, 'They insist we wear this. I'm only 24 and I feel a total plonker!' Getting the exactly right apparently casual look can take a lot of effort in the media sector. The chief executive may be wearing jeans but they will be a premium brand and the buttery-leather loafers, worn without socks, will be handmade.

Clothing and make-up is just one part of the defences we construct against the world but it's an important one. I think of this when I see a local woman who, decades ago, had a role in a popular sitcom. She is never without the kooky make-up and cheerfully garish clothing that she wore on TV, despite the probability that few people will now recognise her. She seems to have become the character she played. Clients sometimes have sessions on a day off when they appear in more relaxed attire. Men arrive wearing jeans, women come without their usual make-up. It is no surprise that the sessions immediately have a more relaxed air.

Coaching is the opposite of the 'blank mirror' of psychoanalysis where the patient (sic) may still lie on a couch while the analyst sits behind their head. The idea is to encourage free association where the patient, undistracted by the therapist's nods, frowns or smiles, can say whatever comes into their mind, and where 'transference' can happen, that is, the patient begins to relive relationships from their early life by recreating them with the therapist. Freud himself was very far from always practising the remoteness that all of this implies and once admitted that he could not bear being stared at all day, so the couch came in handy.

People whose stock-in-trade is their expert wisdom may choose distinctly sterile, bland or opulent environments for their work. I meet my solicitor in a glass box with hard chairs. The room conveys 'please don't stay too long'. When I had a session with a Harley Street doctor, famous in his field, he sat enthroned behind a massive oak desk at one end of a cavernous room, while I sat on a smaller and slightly lower chair in front of him. He had a tiny frown on his face while he wrote notes – so not looking at me – with a Montblanc pen in a large Smythson leather notebook. Perhaps he was writing his journal. A meeting with a head-hunter took place in a stylish Mayfair office with subtle lighting, squashy leather sofas, soft carpets and large-scale, quirky artwork on the walls. Often, some power differential is implied in these rooms. The stage is set for a petitioner–authority exchange.

It's true that some of us work in hired rooms at business centres where all individuality has been carefully stripped away because that makes it so much easier to let the room to anyone and everyone. Or we may work at bookable tables in big hotels. Many of us work from home where we have striven to create and convey equality and ease in how the coaching room is arranged. The two chairs will match, they will be a cross between slouchy armchair comfort and the rectitude of an upright chair and there will be a low coffee table between them. There will probably be cushions, books and pictures. As people arrive and I take them to my coaching space for the first time, I always say, 'pick whichever chair you like, there's no mine and yours here...' I have a cashmere blanket within easy reach so that clients can pick it up if they want to hold something soft and comforting.

The room symbolises my belief that a core principle of coaching is that it is a relationship of equals. The client is the expert on themselves, while we are the experts in human psychology as it manifests in the coaching process. If we are executive coaches, we are also experts in organisation behaviour whose tortuous dynamics can often resemble life in a Renaissance court. While there is sometimes a case for offering information and for giving advice, mostly our role is to ask the right questions, not to come up with clever answers. 'Equal' does not mean 'the same', only that, in our different roles, we and the client share the power.

In coaching, we face our clients. As a pair of people, we are exchanging data about each other throughout the conversation; we are each under close scrutiny. Discussing this with a fellow coach in supervision, he suddenly blurted, 'The trouble is that when I show people my real self, they don't like me very much.' No wonder then that his main issue in supervision was how to manage the overwhelming feeling that he was an impostor. In his classic book, *I'm OK, You're OK* (Arrow, 1995), still in print after over 50 years and many millions of sales, Thomas Harris makes the point that positively accepting ourselves while positively accepting other people is a life position that has to be learnt. It is not a natural state because, as small children, we all absorb the impression that our parents are OK but we are not. For coaches, the I'm OK, You're OK process starts and carries on in perpetuity as the courage to take a good look at ourselves.

There is no better way to begin than to take the same psychometric questionnaires/assessments that we recommend for our clients. A single questionnaire is never enough. Three is the minimum. A Jungian Type questionnaire such as the Myers Briggs Type Indicator (MBTI) will suggest a baseline way of looking at your preferences on four dimensions and will instantly show you how certain people, radically different from you, might provoke puzzlement or hostility on your part and you on theirs. These questionnaires do not, as some people assume, stereotype, but pose searching questions about how well or badly you are using your four preferences of choice. When you take the FIRO-B, an assessment of interpersonal need and style, it can suggest what kind of impression you are making and why you may not be getting what you want in life. A trait-based questionnaire such as the NEO will assess you against the so-called Big Five personality factors: Openness, Conscientiousness, Extraversion, Agreeableness and Neuroticism.

When you put these three instruments together, it is highly likely that you will get a pleasing affirmation of your strengths, along with some surprises, plus many questions about how you interact with clients. For instance, let's suppose that you have a preference for Feeling and Judging on the MBTI, high scores on Extraversion, as revealed on the MBTI and the NEO, a highish anxiety (Neuroticism) score and a high score for Openness on the NEO, with the high needs for control and for wanting to offer and receive affection suggested by the FIRO-B. What does this mean for being authentic? These were the results of a colleague when she took these questionnaires. They told her that her authentic self was a vivid presence: sociable, likeable, open-minded but not as confident as she looked. They told her that she could talk too much and needed to work on her listening skills. They suggested that she might overwhelm clients if her eager offer of friendliness was poorly matched to clients with a cooler style: it could look needy and anxious. 'I need to calm down', she said, 'and I need to stop taking everything too personally as well as trying to put too much structure into my sessions'. This coach had high levels of honesty and compassion, for herself and for others. She was able to look at how and why she had made mistakes and she had the courage to be imperfect. She was embarked, as we all need to be, on a lifetime's quest to build on the strengths and to manage the imperfections.

That is why a key part of being authentic as a coach is to understand the importance of forgiveness. Forgiveness starts with self-forgiveness and with accepting that perfection is impossible. You are just one human being working with another and doing your best. A few years ago, I made an inadvertent but serious professional mistake. It could have had grave consequences and I still don't know for sure whether it did. The process of coming to terms with my blunder was painfully slow. I cringed when I remembered it and I remembered it many times a day for many weeks, berating myself for my stupidity and thoughtlessness. Slowly, I realised that there was learning in this incident and that it did not define me as a human being or as a coach. I could move on.

Seeking and listening to feedback is as important for us as coaches as it is when we recommend it to clients. When you ask clients for feedback at the end of a session, it is unlikely that you will get much that is detailed, though every now and again, if you ask for specifics, you might hear some gems. Feedback that is collected by a third party or carefully moderated in group supervision is far more likely to be candid. Like colleagues, I have a variety of ways around this issue. Survey Monkey is a free or cheap way of sending an anonymous questionnaire to former clients as long as you can construct the items simply and in a way that will give you something meaningful. When you are on a preferred suppliers list, the organisation may be collecting feedback on you, though you will probably have to press to see it. Again, this may just consist of bland statements which tell you little, but just occasionally there may be some nuggets of treasure. This was how I discovered that one civil service client judged my coaching the best development experience he had ever had because 'she is direct and doesn't faff about or constantly ask "How does that make you feel?"' Another spotted that I had over-used summarising in the dying phases of our coaching. She was quite right – I had – a sure sign that we should have ended the engagement long before we did. Too much summarising was a trustworthy sign of an exhausted agenda.

The most reliable way to get feedback is to ask a fellow coach to collect it for you, ideally by interviewing clients in the same way that you would collect feedback yourself for them (Chapter 20) or through an email process. People will always be more frank when they know that anonymity is guaranteed. You might offer a fellow coach the same service in return so that no money needs to change hands. The questions are simple:

- What did you gain from coaching with X?
- How are you using these gains in your everyday and work life?
- What would you say X's strengths are as a coach? Please give specific examples.
- No coach is perfect, so what would you say X does less well? Please give specific examples.
- On a scale of 1–10, with 10 being extremely ready, how ready would you be to recommend X to a colleague or friend?

All of these are ways of preparing yourself for circumstances that you know could create self-doubt and uncertainty for you, such as a first session for a very senior client from a new organisation or making a pitch for new work. In such situations, the temptation to fall back on our inauthentic selves can be strong, but you will already know from your client work that the more you live inauthentically, the greater the potential for distress. In the end, it is about openness, an ability to empathise with people who are different, and a constant process of ruthless, merciful, unbiased self-examination.

11

Exploring the Backstory

Coaches can be nervous about asking for the backstory: an account of the client's early life. We can worry about how the client will receive the request. What if a highly paid senior executive stares at you with hostility, saying, 'I've come here for coaching, not for psychotherapy'? What if they start at age 18 and entirely leave out their childhood? Then there is the danger of asking a question where you might not know what to do with the answer. What if the client tells you an horrific tale of sexual abuse or breaks down as they give you a bleak narrative of deprivation and sadness? What if the client starts crying and can't stop: have you caused this distress? What do you do about it? What if they just refuse? What is the point of it anyway?

Despite this common uneasiness, I am still surprised to encounter coaches whose training has omitted any reference to soliciting autobiography. The case for including it seems to be so strong. In coaching, we are working with clients who say they want something to change. It is usually important enough to dominate their lives: they have already consulted their friends, colleagues and family and are still no nearer to making the changes they say they want. Just stating the issue will often suggest what the answer should be:

I'm miserable in my job. Solution: change jobs.

I'm working too hard. Solution: work less.

My relationship is making me unhappy. Solution: improve it or end it.

I'm being bullied. Solution: confront the bully or leave.

If the solution were as easy to implement as it is to describe, then the client would not be sitting in front of you because they would already be doing whatever they needed to do. The client who, in theory, needs to change jobs will tell you that the known misery of a job they hate is better than taking the risk of moving to the unknown which, for all they know, might be ten times worse. The client who complains of overwork will describe a culture where anyone who appears unwilling to answer emails at midnight is considered to be uncommitted and will be rapidly sidelined. The client in a miserable relationship may fear causing multiple hurts to others, where the guilt would be worse than living with their own hurt. The client who is the target of a bully may tell you that the possibility of retribution is more than enough to keep them compliant with the bully's behaviour.

We give ourselves multiple reasons why we can't change and almost all of them will have a direct connection with attitudes we acquired in childhood. The person who fears changing their job may have lived in a household where parents fretted about the possibility of a descent into crippling poverty if you took a risk by finding new employment: 'Better the devil you know' might have been their mantra. People who overwork may have learnt that love depended on achievement. Someone who stays in an unrewarding relationship may have learnt from their parents that pleasing others is more important than pleasing yourself. The bully's target may have been dominated as a child by a harsh parent and learnt that acquiescence was safer than confrontation. I find repeatedly that clients have never made these connections. Rather, they believe that their attitudes and assumptions are self-evidently true. Sometimes they see these beliefs as having the force of superstition. They think that if they are disregarded, some nameless horror will follow. As implicit rules for living, they have been totally taken for granted.

Unless you draw out this material, it will potentially lead you to the kind of coaching where the client plays along with the 'obvious' solution and then, mysteriously, never makes those changes. Or, in your frustration at the client's lack of progress, you find yourself giving them a little lecture, for instance on the principles of time management or your own interpretation of why organisations appear to tolerate bullies.

I have never yet worked with a client who refused to tell me about their childhood, but what they say may be heavily edited, with the most important data censored, either permanently or until the point where the client feels that they can trust you. The give-away that you are not hearing the full story could be fractional hesitations as they speak, or the client appearing to hurry over their account of their early years, or telling you that it was the kind of unremarkable and happy childhood that is not worth talking about. Sometimes they will say frankly that there is more to the story and that they will tell you what it is at some later stage. You may want to enquire into the reasons for their reticence or just nod and let it go, noting that the client is probably giving you permission to ask later for more detail, or that they will do it unbidden when they are ready.

It was in this spirit that I learnt in her first session that a client had been the daughter in a military family and that she had moved schools five times before she was 12 years old. It was a full six months into our work before she said that she had developed obsessive compulsive disorder (OCD) at the age of 11. It had been so severe that she had missed a whole year of school. I asked her how this had shaped who she was as an adult. Her reply was that it had given her insight into and tolerance for anyone with a mental health issue, including people in her team. Treatment had made a difference but OCD was still a problem. She explained how it might intrude into our sessions, for instance with what might otherwise have seemed puzzling requests to repeat some of the comments I was making to her.

I worked with one client for eight months before he told me that he had been adopted as a baby. His parents were people who, as he put it, 'would never, ever, be approved as adopters today', saying that the adoption had been about their needs as an infertile couple rather than about his needs as the child. I already knew that he had cut off communication with his parents. He had described their cold, controlling style of parenting, but the full horror of his life as a doubly rejected small child had to wait to be told. He needed to be certain that we could link it with his dawning understanding that it held the key to so much that was preventing him from doing his job well.

There is no one right way of asking for autobiographical material. Your choice will depend on how much time you are likely to have with the client, their stated goals, your own preferences and your assessment of what might help this particular client tell their story. Where the coaching programme is short, then the 'lifeline' approach can work well: a simple graph where the horizontal axis is time and the vertical axis goes from 'low points' to 'high points'. You can send it in advance so that the client brings it to the session with some of their thinking already done and with plenty of time to consider what they are prepared to disclose. Some coaches get impressive results from sending clients a brief questionnaire with ample space for the replies. This might include questions like:

- What's the immediate trigger for coaching?
- What would you like to change in your life in the longer term?
- What do I need to know about you in order for us to work well together?
- When you are at your best, what is happening?
- When you are at your worst, what is happening?
- What feedback do people give you about what it's like to work with you?
- What do you like best about your life?
- What do you like least about your life?
- What's the hardest decision you have ever made?
- Which relationships in your past have had most impact on you?
- What motivates you?
- What scares you?
- If there was one thing in your life that could improve it, what would that be?

These questions get at autobiographical material sideways because almost every client will talk about how the past has shaped their present. Alternatively, you may have your own list of favourite questions. These might be about birth order, parents' occupations, parenting style, the relationship between parents, which parent the client was closer to and why, sibling relationships, what was encouraged and discouraged in the household. A powerful question here is, 'How safe and loved did you feel as a child?'

For clients who seem as if they might appreciate a more creative approach, I have a box of dolls made to scale for dolls' houses. They include adult men and women of a variety of types, dress styles and ages, children of both sexes, a baby, dog and cat. I ask clients to represent their family 'system' by choosing and then setting out and moving these little figures. Although I have never done it myself, I know of coaches who have asked clients to draw their childhood as a kind of screenplay – no artistic ability required, just a series of 'frames' – or to bring a selection of family photographs, easily done now by putting them on to a phone.

Some coaches get good results simply from asking the client to draw a family portrait, looking, in the discussion that follows, at who is in the picture, their relative size, their configuration, facial expressions, body language and clothing. One coach told me of the excellent results she gets from having a flip chart sheet, a pile of magazines, scissors and some glue, then inviting the client to make a collage of their life story. Yet another approach is to reach for the same material through asking about role models when the client was growing up: Which stories did they love? Who were the heroes or heroines of these stories? What was it that they liked about the story? If they could have a dinner party where they could invite anyone, living or dead, fictional or real, who would be there? What is it about these people that appeals? If they were telling the story of their life as a film or as a TV show in eight or nine episodes, where would the dramas and twists be?

Whichever approach you use, you need to tell the client why you are asking these questions at all, explaining the link between childhood and current beliefs. You might want to explain how neuroscience shows that childhood experience shapes our brain, nervous system, cardiovascular system and immune system as well as our mind. The body remembers, even when we have no explicit memories to draw on because we were too young. In the extremely rare event that the client baulks, then just accept it calmly and move on. Some clients may worry that their story is 'boring' or that they can't tell it 'well'. Reassure them that no life is 'boring', though a client who starts apologising in this way is inadvertently giving you many clues about their seemingly anxious attitude and their fear that others will be judging them as inadequate.

Be clear what you are listening for. Our experience of growing up is our first exposure to the politics of power, so who made the rules and how were they enforced? Childhood is our first experience of living inside a system, so what was the interplay between parents, parents and the rest of their families and then between parents and children? How were conflicts resolved or not resolved? How safe did we feel? When we felt unsafe, as all of us will have felt at some point, what was going on? How secure did we generally feel? What rules for living were overtly and covertly enforced in the household, for instance over how to treat other people, attitudes to achievement, education, religious faith, authority and work? Where clients have come for career coaching, there is much to be said for enquiring more closely into family traditions around work. This can be especially relevant when clients are from professions where there can be dynastic expectations, for instance farming, the law, media, acting, architecture. Would that 18-year-old make the same decision today to follow a mother, father and grandfather into medicine?

If you have yet to do an autobiographical exercise yourself, then it may be worth giving it a try, perhaps with a fellow coach or your supervisor, using the method of your choice. With my friend and colleague, Jane Cook, before we settled down recently to a pleasant supper at my apartment, I opened my box of dolls with a flourish and suggested that we should take it in turns to tell our stories through these mini puppet theatre 'plays'. Our question to each other was, 'What helped form the coach I am today?' Although we had both done similar exercises previously, each of us was astonished at the new insights that this tactile and visual experience gave us.

In the telling of and listening to this story, it's the client who makes any interpretations, not the coach. Few of us have told our life story this way before and most find it enjoyable. After all, we are talking about our favourite subject – ourselves. Ask, 'what themes do you see here?' or 'How do you feel these experiences have shaped who you are now?' The answers may surprise and move you:

> 'I realise I have always been an under-achiever and I need to stop sabotaging myself – it's why I'm here with you now.'

> 'I'd love the opportunity to tell Mr X, the one teacher who helped me so much, how greatly I appreciate everything he did for me.'

> 'I had the incomparable gift of loving parents who have always supported me.'

> 'I would like to go back to that 14-year-old to reassure her that she will be OK.'

You will be looking for clues to the client's attachment style and how it was shaped in childhood, and listening out for any experience that might have been traumatising, the subject of the next two chapters. Asking these questions and listening to the replies remind me, as so often in coaching, that we are looking for what clients can teach us, rather than for what we can teach them.

12

Understanding Attachment

In the 1930s, a young psychiatrist was beginning the research that would permanently change attitudes and practices towards what it meant to raise a child successfully in the western world, including what was likely to happen if you separated children from their parents. He had ample reason to know much of this at first hand. He was the fourth of six children in a wealthy family whose mother delegated virtually all of their care to nannies and nursemaids. He rarely saw his father. He was sent to boarding school as a 7-year-old, a practice that has chillingly been described as 'privileged abandonment'. His name was John Bowlby. His work into what was then known as 'maternal attachment' was taken further by his colleague, Mary Ainsworth, who first identified 'attachment styles'. In the many decades of research that have followed, including by neuroscientists, it is clear that brain, body and behaviour are shaped by our earliest attachment experiences. As coaches, we simply can't afford to be unaware of this work, starting with its impact on ourselves.

To understand the radical influence of these ideas, you have to look to the popular childcare books of the early 20th century. The assumptions were that children became attached to their mothers as a response to getting food. If you provided food, you were proving care. To raise an independent and 'unspoilt' child, you would deliberately withdraw your attention. Children were left to cry because, if you rushed to comfort them, they would believe that they were little emperors, becoming demanding and selfish. This regime did produce independent people but not in quite the positive way that its proponents imagined. Everything was about routine that suited the parent: food, sleep, attention, bowels and bladder. Few thought it odd to exclude parents from visiting their children in hospital, a policy justified on the grounds that such visits made the children 'upset'. Nor did the government worry too much about the emotional and physical impact on thousands of children who were abruptly evacuated during the London Blitz of the Second World War to be fostered in physically, but not necessarily psychologically, safer places by strangers.

Bowlby and Ainsworth showed that the need for long-term physical and emotional attachment to a few primary caregivers is instinctive in humans as it is in other mammals. Humans who could attach and be attached would have a survival advantage because they would not have to operate alone. Ainsworth's research suggested that we develop different attachment 'styles'. These are the result of interaction with our primary caregiver, in their turn the result of his or her attachment experience. Attachment styles are not necessarily fixed, nor are they the sole result of our primary carer's style. Inborn temperament plays a part and early experiences can be modified by what happens later in life. Nonetheless, attachment experience is a crucially shaping part of who we are. Attachment is about security: could we express our feelings, did our carers respond kindly and consistently, did we have a stable base from which we could explore the world? Attachment experience is likely to affect our mental health, ability to communicate, attitudes to love, sex, authority and career. It is increasingly clear that it also affects our physical health. Adults who had unfailingly stressful and chaotic attachment experiences in childhood are more impulsive and less able to self-regulate. They tend to take more risks, have many more illnesses and die much younger than people whose carers were loving, dependable and stable. The worse the childhood story, the more obvious the impact on the brain – for instance, a smaller prefrontal cortex and hippocampus.

Attachment is about our ability to be emotionally close to another person without creating a mask or becoming unhealthily dependent. Its essence is how we manage intimacy. Can we give it and receive it with grace? Are we so anxious to have it that we swamp others with our neediness? Has our experience been so damaging that we push others away?

As coaches, our first task is to interrogate our own experience.

Secure attachment: roughly 50% of the general population will demonstrate this style. Your primary caregiver was centred, steady, responsive and loving. You believed your caregivers were emotionally available and reliable so this is how you face the world. You can balance the need to be dependent with the need for autonomy. You have realistic views of yourself and high levels of intellectual openness with a tolerance for ambiguity. You will believe in the possibility of self-growth; your relationships will be long term, characterised by mutual trust. As a coach, you will be flexible, you can compromise. If you don't see a client for a while, you feel sure that they will get in touch at some point and if they don't, then there will be some ordinary explanation. You can stay on friendly terms with former clients but you don't feel stabbed by resentment if they move on to another coach or if you fail to be the chosen coach after a 'chemistry' session. You don't see coaching as hard work, there are few dramas in your coaching life and you don't play manipulative games with clients.

Insecure-anxious attachment: about a quarter of the population might have an anxious style. Your primary caregiver was preoccupied, inconsistent and often unavailable: physically, emotionally or both. Sometimes they were affectionate, sometimes they were cool or angry; sometimes they were over-demanding of your love; it was hard to know which version you would meet at any one time. You are engulfed by your need to be loved and you want people to prove their love overtly. You are preoccupied with wanting to get close to people but may find that they experience you as overwhelming and needy. You want instant intimacy. You worry all the time about being rejected and abandoned, seeing relationships as fragile and unstable. If you fear this is happening, you may lash out or threaten. You find it hard to listen to critical feedback because it feels like a personal attack.

A client came to me for coaching where her agenda was about being more assertive. I noticed that she was never without a tightly balled-up cotton handkerchief in her hand and that she touched her nose with it constantly. In these days of throw-away tissues, handkerchiefs are rare. Asking gently about the handkerchief led to telling me more of the story. This client's mother had experienced a postnatal psychosis that had been severe enough for her to have been hospitalised and her baby daughter fostered for her first year by a grandmother. Her mother recovered but the client described the entire family as 'tip-toeing around'. The constant phrase in the house was 'Don't upset your mother'. The client said, 'Sometimes it was fine, she felt well and she'd be lovely, other times it was like no one was at home. Her needs always had to come first and I spent my childhood trying to please her.' The handkerchief habit had started as a self-soothing bedtime ritual and she had been unable to give it up as an adult in situations where she felt she might be being judged. This client was unnervingly anxious with me. It was a long time before the handkerchief could be put away and she stopped saying what she thought I wanted to hear.

When you are a coach whose attachment style is anxious, you will probably find it easy to create rapport with people. They will experience you as open; transparency may be one of the qualities they admire. Being a coach may awaken your neediness; in response, you may be tempted into rescuing, colluding with clients by agreeing that all their problems are other people's fault, or offering extra sessions unpaid. Anything might be better than feeling that clients don't like you. It's hard to avoid wanting to talk about yourself, sharing your own experiences when they seem to be parallel to the ones the client is describing. You constantly worry about causing offence and yet sometimes you are tempted to play games with a client as a way of keeping their attention. You may misjudge clients, pushing them too hard to talk about their most upsetting worries; secretly, you feel connected when they cry. You may have problems with boundaries, perhaps trying to be a therapist when you do not have the training, or struggling to turn a client into a friend when they are giving you clear signals that this is not what they want.

Insecure-avoidant attachment: about a quarter of people in any given population may have an avoidant style. Your caregiver was aggressive and cold a lot of the time. They may have been demanding, critical, chilly and dismissive, emotionally and physically absent, pushing you away. Alternatively, you may have experienced a kind of benign neglect. This was the case for a client whose Indian parents were forced out of Uganda by Idi Amin. They abandoned a prosperous life there, arriving in the UK as a penniless young couple. They started with a single corner shop and built the business into a chain that was part of a mini property empire. My client was the youngest of five brothers. He said, 'We always had decent food; they took care that we went to good schools but that was where it began and ended. I'll never know why they had so many children when they showed no interest in us: they worked 24/7 and we were expected to work too, either in the shops or collecting rents. There was no tenderness.' This client had intellectual insight into his parents' trauma but he was steely in his indifference to them. At work, he puzzled and alarmed people with his cool, over-formal style.

When you grew up with parents who were remote and preoccupied, you learnt that you would be rebuffed if you asked for love so to protect yourself you became impassive and distant. As an adult, you dread being enmeshed in other people's feelings because your aim is to be self-sufficient. If things get too emotional, especially if other people get clingy, you feel a strong wish to escape. You need time alone. You see feelings as mawkishness, as a weakness; you can't bear sentimentality.

As a coach, you can stay steady in the face of a lot of intensity from a client. You bring your analytical skills to bear on their problems and your objectivity can be welcome. You are drawn to performance coaching or mentoring because the goals seem objective and measurable; you are less interested in your own or your clients' internal dialogue. You may be inclined to dismiss psychological explanations of behaviour as 'fluffy' or 'psychobabble'. If clients make distressing revelations, you can listen calmly without thinking that it is your duty to get involved. You see a clear boundary with therapy and sometimes you miss signals that the client wants more. Some clients may find you too detached, your approach too forensic.

These portraits are maybe a little crude. Many of us will have more nuanced attitudes which blend more than one attachment style, but I do see these patterns all the time in the coaches I teach and supervise. A promising coach came to me for supervision specifically to discuss her attachment style, aware that it might need managing. As a 6-year-old, she had been trapped in a house fire and had survived burns to her face, torso and hands. She had been in hospital for many months at the tag end of the policy forbidding parents to visit. Her comment was, 'I learnt that no matter how hard you cried, no one came, or they just told you to be a brave girl. I've kept up that I'm-no-trouble smile, but all the time I dread that clients will reject me. I overdo the helping, I'm constantly looking for ways to show them that I'm not an impostor, I get into rescuing and I need to stop.'

Another coach and I agreed that he protected himself with his avoidant style. He was the only child of parents who had been in their late 40s when he was born. They had discouraged closeness; he had never experienced hugs and kisses. As a teenager, he was sent to a famous boarding school where he cultivated a jolly sportsman exterior and became an elite athlete. He trained as a coach at the point where his active sporting career was coming to an end.

He was troubled by the notion that clients, especially the women athletes he was coaching, would do what he called 'over-confiding'. He confessed that his wife constantly looked for overt signs that he loved her and that he had no idea how to say the words that would reassure her. He was puzzled: 'I don't have those words in my vocabulary.'

Everyone has an attachment style, so what happens when the attachment styles of coach and client meet?

A coach with a secure attachment style will probably be able to work with any client, whatever their attachment style. A securely attached coach with a securely attached client is already off to a positive start. Both will be able to create rapport and trust. Each will be flexible about how much depth and intimacy they need in the relationship. They will be comfortable with giving and receiving feedback and there will be a high level of openness in the coaching conversation. These are the partnerships that get renewed, sometimes stretching over several years when the client changes job or faces new challenges in an existing job. It would not occur to either client or coach that there was any worrying dependency in the relationship. When the coaching has run its course, coach and client might become friends.

The secure coach will find it more taxing to work with either anxious or avoidant clients. Anxious clients may need to learn what the boundaries are about contact between sessions so it will repay the small investment in time to discuss and clarify how much contact you feel is appropriate. Feedback will need to be carefully calibrated so that it does not appear to be a personal attack. The client may ask for a style of coaching which is nearer to psychotherapy and each coach will have to decide where their personal boundaries are here. I have observed from my own work with anxious clients that they can sometimes relax and learn how to be less anxious simply by how they work with us. I might discuss attachment styles with this kind of client when it becomes obvious that many of their relationship problems, at work or at home, stem from their fear of abandonment, criticism and rejection. I might then raise this issue as part of the 'how are we doing, you and me?' discussion at the end of each session. This could involve, for instance, discouraging them from trying to please me with vague flattery. I might ask for some more honest comment instead.

It would be common for executive coaches to work with clients whose attachment style is avoidant. Avoidant behaviour is characteristic of the senior levels in many organisations and people may be hired specifically for their ability to stay aloof or to be 'robust'. Staff may be explicitly told that they should leave their personal problems at home. A chief executive might operate through cultivating one-to-one relationships, generating a culture of suspicion and criticism, explicitly avoiding the interdependency involved in creating a team. Managers will often espouse policies on issues such as bullying, diversity, safeguarding and whistleblowing which say the right thing, while everyone in the organisation understands that this is merely paying lip-service. This may be linked with giving the appearance of emotional intelligence, the phenomenon which is sometimes called *cognitive empathy*, meaning that the person can simulate empathy but it is entirely an intellectual process, as feelings are not genuinely involved. These clients can be demanding (see Chapter 17) because they can be determined not to let you see their vulnerability. A secure coach working with an avoidant client will struggle to establish a personal connection and the work might feel frustrating and superficial. With these clients, staying centred and waiting patiently may often produce positive change. One danger is that a secure coach might tolerate unacceptable behaviour for too long from either anxious or avoidant clients, giving them the benefit of the doubt when respectful confrontation might produce a better result.

Anxious–avoidant is the tricky pairing because whichever party has which-ever style, their needs for closeness are always at odds. One party yearns for more intimacy and the more they press, the more the other will protest by creating yet more space. I observed a trainee coach getting into this fated dance with a client. Her own attachment style was anxious; it seemed to me that the client's style was avoidant. The client started the session by saying that he wanted to discuss how to persuade his wife to abandon their latest attempt at IVF. The coach rightly objected, saying earnestly that the choice was down to the two of them and she only had one of them in the room. The client scowled a little so the coach then said, unnecessarily, 'I'm sorry if I've offended you'. When he made no reply, she apologised again. Stumbling over her words, she suggested that the decision was intricately connected with the health of the couple's relationship generally, a perfectly reasonable conclusion but one that seemed to suggest wanting to discuss the client's marriage.

'I don't want marital counselling; I came here for coaching!'

'Oh gosh, I'm sorry, I've done it again...'

The coach looked flustered and launched into an account of her frustration and disappointment at the delay in conceiving her own second child. In her panic, she had entirely missed the point of the client's problem and was making a clumsy bid for intimacy through this unwanted revelation. The session wob-bled on. Later, when the client had made a pantomime performance of looking at his phone and of announcing that he had to leave early, the coach sat with me in tears. Over the next few days, she emailed the client several times with a mixture of further apologies and unsubtle hints that his own reticence was at the core of what had gone wrong, despite my strongly worded advice not to do so. I was certain that he would have read these emails as accusations.

This coach and client were in the unhappy situation of unwittingly trigger-ing each other's rawest insecurities. They were never able to find the neutral ground where coaching could have been valuable. A further issue is that trying to resolve the problem through a direct discussion will rarely appeal to some-one whose attachment style is avoidant because the resolution process itself will feel threatening.

When an anxiously attached coach meets an anxiously attached client, the coaching may be problematical. Both parties could be obsessively monitoring the other for signs that they are liked. There may be too much sharing too soon of personal information, too much smiling, too many pleasantries, too much time spent on enquiring into each other's health and wellbeing. Despite eager exploration of the various problems, it seems that no action is happening. At this point, each might fret that they are to blame, yet continue with the coaching for fear of being disliked. Collusion is likely, with the coach dreading challenging the client and the client hesitating to express doubts about whether the coaching has value for them. Sometimes there may be some co-dependency, where the relationship begins to have the external appearance of being a friendship, with too many out-of-session conversations and a great deal of indiscreet gossiping where boundaries are constantly breached on both sides. Despite the appearance of intimacy, there will be a lack of honesty in the conversations and ultimately the coaching is likely to peter out because it is neither a friendship nor a professional partnership.

An avoidant client working with an avoidant coach will most probably be a doomed relationship for different reasons. Both may agree to limit the length of sessions or seek to have them via virtual means so that they do not have to be in the same room. Dates may be changed at the last minute. When the client does this, the coach may feel relieved: *thank goodness I don't have to meet that person.* Sessions may seem like role plays, with both parties straining to appear the good coach or good client, but neither side will be fully present. It will be difficult to have honest conversations about what is going on in the relationship itself: both will be eager to avoid it. Much of the coaching time may be spent on externally based issues such as the dysfunctional behaviour of others in the client's team or of the allegedly toxic nature of the organisation's culture. There may be extensive discussions of theoretical models, their validity, rival models, the history of leadership, books the coach or client have read, which throw light on all of these ideas. Real progress is unlikely.

There is a fourth possible attachment style, usually described as *disorganised*, the result of protracted abuse in childhood. I have only worked with one client who fell into this category. Her account of the sexual abuse she experienced in childhood was horrifying to hear and she recounted it as if it had happened to someone else. She combined explosive accusations about my lack of skill as a coach with, only a few moments later, tearful pleas not to abandon her. She was a highly paid young executive and the coaching help I could give her was minimal and mercifully brief.

Learning about attachment styles has many benefits. It is a further way of understanding yourself. All good coaching starts here. It gives you a framework for understanding your own conflicts at home or work, as well as those same issues that clients bring to you. You may decide to share attachment theory with clients: it will depend on the client, on how much time is available and your judgement about whether a theoretical explanation will help. It probably will. Some clients are intrigued enough to put it on our agenda as work in progress after I have reassured them that these styles are not fixed. They can change through insight and through committing to the hard work of learning new ways of thinking and behaving.

Attachment experience is closely linked to understanding trauma, the subject of the next chapter.

13
Becoming Trauma-aware

Perhaps you've been a coach for a few years now. Starting from a modest base, you feel that your reputation is building well. Clients recommend you and several of them return for further coaching. You are enjoying the work, you like your clients and they like you. Yet there's a niggle; something is lacking. When those clients come back for more coaching, you can get that sense of déjà vu: haven't we been here before? Sometimes the sessions run out of energy and end early. The smaller problems have certainly been dealt with but the bigger ones still lurk – repeated patterns of behaviour that create dysfunction, yet the client is an outstandingly successful professional. Alternatively, there may have been some coaching sessions where the client has unexpectedly raised a personal issue and this has evoked a level of emotional turbulence in you which it has felt taxing to manage. Progress feels slow; you suspect that there are slippery invisible blocks that you cannot quite grip.

If these scenarios seem familiar then perhaps it is time to take the leap, as I have myself, into bringing an awareness of trauma to your work. I have been lucky to count Julia Vaughan Smith a friend and colleague for more than 20 years. She is an experienced executive coach alongside being a fully qualified and experienced psychotherapist. Some years ago, she began to study with Franz Ruppert, Professor of Psychology at Munich University of Applied Sciences, and has brought his theories about trauma into the coaching world. She and I now run masterclasses for coaches and therapists alike to introduce them to these ideas.

The word trauma can terrify coaches. Isn't this exactly the sort of thing that coaches are constantly warned to leave severely alone? Be assured that being a trauma-informed coach does NOT mean being a trauma therapist. It does mean understanding the wholly common impact of childhood trauma, so common that, in most of my own clients, it will be playing at least some part in the issues they bring to me.

There are five myths about trauma and coaching which it is as well to name and dispense with immediately.

Myth 1: Trauma is about post-traumatic stress disorder (PTSD) associated with war veterans, or people who have had a serious accident.

Truth: War and accidents can certainly be traumatising but trauma-informed coaching means interpreting trauma in a more everyday way as the lasting effect of attachment failures in early life with a permanent impact on our neuro-physiology. It is not an event, but the result of a series of events. It doesn't go away over time but might become more intense through being ignored or denied.

Myth 2: Trauma wrecks people's lives.

Truth: It does for some people, but, paradoxically, when you interpret trauma the way it is described above, it can be associated with success. People who overwork as a result of traumatising experiences in childhood can often reach the highest levels in organisations.

Myth 3: Trauma from childhood experience is rare.

Truth: It is extremely common. Most of us will have some kind of 'trauma biography' because our parents might, despite their best intentions, have exposed us to feeling unsafe; or else life events, over which they had no control, might have created traumatising experiences. These might include serious mental or physical illness, unemployment, poverty and bereavement. Trauma results from our earliest experience, from conception onwards. It arises from any severe stress a mother might have experienced in pregnancy and from the relationships with our earliest and closest caregivers. All forms of insecure attachment are examples of trauma survival.

Myth 4: If you've been traumatised, you will remember it clearly.

Truth: The memory centre of the brain develops slowly and it is probable that when we have experienced trauma as young children, we will have no specific memory of what happened. We may have little idea of the impact it has had on us.

Myth 5: Coaching has nothing to do with trauma.

Truth: Trauma is most likely there in our coaching rooms every week, so it is essential to know it and recognise it and to know what to do when we meet it.

It is confusing that the word trauma is correctly used to describe a physical injury, the result of an accident or surgery. This is easy to understand because you can see the wound. Psychological trauma is different. It is why, in the First World War, traumatised soldiers were accused of cowardice or their behaviour was described as 'shell shock'. In my husband's family, a grandfather returning from this war received sympathy for his severely gas-damaged lungs, but his lasting withdrawal into numbed silence met bewilderment and hostility.

Psychological trauma happens when we feel threatened and unsafe. We cannot escape so the fight-or-flight response is stifled and we freeze. As infants, we are helpless so any interaction with carers which persistently denies us love, attention, recognition, holding and soothing can trigger this freeze response. Witnessing the kind of constant arguing and shouting which is frightening to young children may have the same effect. All our bodily systems respond, including nervous, endocrine, digestive and cardiovascular systems. Psychologically, we try to manage the distress by shutting it off with distraction or with other behaviours which appear to keep the pain at bay and which may persist into adult life:

> Client A grew up in an affluent family where his parents referred to him as The Mistake. His older sister was adored and admired. He was the child they had never wanted, who should never have existed. His defence was to walk with a pronounced stoop, to speak in a barely audible voice and to avoid eye contact. As a teenager, he developed anorexia, further exasperating his parents by this allegedly 'ridiculous and inconsiderate' behaviour. He had a first-class degree from Oxford and 15 years' experience as a lawyer, but was repeatedly failing to get jobs that should have been well within his scope, and came to me for career coaching.
> Client B was the son of a well-known entrepreneur. His father had left the family when B was aged 6 after years of what B called 'parental fighting on a grand scale'. B still felt that he was somehow responsible for the failure of his parents' marriage and said he 'hated' his father. B's problems concerned his immoderate responses to authority where he combined pranks with outbursts of anger.
> Client C grew up in a household governed by rigid rules. Her parents believed that too much attention led to a 'spoilt' child, so C was put to bed early, was never picked up when she cried and was punished with slaps if she was 'defiant' or 'showed off'. She said she had been 'a difficult child', the way she had been constantly described as a small girl. C escaped from this regime at 17 but her staff experienced her as strangely passive, unable to make decisions and given to bouts of crying.

If we were able to enquire into what the parents of Clients A, B and C had themselves experienced as children, we would most probably discover that they had been traumatised by their own parents in a similar fashion. This is how trauma is passed through generations.

Trauma is an inescapable part of being human. We are all traumatised to some extent. It is wrong to believe that there is a traumatised population, 'Them', needing treatment and an 'Us' who are healthy and untraumatised. It's a lengthy continuum. It is inevitable that we will meet trauma in our coaching rooms and it affects us as coaches as much as it affects our clients. This is where Franz Ruppert's model of the 'split psyche' is so helpful. He represents the psyche as a pie chart with three segments: a traumatised self, a survival self and a healthy self. The relative size of the three wedges will vary according to the individual. The traumatised self is the part of us that is well hidden. It represents feelings of fury, abandonment and hurt. We rarely see this self in coaching and dealing with it is the business of therapy not coaching.

The survival self is the defence we construct against feelings which would otherwise be overwhelming. It is always associated with high levels of stress because of the effort it takes to maintain the emotional shield. We lose touch with our bodies, and we deny the connection between the behaviours that are keeping us stuck and their origins in trauma. The whole purpose of the survival self is to keep us exactly as we are because that defensive shield helped us in the past and we believe that without it we will be lost in the present. The survival self takes flight from distressing feelings by seeking distraction in alcohol, gambling, shopping, an overuse of opioids, an obsession with social media, an over-concern with appearance, overwork, gaming, relentless exercise regimes, sexual promiscuity or eating disorders: this is not a complete list. It may show itself in any of these behaviours or through mental illness and the kinds of physical illness that result from suppressing intolerable feelings. The function of the survival self is to keep us stuck and the attempt to coach it is why so much coaching fails.

Then there is the healthy self, the part of us that can acknowledge the whole gamut of feelings, 'good' and 'bad', that is open to feedback and change; we accept ourselves, we are undefended, confident, resilient and authentic.

In coaching, we meet the healthy self but we are frequently working with the survival self and this may explain why progress can seem to be so slow. Signs that this might be happening are that the client cannot confront or change any behaviour that is clearly damaging. They may unconsciously have sought out an exact mirror of the toxic relationships from their past and be stuck either in fruitless attempts to control others through bullying or in seeking approval and recognition from people who are trying to bully and control them. They may assure you that the problems in their lives are all about the behaviour of others, for instance the team members who won't take responsibility or the boss who is unreasonable or the organisation where exceptionally long hours are the norm. When you challenge these beliefs, they may frown and tell you that you don't understand or try to distract you with further tales of horror.

The place to start is with our own trauma biography as coaches, ideally with a supervisor who is trauma-aware. One question that I have found fruitful is, 'What kind of child did your parents want you to be?' I follow this with, 'What kind of effort did it take to try to conform?' Asking these questions of yourself will most probably lead you to your own survival identity. In my own case, I was the much wanted, cherished and only child of a loving marriage. My parents' education had been wrecked by poverty in one case and by a mother with mental health problems in the other. There was little privacy in our house and money was always short, partly because my parents were supporting my mother's father and a foster child. I grew up knowing, or perhaps believing is a better word, that my role was to succeed where their hopes had been destroyed. Carl Jung wrote that what he called 'the unlived life' of our parents is one of the strongest influences on us. The child my parents wanted me to be was the one who was 'clever' and who would be able to use education as the ladder to a better life. I believed that love depended on success at school. My own survival identity is inextricably linked with the lure of over-achieving.

Therapy, reading, training, coaching and supervision have hugely helped me deal with how this may continue to warp my thinking and behaviour.

As a coach, you will be able to work with literally any client as long as you are coaching from your healthy self: much easier said than done. It's all too possible to be pulled out of shape when your own survival self meets the survival self of the client because your well-meant coaching interventions have not worked. Anxiety quickly sets in. You stiffen mentally and physically, you may try to impose advice on the client, introduce a tool or technique, collude with the client in blaming everyone and everything else in their lives for their problems, rescue, indulge the client in hearing yet again their much-repeated stories about the indignities of their lives, or feel so overwhelmed that you look for ways to end the coaching programme early. When you are coaching from your healthy self, none of this will happen. You need no fancy techniques to be trauma-aware. Classic coaching is what is needed: great rapport, suspending judgement, good questions.

What do you do with this awareness? At one level, your answer might be 'nothing' other than noticing what is happening, keeping your understanding as a silent reminder that if you are in the presence of the client's survival self then it is critical not to get involved in trying to coach it. You might merely say, 'These habitual ways of behaving can be hard to shift. At your most resourceful, what would you do?' Your most important question to the client is, 'What do you need from me in relation to this issue?' If what the client needs is not what you can offer because you lack the appropriate confidence, skill or experience, then you will use your coaching skills to explore this with the client and later with your supervisor. I am reminded here of a former client who came to me after a disastrous previous attempt to find a coach. His wry comment was, 'She was always trying to bring things back to my mother, everything led there, even when it didn't. It freaked me out, I had to get away from her!'

Assuming that you do have that confidence and that you know you are not trying to be some kind of faux therapist, then you might want to use the Ruppert model overtly. I have found clients immediately appreciative of it. It is simple to understand while also having depth and subtlety. I have introduced it to a wide range of people, for instance fund managers, fellow coaches, academics, chief executives in healthcare and charities, entrepreneurs, HR directors, media executives, and to people looking to recalibrate their lives as they head into retirement. I explain it and then ask how it may be playing out for them, especially over those areas of their life where they feel that they are teetering on the brink of losing control or of feeling that they might be 'impostors'. I stress that I am not inviting them to see me as a therapist and that if the original traumatising experiences need attention then I can recommend someone who specialises in this field. Clients usually understand that 'trauma' seen in this way does not mean blaming their parents: most see straight away that the reason for their parents' behaviour was the trauma they themselves had experienced.

As part of our conversation, I might say, 'Which self am I talking to now?' or 'What would your healthy self do here?' or, 'How can we bring your healthy self back into the picture?' Clients learn to monitor themselves, for instance saying things like, 'I felt the siren voices of my survival self; they were luring me into losing my temper at that meeting, and I stopped just in time!'

You will listen attentively for the language that clients use, looking out for words that indicate imperatives such as 'must', 'always', 'never', 'can't'. Some of their more metaphorical language may be heart-breaking. One client grew up with parents obsessed by the constant threat of imagined social disgrace if their rigid rules were challenged, especially by anything that might look like sexual indiscretion. The client described them as 'bigoted and controlling'. He realised early on that he was gay. He said of his childhood, 'It was like always being at the station waiting to be met and knowing that no one was coming.' He struggles even now with feelings of loneliness, despite being happily married to his partner of many years. Another client described her upbringing as the daughter of a violent mother: 'I was my mother's dancing bear where she jerked my chain and then whipped me for not dancing well enough to her tune.'

We know now that sexual abuse in childhood is far more common than used to be thought. This makes it likely that you will work at some point with clients who disclose that this is what happened to them. At the height of the pandemic lockdown in 2020, I worked with a client who had already hinted in an email that there were 'issues' in his childhood. He was asking me for help on getting through job interviews. The presenting scenario was that, despite a seemingly successful career, he was failing to get through to the highest level in his profession. 'It's disastrous. I flail about, I don't prepare properly and I'm struck dumb at the interviews', he wrote. 'It's humiliating.'

We had never met face to face. Possibly it was the odd combination of intimacy and remoteness created by Zoom that made it possible for him to tell me, with great calmness and articulacy, only 20 minutes into the first session that as a young child he was sexually abused by a teacher. This man groomed the client's parents as much as he had groomed the child. He strung them along with talk of 'outstanding talent' and 'scholarships', telling the boy that he was a 'special friend', taking him to 'training camps' or to his own home. The client kept this terrible secret for 15 years. He spoke of it only when several other men came forward to accuse the teacher. My client was interviewed by the police but did not give evidence in court. The perpetrator showed no remorse and claimed that the accusations were 'lies for money'. He served four years of a custodial sentence.

Many coaches have asked for advice about what to do were a client to tell this kind of story. Mostly the answer is that you need do nothing more than quietly acknowledge the client's courage and candour. Inside, you are remembering that people who have been abused will often confuse perpetration with love because this is how their abusers operate. They will blame themselves, will feel confusion about why their parents did not protect them and may never have addressed the trauma. When at last they have spoken up, they have routinely not been believed; they have been silenced. I reminded myself of this, listening to this client. I realised that his notable calm was a healthy sign of keeping himself safe from being re-traumatised. He had seen the perpetrator punished. In asking me to work with him and telling me his story at such an early stage of the coaching relationship, he had probably already made some kind of connection between the damage created by his childhood experience and his current problems, but I wanted to check this out.

'What links do you see between that whole horrifying time, including the court case, your difficulty at interview and your decision to come for coaching?'

I was aware of the long silence and the importance of not entering it. 'I think', he said slowly, 'that I felt just like I did when I told my parents and later when I was interviewed by the police. I met doubt, I met scepticism, I felt it was my fault. With my parents I met anger and denial.'

'What was going through your mind just before the latest job interview and then during it?'

'That I was on trial, that I couldn't be me. I didn't know who "me" was. I felt 7 years old again.'

'That's our cue. Our work is going to be about who that adult "me" is, all his many strengths, his resourcefulness, his impressive experience, his reputation among colleagues for doing such excellent work. Then it will be about how to bring all of that to the interview.'

The work we did was entirely along these lines and it had a positive outcome: the client was offered the next job for which he was interviewed. Even so, I was more than aware of the many chronic problems in his life: the narrow escape from alcoholism, the uneasy relationship with his parents, an unstable marriage and the challenge of forming loving attachments with his own children. None of these was my business in this assignment: they were boundaries I knew I should not cross. This was territory for the skilled trauma therapist we had agreed that it would be vital to engage once the new role was safely in the bag.

Unless we are trauma-aware, we will miss the information the client is giving us about what created their problems in the past and be unable to help them make links with what is going on in the present. We will fail to focus the work on their healthy, non-traumatised resources which are able to challenge the survival narratives they have developed and the survival behaviour they say they want to change. As ever, we need to understand our boundaries, in itself a strong argument for becoming trauma-aware.

Franz Ruppert is one of many psychologists and thinkers to have named different 'selves' in human personality. For instance, Sigmund Freud described the Id, the Ego and the Superego; Donald Winnicott proposed a 'true self' and a 'false self' where the false self is a defensive façade. Carl Jung's concept of the 'persona' has some similarities to Winnicott's false self. The contemporary writer and psychotherapist Susie Orbach has explored the idea of a false self in relation to women's feelings about their bodies. The idea of a pseudo self appears frequently in fiction, for instance in Charles Dickens' novel,

Great Expectations, where the hero, Pip, denies his humble social origins. Seen through the lens of the Ruppert model, the book is about the crushing cost of living through a survival self. The advantage of the Ruppert framework is that it is easy to understand and that, unlike many others which may look similar, it is not judgemental: the survival self can be thanked for its efforts on our behalf.

In subsequent chapters, I look at how trauma may show itself in common phenomena such as rescuing and perfectionism.

14

Avoiding the Lure of Rescuing

It's a dark winter afternoon in North London and I'm standing at a noisy junction with cars and buses swirling towards me from two directions, with no traffic lights or pedestrian crossing. Out of nowhere, a young man I had just seen darting and dodging between the flow and laughing merrily with his friends, appeared from behind me. He grasped my elbow. 'I'll take you across the road', he cried. I was furious. Shaking off his hand, I said stiffly, 'I'm fine, thank you.' Indignantly recounting this incident to a friend, she chided me for my ungraciousness: 'He only wanted to help.' Maybe, but I didn't need help. He was rescuing me to impress his friends with his gallantry and I saw him as patronising and impertinent. If I get to the stage of decrepitude where I need help in crossing the road, I hope I will be humble enough to ask for it.

Rescuing has allure for coaches too. We go into coaching because we *like people* and *want to help*, perhaps not stopping to think about how few of us own up to disliking people and wanting to be unhelpful. The wish to help is noble. It's what often draws people into coaching as a third or fourth career after first and second careers where *helping* was not built into the role. These coaches have often been well paid for work that was essentially unsatisfying. They leave corporate life thankfully.

Helping and rescuing are different. The genuine helper responds to a request and acts on what will be best for the other person. In an emergency, there's no time to stop to ask how people feel. If the building is on fire, people need to be directed to safety as quickly and crisply as possible. This is why the word *rescuing* has dramatic appeal: it is a physical process. Psychological rescuing is about the needs of the rescuer. At heart, it is a bargaining chip: if I rescue you, in return you will give me gratitude and love. Rescuing is underpinned by pity. From your stance as rescuer, you see the other person as in some way incapable. They have lost their sense of agency and they need you to sort them out. The rescuer needs to feel needed.

When you fall into the rescuer trap as a coach, you have forgotten that you can't truly be a *helper*. It is impossible because all effective help is self-help. What works best is the help we give ourselves when we make a decision that is based on our own beliefs and values. This is true even when we make poor decisions, for instance to pursue a self-destructive path with drugs or alcohol, to continue with an abusive love affair or to invest money in a project which at heart we may know is too good to be true. The need to be liked is overwhelming in rescuers. When the need to be liked gets out of control, it is a serious handicap to effectiveness as a coach.

Here is some of what can happen

The most common scenario is the one where the coach over-identifies with the client. The client has a tale of infinite distress, often about being bullied. This was the case with a coach who shared a background with her client as a clinical practitioner. The coach knew the organisation well, including the boss whose behaviour was upsetting her client so much. The coach had never much liked the boss either. The coach found herself listening patiently to hours of complaining about the insults, provocations, overwork and humiliations that her client said she was enduring. She found herself making the fatal mistake of rolling her eyes and heartily agreeing about how wrong it all was. The client emailed and texted her frequently and both parties were ending their messages with 'xx'. In supervision, this coach began to realise that she had become helplessly complicit with her client. She had been telling herself that it was 'useful' for her client to do what she called 'venting'. But, strangely, many hours of venting did not seem to be working as a way for the client to take control of her situation and the coach had come to feel as powerless as her client. The client was utterly committed to her role as victim and the coach to her role as rescuer.

For people who fall so readily into the victim role, their fear of taking responsibility for themselves trumps everything else. It is easier to blame external factors. These might include the culture of the organisation, the appalling behaviour of their colleagues or any handicaps inflicted on them, as they see it, by a malign Fate. 'If only I didn't have red hair', I remember one man telling me solemnly, 'people would take me more seriously.'

In another version of the same scenario, the coach's client was accused of racism and a formal grievance had been laid against him. This coach and client had worked together on and off for some years and the coach found herself indignant that a man she regarded as an honourable, decent human being could be the focus of something so palpably unfair. Soon the client was sending her a mass of legal documents. Despite her own lack of legal background, the coach was offering opinions and advice, describing herself as being 'desperate to help him'. Something similar happened with a coach whose client was constantly in difficulty at work: the problems all centred around activity rates and getting projects finished. Wherever the client carried out her series of short-term assignments, it seemed that bosses would make the same complaints. The client believed that this was prejudice and that what she called the organisation's 'jungle drums' were determined to sabotage her. The client constantly referred decisions to the coach, complimenting and thanking her, texting or calling many times a week, asking anxiously for reassurance and advice about smaller and smaller matters. That client lost her job and the coach never obtained any further work with the organisation.

It is so easy to slide into this kind of relationship with a client whom you like and who likes you. I was asked to accompany someone I had known slightly some years before, to a meeting with his boss. I accepted, believing that this was just another version of a three-way session (Chapter 3). The client asked if we could get together half an hour ahead for a briefing in the organisation's restaurant. He had presented it to me as an opportunity to sketch out what he needed from a potential coaching programme, but, as we continued the discussion, I realised with dismay that his true purpose was different. He wanted to be sent on an expensive leadership programme at Stanford University. My coaching was to be an adjunct to this programme and my role in the meeting was that I was to make the pitch to his boss. As my tea grew colder and colder, my potential client's face heated up and acquired a sheen of sweat. He described his boss as 'terrifying'. By the time we joined the boss, he was still sweating but had become ashen and was visibly shaking. In the meeting itself, he seemed to disappear, binding his arms tightly across his chest, hunching in his chair, avoiding eye contact and unable to finish a sentence. The boss himself seemed perfectly ordinary to me, forceful and loud yes, but otherwise harmless. Later, my guess was that this boss had somehow transmogrified into some extremely frightening male figure from my would-be client's past to the point where he had entered a dissociative state. I never had the chance to test this assumption, nor to carry out my virtuous decision to refuse the assignment should it happen, as it never did. On reflection, this was the most naked bid for rescuing that I have ever encountered. A milder version of the same trap was the coach whose client, in a large and rich US corporation, wished to renew his coaching programme, but who could not bring himself to ask his boss for the extra budget and wanted the coach to do it for him.

Over the last few years, I have noticed an increase in the number of clients involved in grievance claims. They may be the alleged perpetrator or the alleged victim. I am careful to write *alleged* because, however open the client believes they are being with you, including confessing where they did make mistakes, their story is always partial. They may want to enrol you psychologically as part of their defence team. A case that cannot be settled through mediation may go to a tribunal where a more complex set of evidence is probably going to be revealed. It's not our role to judge. Clients who get involved in such a suit can suffer intense misery; their energy is consumed by it, their resilience is sorely tested and there is frequently nowhere they can safely take their feelings. You can certainly listen attentively and offer coaching support for their distress, but it is a mistake to get drawn into the rights and wrongs of their case.

Attempts to rescue are doomed. Coaches who embark on a rescuing mission will find that clients never make any progress. They will promise to carry out the actions that are seemingly agreed in the coaching session but, oddly enough, events always get in the way and often these events are caused by the alleged intransigence and failings of other people. By this stage, it will be almost impossible for the coach to challenge. If, belatedly, you do, the consequences will be uncomfortable. You will be accused of letting the client down; you have taken the side of their enemy and you may find yourself treated coldly: 'I thought your role was to support me.' Emails remain unanswered or the replies have a curt tone. You and the client have swapped places – the client is now the persecutor and you are the intended victim. Emails and texts no longer end with 'xx'.

There are few ways for you to know where the truth lies in any of the allegations that clients make about behaviour in their workplace. You never or rarely see them at work. Unless you gather bespoke feedback for them (Chapter 20), all you have to go on is what they tell you and their behaviour with you. Your role is always that subtle blend of challenge and support. If it's all support, then you have become their friend and cannot be their coach.

With hindsight, the danger signals are obvious. You come to believe that the client cannot operate without you, so when you hear that they have had a job interview without asking you for coaching to prepare for it, you are indignant – surely they needed you? When the client appears unduly deferential, you experience irritation at their dependency at the same time as feeling secretly gratified. The client promises to contact you to arrange the next session and yet you hear nothing. Instead of assuming that there is a myriad possible reasons, you are hurt: surely you meant more to them than this silence? If you find yourself thinking about clients all the time, the probability is that they have become more important to you than you to them.

Another worrying sign is that boundaries become loose: you find yourself extending the session on flimsy grounds. One such coach told me, 'We came to the end of the allotted time, but just as we were wrapping up he suddenly mentioned a serious health problem. Before I knew it another hour had passed but I felt I just had to do it.' Later, this coach discovered that the client had felt uncomfortable and embarrassed at what he interpreted, probably rightly, as intrusive and unnecessary but had not insisted on leaving, saying, 'I felt sorry for the coach.' The client had clearly seen that this was about the coach's needs and not his own. The same phenomenon may be at work when a coach offers to work pro bono after a coaching programme has ended, even though the client can well afford to pay.

Underneath the appearance of kindness and generosity, there is a different story in coaches who are compulsive rescuers. They are constantly suppressing their own legitimate needs. They fear to put themselves first because they often associate doing so with pain, with threats and with the ending of a relationship. They will talk about their wish to serve others but, in supervision, their true feelings will emerge: irritation, fear, spite, envy, all amounting to a boiling cauldron of resentment. Indignation dominates: 'After all I've done for them!' Sooner or later, this emerges as dislike of clients who seem so unappreciative of the enormous efforts the coach is making on their behalf. Stress increases and may show itself as depression or physical illness such as hypertension or chronic migraines.

When you notice this as a pattern, it is time to ask yourself about your own attachment style and to interrogate your personal history. There is much evidence that people who enter the caring professions have often had unsatisfactory experiences of being cared for as children. One of my supervisees started her account with the coolly spoken comment, 'My parents didn't do a very good job of looking after me.' She went on to describe a dysfunctional family where her mother had had early-onset Parkinson's disease and her father had been a violent alcoholic. As an only child, she had turned into a carer for her mother and had made futile attempts to stop her father from drinking. She had learnt that her own needs were unimportant and that it was 'selfish' to try to put these first, along with a nagging feeling that if only she had tried harder and been a better daughter, she could have solved all the problems in her family.

Equally common is the family where love was dependent on achievement. Children may have been told repeatedly that it was only acceptable to be top of the class and then upbraided if they appeared to 'fail'. The need for approval from authority figures becomes overwhelming so that once again it is impossible to say no. Coaches from this kind of background can find themselves over-performing for clients. They are always trying to offer 'helpful' handouts, links to websites, books, models, over-dramatising the severity of their clients' problems and pressing advice on to clients who have not asked for it.

Many of us can find ourselves occasionally falling into the rescuer trap but, if it becomes the dominant way of being a coach, it can only end unhappily. It is plausible to assume that coaches who become compulsive rescuers are doing so as a way of dealing with a feeling of uselessness, a lack of healthy self-confidence and a fear of being rejected. They have become faux-altruists, constantly feeling martyred, tired and unappreciated, not understanding that their behaviour is a doomed attempt to control people. This can be an especially toxic mix if, as a coach, you are drawn to needy people where the chances are that, at an unconscious level, your wish is to merge with your client. You see their distress because you have experienced it yourself. You know what it is like to feel the guilt associated with being unable to do enough for those shadowy people from your past. But you cannot put right those old apparent wrongs by acting once more as carer and rescuer. It didn't work in the past, so why would it work any better now?

There can be few of us who have not done at least some of the rescuing I have described here. Self-awareness is the key to managing it, plus regular supervision where a supervisor may spot what is invisible to you. I was discussing this with a colleague specialising in people who have been made redundant from high-profile jobs, and who works brilliantly with them. His comment was, 'I fully recognise that I'm drawn to this work because after my mother died and my father remarried, I became the rejected son, regarded as inferior to my half-siblings. But I've done the therapy, I get regular sessions from a seasoned supervisor who takes no rubbish from me, I'm alert to the dangers of over-identifying, I've got it to the point where it's a plus rather than a handicap.'

15
Working with Rescuers

It's the first session with a new client. We've spoken on the phone but have never met in person. She has just been promoted to a more senior role and we have had a slightly dispiriting discussion about the challenges of the job before moving on to what is happening in the rest of her life, including health. She is slim and noticeably pale.

'Health is OK. No major illnesses – yet.'

'And your mental health?'

The client stares into a space somewhere above my head.

'I've often thought about ending it.'

We could not go on until we had talked through this worrying disclosure: how serious was her wish to 'end it'? Had she actually made plans for taking her life? If so, how detailed were they? They were not detailed. She wished to 'end the pain' rather than to end her life, but what was 'the pain'?

That was a testing beginning to our work.

This client grew up as the eldest of four daughters in a prosperous professional family. Her father died suddenly when she was 14, leaving the family financially stable but emotionally shattered. As a teenager, she described herself as 'the only adult in a world of out-of-control children, and one of them was my mother'. Her mother retreated into depression and this academically gifted, dutiful girl assumed responsibility for the household. At the same time, she continued to do well at school and got herself to Cambridge from where she went on to a well-paid management career in healthcare. When I met her, she was exhausted and irritable, saying, 'I'm running on empty'. She was annoyed with her work team, annoyed with a husband who was disabled by depression and had given up work, annoyed with her two young daughters, annoyed with her sisters and her mother, all of whom she found 'exasperating'. She readily confessed that she was drinking too much and that vodka had become her crutch – 'it's the only time and place I get time for me, but I think I'm dependent on it now and I feel ashamed and guilty. I'm often hungover in the mornings but I still have to get to work.'

The issues she presented for coaching were the 'impossibility' of managing her workload and the 'impossibility' of managing her boss. Many clients have solemnly assured me that their massive workload is a given and that the demands on their time are non-negotiable. I frequently shock them by saying that I do not believe a word of it. I offer them the idea that workload is always negotiable and that people who overwork are making a choice and are, more often than not, training others to think that overworking is what they want.

At home, this client organised the shopping and cleaning and she did the cooking, just as she had done as a teenager. She acted as chauffeur for her daughters, driving them to and from ballet lessons and playdates. If staff brought her a draft document, she spent precious time rewriting it herself. When team members came to discuss a problem, she made the decision for them or said, 'leave it with me'. She was routinely working 12-hour days. There had been two 'Serious Untoward Incidents' in one of the facilities managed by her team and the regulator had been severely critical, pointing out that signs of trouble had been visible for some time without anyone taking action.

All executive coaches meet people who have difficulty delegating. The problem is rarely that such people do not know the theory. The real question is why they are not acting on it. Answers range from the alleged incompetence of their team members, a belief that if you want something done well it is better to do it yourself, to it being 'unfair' to ask busy people to do yet more; it shows your own good-heartedness that you are willing to step in. Sometimes the underlying cause of failure to delegate is fear about whether you are up to the demands of your own job. It is simpler to do the familiar and easier work of more junior people. Sometimes, as with this client, the problem is an addiction to rescuing. This client was a super-rescuer, initially unaware that she had expertly created the very environment at work and at home that she claimed to dislike so much.

The rescuer believes that they are being helpful, even when it is clear that the target of the rescuing does not want their help. Rescuers can be unaware that their rescuing comes with a price tag, designed to provide the appreciation and care that is so lacking in their own lives: *if I look after you, you'll look after me*. They may attract people who enjoy the dependency that the rescuer is so eager to create, creating a desperately entangled relationship where both parties dislike what is happening and yet cannot seem to escape it. At work, the compulsive rescuer is likely to alienate and undermine by constantly implying that other people are not up to their job. When I have carried out feedback surveys for such bosses (Chapter 20), it would be common to hear their team members say with a shrug, 'I'm fed up with protesting; if he wants to do my work as well as his own, then let him get on with it.' Rescuing infantilises people; they will not grow if they have a boss who cannot let them have the autonomy to make mistakes or take risks. I have sometimes seen whole executive teams where rescuing has become the dominant management style. The real work of such teams is neglected, they become collectively a decision bottleneck for their staff while they busy themselves with the tasks of their juniors, leaving the organisation critically exposed at the top.

At that first session, the client and I explored some of the feelings she had rarely or never expressed: her grief at the loss of her father ('there was too much to do, too many other people who seemed in a worse state than I was'), her resentment and frustration, her belief that other people's feelings always had to dominate, her reluctance to say no, her fear of being disliked or of being seen as unkind. We talked about her explosive temper at home where she often shouted and swore. We discussed which of her own needs she had set aside and what the considerable cost had been.

In our second session, I introduced the idea of rescuing. We discussed the positive impulses that lie behind it, the undeniable fact that human society depends on our willingness to help each other and how easily we can misdiagnose what we believe others need. I asked what healthy ways she had of looking after herself and there were several: walking, reading, listening to music, going to concerts. In subsequent sessions, we looked at how her willingness to take over responsibility for her bereaved family had been an essential short-term strategy that had needed courageous leadership at that time. I asked her how well it seemed to suit her purposes now, correctly guessing that the answer would be that it did not. We looked at what her boss needed from her in a senior leadership role and repositioned his 'asks' as reasonable requests rather than as wildly unfair demands that could not be negotiated. We looked at what authentic delegation would look like, sound like and feel like, examining her actual practice against a template that she described for herself. We looked at how to ask the questions which would uncover the differences between people who genuinely did not know what to do and those who needed coaching and encouragement rather than telling and directing.

Where there is an inveterate rescuer, there is usually also a person who yearns to be rescued. This person has had a difficult past, often involving abuse. Their feelings of worthlessness and anger can lead to depression or chronic anxiety. At some level, both parties in what can become a tangle of co-dependence, believe that this time, unlike the way it was in childhood, their needs will be met. Unfortunately, this is unlikely. The malign dynamic of victim-persecutor-rescuer soon takes over. The victim's needs are bottomless because of their profound terror of taking responsibility for themselves. The rescuer's needs for love and care can never be met by the helplessness of the victim. The phrase, 'After all I've done for you!' intrudes into much of the conversation.

I introduced this client to Eric Berne's ideas about 'games' and then to Stephen Karpman's Drama Triangle. The Drama Triangle plays out with each 'player' moving around the different roles of Victim, Persecutor and Rescuer.

The faux excitement of the 'game' handily prevents either party stating what their real needs are, keeping genuine intimacy at bay. The game itself is repeatedly played, always with the same stalemate result.

The client gave me an example of a typical husband–wife exchange in her household:

> She (Persecutor): I've been working flat out all day and you've been here doing nothing. The butter knife is still on the table from breakfast!
>
> He (Victim): You don't understand. This has been a terrible day for me. I could hardly get out of bed this morning and you go on about butter knives.
>
> She (Rescuer): Oh, I'm sorry. I'm sure it's been horrible; let me make you a cup of tea.
>
> He (Persecutor): A cup of tea won't do it for me. You never understand. You're just thinking about yourself.
>
> She (Persecutor): I have to think about myself because no one else will. I've kept this whole household afloat for years and this is how you reward me…!

The client talked about her husband's childhood, a story of physical abuse and neglect from both parents and the impact on his mental health. We considered how she might unwittingly be sustaining his fragility. We talked through the idea that such unhelpful games can only continue if both parties collude in playing them. We discussed how to disrupt them. The underlying message in all our work was this: 'I am not stronger, better, cleverer or more resourceful than any of the other people in my life at work and at home.'

Christmas was approaching. We had already agreed that the rescuer dynamic had been the dominant one in her home life. Now it was changing. The family had acquired a young dog that needed exercise, forcing her husband to get out of the house. He was already driving the girls to their dance lessons and playing a bigger role in managing the domestic chores. He was getting the psychiatric help that he had previously refused in managing his depression. He was actively looking for a job. She suggested that we devote the whole of our December coaching session to discussing what she called her Grand Strategic Plan for Christmas. This involved being Christmas Director rather than Christmas Skivvy and meant doing none of the actual work because it would all be delegated to others. And so it transpired. Her sisters brought and cooked the turkey, her mother did the puddings, her husband prepared the house, bought and set up the tree. Her daughters peeled the vegetables and provided the waiting service. It was agreed that another member of the family would host the next Christmas. From January of that year, she gave up alcohol for good.

The breakthrough for this client was probably not so much any of the work we did in the sessions, satisfying though this seemed to me and helpful though I hope it was to her. The truly decisive moment was nothing to do with me; it was her decision to ask for coaching in the first place, the very thing that so many compulsive rescuers find difficult. Secretly, they don't believe they deserve help; help should go to other people, as it is something you give rather than receive. Nor did we ever tackle head-on the lack of self-confidence that all rescuers feel. That would have felt somehow fluffy and elusive. At exactly the right moment, her insightful boss, someone towards whom she had felt in equal parts liking, suspicion and envy, had spotted that coaching might help and had expressed his willingness to fund it. She had accepted. The safety of the coaching room was a new experience for someone who had felt unsafe for so much of her life, and for whatever reason she was ready to benefit from it.

Our work consciously modelled what 'effective helping' meant. Although I was moved by the level of her distress, I felt no temptation to rescue her in return. I asked coaching questions, I did a lot of listening, I made suggestions, I offered new ideas tentatively and accepted her reservations. Unlike the rescuing patterns in her life, it was a partnership of peers. The content of what we did was probably a lot less important than the quality of the relationship we established, something in which she was absolutely an equal player.

To work with rescuers, my suggestions are to look beneath the presenting issues. I would always consider 'overwork' to be a candidate for masking a rescuer. Ask for the backstory as it will often reveal that the client had an upbringing where they were expected to subjugate their own wishes in order to serve those of more powerful people. These clients should be able to see that it is not 'selfish' to have needs and ambitions of their own and they may want your help in uncovering what these are. They need to acknowledge their anger and resentment. They need to be able to turn their wish to help into a strength – an ability to release the other person from dependency rather than latching them to the rescuer. It is often useful for them to practise saying 'no' in informal role plays during their sessions with you, or doing some 'empty chair' work where they sit in a different chair 'as' the other person in the relationship and 'see' the relationship from that person's perspective.

Clients who have assumed the rescuer identity will frequently come to coaching looking for more effective ways of rescuing. They will talk about their heroic striving to save the world as political activists for lost causes. They will describe their attempts to encourage their team, to persuade an exasperating elderly parent to use a computer, to set an example to colleagues by putting in long hours on a problematical project. They will tell you that none of their previous efforts has worked so, obviously, they need to try harder; their rescuing endeavours need to be stepped up.

'What happens when you've tried this?'

The client frowns. 'They go all helpless on me or say I don't understand.'

'What would happen if you knew for certain that all your attempts to help them were pointless? That you were making it worse?'

The client looks appalled and often cannot speak. There is a long silence. 'I'd be distraught; I'd feel helpless.'

Helplessness is the core of the issue. The rescuer has lived with the possibility of their own helplessness since childhood and the thought of it is horrifying.

You might spend a whole session exploring how and why this has happened, following it with a discussion about how to identify which part of any issue is actually their responsibility. A good question here is, 'Which bit of this problem do you own?' The answer is always that it is a fraction of the responsibility which the client has been assuming up to that point.

Rescuing is underpinned by bitterness, sometimes well concealed, but as a coach it's important to avoid joining in a festival of blame at the witless team or the useless family members who allegedly can do nothing for themselves. The question, 'What might you be contributing to this?' is vital. Look at the consequences of everything carrying on as it is: usually, the thought of doing more of what is already not working is intolerable and can create energy for change. Make rescuing part of the vocabulary of your work: this need not be deadly serious, it is better if it is light-hearted. Point out that rescuers are often guilty of digital thinking: it's on or it's off, it's either rescue or abandon, but this is a false dichotomy. Discuss how some small pilot projects might show what could work instead and then review them at your next session.

Sometimes you will work with clients where rescuing will prove to be the key that unlocks so much else in their lives. One client grew up as the youngest of three brothers in an impoverished family. Their father left and the young client was recruited by his mother to run errands, to do household chores and to soothe her when she was upset. He was mocked for this by his older brothers as 'Mummy's Little Helper'. As an adult, he was drawn to humanitarian work and came to me for coaching in his first senior leadership role. Bespoke 360-degree feedback revealed the dismay of his boss and the high levels of irritation in his team created by his insistence on doing their jobs as well as his own. He was exhausted by the perpetual international travel. His marriage was collapsing, and he was overweight and unfit. In our final session, we reviewed what had changed over the year of coaching: 'I've retired Mummy's Little Helper', he said. 'I'm not flying anywhere if I can do a virtual session instead. I'm taking taxis instead of lugging my heavy suitcases to save the organisation a few dollars. My team are doing their proper jobs without that dire "help" from me. I'm not comfort-eating anymore and I've lost 13kg without dieting. My wife and I are talking properly again.'

Rescuers love to be needed but their real need is to be loved. If your coaching succeeds to even a small extent in clients working out how to achieve this without rescuing, then together you will have done good work.

16

Coaching the Perfectionist

I'm noticing the clenched fists, twitching left foot and the furrow between her eyes. I'm meeting her for the first time for a three-way discussion: the potential client I'll call Charlotte, me and her boss.

Charlotte is in line for promotion and I have been suggested as the coach to prepare her for the selection process. In this conversation, her boss, a man some years younger than she is, calmly commented that Charlotte 'can seem a bit tense'. To be promoted, the message seems to be that she needs to be less tense.

'What does tense mean in terms of Charlotte's actual behaviour?' I asked, including her with a smile as I asked the question.

'She's very hard on herself – she often does more than she needs to. For instance, when we had an Awayday recently she offered to take notes, even though I said I didn't think we needed them. But she did it anyway and then spent a long time typing them up and then she complained that she was over-worked! It wasn't necessary though of course I thanked her. If people don't reach what she thinks is the right standard', he glanced at her, 'she can snap at them.' Then looking straight at her he said, 'We've had this conversation, haven't we Charlotte, but nothing much has changed.'

Charlotte looked down. 'Standards matter.'

'Yes', said the boss pleasantly, ignoring her comment, 'and I'd like you to explore with Jenny what's going on for you, why it is important to you and what to do instead so that you make the best possible bid for that promotion.'

Perfectionists come in many forms, but their most obviously distinguishing features are their refusal to compromise and their need for control. They are as harsh, if not harsher, on themselves as they are on others. A friend whose efficiency is legendary forgot to renew his passport until the day before an important business trip to Canada, and sent an email lambasting himself to 20 of his social circle and then did the same on Twitter. There is an air of compulsion about their need for lists, tick boxes and forward planning. If you make a list, if you plan far, far in advance, you reduce the chances of chaos overwhelming you because, to a perfectionist, chaos and inefficiency are always only just around the corner.

The world needs meticulousness but whether it needs perfectionism is another matter. Perfectionism is meticulousness that has got out of control. When the perfectionist can be 'adaptive', it can be a strength because it can be dialled down when it's not needed. When it is 'maladaptive', it becomes a weakness. It means there is needless checking and re-checking which absorb time and energy that could be better spent elsewhere. There is attention paid to unimportant detail and there is a failure to calibrate energy because the same energy goes into the unimportant as into the important. What is worse is that the perfectionist in a senior role imposes all this on others and then gets upset when people protest. Perfectionists can seem humourless; you can't tease them, as it's all too serious for jokes. In some cases, there is a link with obsessive compulsive disorder (OCD) where the sufferer feels overwhelmed by what they believe is their responsibility for whatever area of life their OCD involves – cleanliness, health, safety and so on, and which can only be kept at bay by incessant rituals.

OCD wasn't Charlotte's problem but, at our first session, she explained how often she was misunderstood: 'I'm not really trying to control those people', she said, 'I'm only interested in the quality of what they do.'

At this first session, Charlotte told me that she had grown up in a single-parent family and that she had huge admiration for a mother who had somehow kept Charlotte and her brother well fed and clothed, despite a chronic shortage of money, juggling parenthood with two humble part-time jobs. She described a household that ran on rigid rules, with both children committed from a young age to a rota of duties. Adhering to these rules earned praise, while deviation was punished with immediate disapproval and a withdrawal of privileges. In such circumstances, the child dreads being criticised, interprets praise as 'love' and comes to believe that love depends on conformity to the rules.

I often ask clients for the two or three outstanding memories from their childhood and the answers are always illuminating. At 10 years old, Charlotte begged her mother for a pet rabbit. Her mother reluctantly agreed, on the strict understanding that the rabbit would be Charlotte's responsibility. She would have to ensure that the animal had food, clean litter, bedding and water. If this did not happen, then the rabbit would disappear. A cheap hutch was built by a neighbour and a pretty young rabbit was bought at a bargain price from the pet shop. The rabbit was named Lara because Charlotte had been reading and enchanted by the novel *Dr Zhivago*. Alas, after two weeks Charlotte reneged on her promises. For two days, these essential duties were neglected. On the third day, Charlotte came home to find that Lara and the hutch had vanished.

> 'You didn't keep your part of the bargain. So the rabbit has gone to the vet and has been put to sleep.'

Charlotte wept as she told me this story. She had absolutely accepted her mother's verdict and sentence. She had been responsible for the death of a beloved pet. I listened to this story sceptically. I did not believe for a moment that a very hard-up mother would have paid a vet to have a baby rabbit euthanised. I understood that a mother in these circumstances could feel that a harsh lesson was necessary, but nonetheless I did not think that this was a proportionate response to what was most probably a very well-behaved 10-year-old girl. I thought that by far the most likely scenario was that the rabbit would have been quietly returned to the pet shop. I expressed these thoughts. Charlotte was astonished. It had never occurred to her that the story about the rabbit's death might have been false.

Perfectionists believe that their behaviour is normal. They have internalised the messages they got as children that achieving what other people want means being repaid with love and approval. They believe that they are in an invisible competition with others and that these shadowy others will always be one step ahead. Their behaviour is driven by fear and shame and their underlying question is always, 'What will people think?' Their conversation is full of the words *should*, *must* and *have to*, often applied to others as well as to themselves. Their thinking is digital: things are on or they're off, they're black or they're white; nuance is difficult, shades of grey impossible. Their expectations are unrealistic and for this reason they are perpetually disappointed in themselves and in others. They evaluate their performance in terms of goals and outcomes rather than in the effort and learning that have been involved in getting there. These goals often assume gigantic proportions because they recede as fast as you look at them; they are never big enough for the perfectionist.

Charlotte was happy to use the word perfectionist about herself because she believed it was, in her words, 'a badge of honour'. We spent 10 minutes exploring what this meant for her, including her reluctant agreement that, despite her initial denial, she experienced high levels of anxiety most of the time.

> 'How anxious are you feeling now?'

> She wriggled a little in her chair. 'Pretty anxious because I think you're about to tell me I'm wrong.'

I kept very still and let the silence run for a few moments, aware that I was consciously refusing the compulsion to copy her tightly folded arms and pinched-together legs.

> 'What do you think I might say?'

'Tell me I'm not a good enough client. Being a failure. Not being senior enough. You must work with better people than me.'

I could not restrain my laughter at this point. 'You mean that I have some kind of ranking list where I judge clients according to their seniority – or what?'

It was hard to make Charlotte smile, but she did, just a little.

I said, 'It's not a coach's job to criticise clients but it is to describe what we see, and here I see a classic perfectionist who is getting in her own way.'

I said, 'I'm going to give you my self-invented Perfectionist's Checklist of Musts.' Now I adopted an exaggeratedly pompous voice. 'Raise your hand or nod if you agree...:

- I must work at my maximum capacity at all times.
- I should offer to do all the unpleasant chores that other people avoid.
- If I make mistakes, I should act quickly before anyone discovers them.
- I should be able to sort things out on my own without needing to ask for help.
- My appearance must be inconspicuously immaculate, neat and groomed at all times.
- It's my job to tell other people when their work falls short of the ideal.'

Now Charlotte was smiling properly because she had raised her hand to every single one of the items on my list.

The first task when you coach a perfectionist is to name it, to challenge their belief that their perfectionism is desirable or that there is no way that they can escape from its clutches, to point out how often the word *should* appears in their speech, and to ask, 'Who says?' There are many ways to do this but it is usually vital to ask them what it costs in mental and physical energy. Often, they have not made the link between perfectionism and their exhaustion, stress and anxiety. Nor have they usually connected it to childhood experience. In Charlotte's case, the immediate hook for coaching was her great desire for promotion and her dawning understanding that this was unlikely if her current behaviour continued unchecked.

Perfectionists believe that 100% brilliance at everything is possible. Unfortunately, 360-degree feedback surveys on bosses unwittingly reinforce this belief, with their long lists of items describing the perfect manager. The perfectionist is then mortified to discover that others see their all-too-human flaws.

There are many ways of coaching perfectionists but, after the initial exploration, my own preference is to start by identifying their strengths. I have a pack of 20 postcards based on Martin Seligman's Values in Action survey. To Charlotte I said, 'Choose your top eight of these cards and tell me what they are. Then discard three, leaving you with your five top strengths.' The point here is that you are, in effect, saying, no one has all 20 of these strengths. It's fine to have five. Let's see how you could make the most of those, acknowledging that other people will be better at the other 15. In the same spirit, I administer the

Myers Briggs Type Indicator psychometric questionnaire (see Chapter 18). Its essence is that it is a forced choice instrument, making it impossible to claim to be equally good at all eight of the preferences it identifies. The challenge is to minimise the downsides and to maximise the upsides of each preference. In Charlotte's case, this led to a discussion about how to get the most from her preferences for Introversion, Sensing, Thinking and Judging (ISTJ), one of 16 such profiles. At their best, ISTJs offer others structure, steadiness, care with detail and respect for proven routine. We followed this with a discussion about how to avoid over-using these strengths to the point that they became weaknesses or, at the extreme, potential career derailers. Then we looked at what the other 15 personality types might offer that Charlotte was unlikely to be able to match.

Sometimes I have explored what I term *constructive imperfectionism* with clients. I ask them to remember times when they were new to a task, were learning, getting things wrong, solving uncomfortable problems or living with uncertainty. Examples are starting a new job, becoming a first-time parent, taking up a new hobby and learning a language. My aim is to encourage the notion that improvement, something dear to the heart of every perfectionist, involves failure, disappointment and trying again. Instant competence is impossible.

People like Charlotte find it hard to admit to getting anything wrong because they dread being exposed as imperfect. This means that potentially they can't learn from mistakes or that, in trying too hard to avoid risk, they never develop. The attempt to cover up or to avoid asking for help almost always leads to poor quality work. Contrary to what the perfectionist believes, I might offer them the mantra that trying to be perfect leads to second-rate work. I might begin, as I did with Charlotte, by raising the question of famous mistakes, which, because they were concealed, led to tragedy, for instance the loss of the Challenger Space Shuttle, the nuclear accident at Three Mile Island and the Hillsborough football stadium disaster.

'What were your four biggest pieces of learning in the last year?' I asked, a version of a question that was likely to be part of the selection process for promotion. She struggled to answer: I could see that it was almost impossible for her to give a single example. In the safety of the coaching room, I coaxed her into talking me through some of her less than successful efforts as well as the many occasions where her work had been outstanding, though she was reluctant so to describe it. In doing this, as a coach, you are modelling a new way of being. You are not going to express horror at the mistakes, nor overdo the praise for the successes.

The 80–20 rule is useful: that 80% of results come from 20% of effort. In my days as an executive producer at the BBC, I met many perfectionists who, if not stopped in their tracks, would cheerfully have booked expensive weekend overtime facilities to make 'one last set of edits' on their film. These would involve tiny changes which no one but they would ever have noticed, but which would have added enormously to costs. Perfectionists don't think 80–20 until they are invited to see the universality of the 80–20 rule. 'Which 20% of your work adds most value?' I asked. 'Maybe that's where to put your effort.'

The heart of learning to moderate maladpative perfectionism is self-compassion. Until you have self-compassion, you can't have compassion for others. I invited Charlotte to think about what she would like to say to that small girl growing up in a stressed household run by a mother who was doing her best in difficult circumstances, but who overdid control. At first, she thought I was inviting her to indulge in self-pity or to criticise her mother. Then there was a thoughtful pause. 'I'd say, "Lighten up, it's OK, you're OK".'

I like the idea of pilot projects because they acknowledge that rapid, wholesale change is impossible. I asked her what she thought a good pilot project would be in the spirit of becoming a less-than-perfect perfectionist. Her answer was to try one week of making a daily to-do list which contained only four items. Only four – down from 30! There was a sting in the tail – that every day in that week she would ask someone for help at least once.

Despite how it might seem to outsiders, Charlotte and her mother, now in her 70s, get on well and see each other often. At her final session, Charlotte recounted a recent conversation. She said, 'I asked her about the rabbit. She reddened a bit and said "best not to ask, it's all a long time ago"'. I persisted and said, "So did you take the rabbit to the vet?" She looked away and gave a little smile. So I knew I'd had my answer.'

17
Getting Away from Endless Intellectualising

Most of my clients are smart and have glossy careers to prove it. I'm using *smart* here the way Americans do, to mean intellectually gifted and sassy with it. There's no British English word which quite conveys the same meaning.

The trouble is that for a sizeable minority of these clients, their smartness is a handicap. It has come to define them in their own eyes. I think here of a client who led a team of forensic scientists in an organisation that took on complex evidence-recovery cases for the police. It was high-profile work involving major crimes. She was an outstanding scientist who specialised in 'cold case' reviews and had a number of successes where offenders had been prosecuted and convicted, thanks to her work. Her bosses found her 'rude and aggressive', and her team were reportedly terrified of her sharp tongue. She was referred to me and at the first session defended herself vigorously by saying that she was merely 'direct' and that, if a man acted the same way, it would be accepted without comment. She followed this with a crisp analysis of how, in her view, sexism affects every workplace. She openly described her own brilliance as a technical expert and said that the people working to her should pull themselves together, stop being so childish and just get on with their work. If they couldn't do this to the required standard, then they should leave. The trouble was that the best people in her team were already leaving. The reason they gave was that they could not stand the climate of intimidation they said she created.

Clients like this can be oblivious to the world of emotional intelligence. Some of them will claim that they have never heard of it. If they have, they will tend to dismiss it as 'soft' or, a favourite put-down, 'psycho-babble'. Being what they will call 'nice' they see as optional, far behind the fierceness of their need to prove their cleverness or their prowess at the technical aspects of their job.

This can be especially true if they have colleagues whose social origins are more obviously privileged than their own. Sometimes they will admit to feeling that they will never quite have what is described so often as 'polish': the flawless English upper-middle-class accent that you acquire from being at the right school and the social connections that go with it; knowing without being told which cutlery to use at a splendid formal dinner; wearing clothes that look tailor made, even if they are not; and sharing the same kinds of jokes. Less privileged people will frequently describe their ascent to seniority by using violent metaphors such as 'clawing my way up the ladder' or 'killing for my place'. Sometimes they feel that their smartness is a talisman against failure.

When people are over-invested in traditional IQ, it can work to their advantage in early career. Without much in the way of track record, employers like cleverness so the bright young person gets promoted. This is especially true of organisations where intellectual capacity is necessary and respected, such as in legal firms, some media occupations and management consultancies.

Later on, when they have to negotiate with peers or manage settled teams rather than short-lived project groups, such clients may appear to lack emotional intelligence. Then they can be in serious trouble, however gifted they are intellectually. One client was known by a variety of nicknames in his role as an editor on a national current affairs programme. These names included 'The Pointy-Headed One' and 'Lord Two Brains'. His programme was renowned for its shrewd analysis of the political scene and for the way it persuaded big-name politicians to take part. It prided itself on being able to set the agenda for national political discussion; in its own eyes, it was an elite production. However, audience numbers were sliding and bosses were alarmed. When they investigated, they found that the production team was riven by open rivalries and rows. Most of the staff were young. They were competing for the favour of Lord Two Brains. If you were 'in', you got the most high-profile work. If you were 'out', you tried to set traps for those who were 'in', for instance failing to fact-check or to make the proper arrangements to greet contributors when they arrived for a broadcast. The client's boss had benefited from coaching herself and believed that it could help him. At the first session with his coach, this client made it clear, as he had in the 'chemistry' discussion, that the coach must first prove that she was his intellectual equal. He demanded to know where she went to university and what her qualifications were. He was openly dubious about what, if anything, she knew about broadcasting or current affairs, and how on earth she thought that his behaviour could have anything whatsoever to do with the precipitous decline in audience figures for his show.

Such people make for challenging clients. They virtually always start a coaching programme by believing that they are performing brilliantly but are unfortunately surrounded by idiots. Their view of leadership is that it is about their technical competence, and their energy goes into proving how very much more competent they are than any of their colleagues. They overwork, they boast, they are short-tempered and sarcastic, they bully. In their own eyes, they are merely setting high standards. The goals they initially bring to coaching are about their frustration: how do they put yet more pressure on their people? The trigger to change is most commonly a new boss who sees clearly what has been resolutely ignored by his or her predecessors, that the price for this alleged brilliance is too high. The boss's straight talking is received with disbelief, with even more disbelief at its tag end: that it's *change or go*. Bespoke feedback carried out by a skilled coach is the back-up tactic. *This is what people feel about you: are you content that they see you like this? Do you understand that you will continue to get poor performance if you carry on in the same way?*

You should note that with clients like this, you are likely to feel much like their staff do: indignant, intimidated, silenced. This is particularly likely if the client is male and the coach is female. Often, such clients have a reputation for allegedly sexist comments; many have been to all-male boarding schools where the only women they met were those of what they might have considered inferior social status – the wives of housemasters, serving staff, teachers. The client hides his gaucheness, resentment and fear of women with patronising banter which women colleagues do not find in the least bit funny and, increasingly, in the wake of #MeToo, are unlikely to tolerate.

If this happens to you as their coach, see it as data; it's not as personal as it seems. Never get into a tussle about who is cleverer. If you find yourself tempted to bandy quotations from the great philosophers or to offer sophisticated opinions on a fashionable book, then you will be unable to work with this client. It's no good engaging with them in the way they engage with everyone else. Your value is that you are different. Underneath the swagger, there is a vulnerable person who may be reachable if you treat them in the right way.

A senior executive client who was renowned for his sharp brain eyed me beadily as he told me in our first session that what he wanted to work on was his ability to do strategic thinking. His job title actually included the word 'strategy'.

> I replied, 'I'm quite sure you're already a great deal better at strategic thinking than I will ever be, so if that's what you want I can't provide it.'

I felt confident saying this as I was sure that he had not chosen me to be his coach because of my expertise in thinking strategically. His real issue was that three staff had separately made official complaints about his allegedly bullying style. His entire career up until that point had been, as he saw it, a resounding success. Now he was threatened with a public failure and, underneath his braggadocio, my assumption was that he was desperate for help. Much later, at our final session, after nine months of hard, enjoyable work together, I brought him a small present. It was Professor Henry Mintzberg and colleagues' amusing and enlightening book *Strategy Bites Back* (Prentice Hall, 2004), a collection of essays by different authors. Some of the points made in the book are that there is no accepted definition of strategy and that what is often claimed immodestly as clever strategic thinking is just post-hoc justification.

Here are some ways of working with this kind of client. Which you choose will depend on the client and on your own style.

Name what is going on: 'I notice you talk a lot about the need for "intellectual robustness"' (or whatever euphemism the client is using to talk about their own excessive gifts); 'I'm finding this tricky – it feels as if I'm at an oral exam where you're inviting me to defend my PhD thesis.' Wait for the response. This will usually be surprise: it would be rare for anyone to speak so candidly to the client. Then say, 'I'm sure you are far cleverer than I am, so I don't think this is a contest I want to enter.' Again, it will most probably be unusual for the client to have their bluff called in this way. Follow this with a statement about your own expertise. For instance, with one such client I said, 'I know your understanding of the political scene is going to be second to none, but my own interest is in how bosses can lead people effectively without either bullying or being a walkover. I think that's probably why you're here.' Offer to collect 360-degree feedback (Chapter 20) as a way of helping the client understand their impact on others.

Since they enjoy engaging in intellectual jousting, you can offer them some rational evidence on how emotional intelligence in leaders links with performance, but note that you are introducing the topic on your terms, not theirs. There is a lot of this evidence about so you can take your pick, for instance from Daniel Goleman's many books and articles on the subject. Ask them if they are willing to hear research evidence on how leadership style affects performance: they are unlikely to say no or to have heard these ideas before.

My own favourite is to describe the innovative experiments of Kurt Lewin, a refugee from Nazi Germany who was the father of action research in social psychology. In 1939, Lewin set up and observed three matched groups of boys who had the same task and materials. The only variable was leadership style. One group was led in what Lewin dubbed an Authoritarian style, with a rigid insistence on rules and do-it-my-way – or else. A second group was led in a Laissez-Faire style, where the leader was overtly friendly and exerted no pressure. The leader of the third group put the emphasis on goals and positive feedback, with a degree of creativity encouraged at the outset. Lewin called this style of leadership Democratic. I have seen the astonishing results of this experiment many times and at first hand when I have run a simulation for managers called The Climate Lab which reproduces Lewin's experiments. This time, actors are briefed, unknown to the groups, to lead them in the three styles. The task is to make paper planes to a tight specification. Each group has identical materials. What invariably happens, even in the bare hour allowed for the task, is that the group led in the Authoritarian style begins well but is soon derailed by sulking, sabotage or mute resistance. The Laissez-Faire group has a pleasant time but its productivity is low. The Democratically-led group outperforms the other two many times over.

I see this part of coaching as being essentially a piece of throat-clearing. It lays down some grounding in a style that these clients will understand and covers material that few will ever have encountered before, but it is not where the fulcrum for change lies.

At some point, it is inevitable that you will raise the question of feelings. When you have explored the client's early life, you will have already legitimised this area as essential for good coaching. But expect the client to be hesitant, dumbstruck or possibly angry when you link this to their current behaviour. They are not on intimate terms with their feelings. They may have an impoverished vocabulary to describe emotion and struggle to name it. Anger is the one emotion they may understand. Anger is deflected outwards: it is the fault of others. These people are idiots; the idiots caused the anger through their own incompetence. I have met much astonishment from clients like this when I have pointed out that expressing anger is a choice; it cannot be 'caused' by other people. In responding like this as a coach, you are deciding that you will not be intimidated. Our role as coaches is to understand how the client thinks, but not necessarily to endorse the client's thinking.

For clients who are over-invested in intellectual achievement, their terrifying anger serves another useful function. So often they are petrified at the thought of real intimacy because that means exposing their vulnerabilities. Many of these clients are lonely. In terms of attachment style, they are Avoidant, the result of harsh parenting (Chapter 11). Their personal relationships are sometimes a wasteland because they are behaving the same way at home that they do at work, but they don't want to experience or admit their loneliness. Their anger serves a purpose: it keeps people at a distance. Your choice as a coach is to decide whether you are going to be whipped into submission, just like others in their lives, possibly deciding that you will end the coaching relationship because working with such people can be exhausting. You may be aware that you dislike them, in which case this may be telling you more about yourself than about the client. Their rage and the helplessness that lies just below the surface can seem overwhelming; you doubt they will ever change, or that if they do, you know that you cannot be their change agent. You tell yourself that they need therapy, even while you know that it is most unlikely they will ever embark upon it.

It is always possible to say, 'this isn't working' but mostly I do decide to continue. I take it as tacit recognition, when they keep coming back, that they know they need the coaching even while they may be telling you, possibly rudely, that they are wondering how it could possibly be helping them. They don't know what the real problem is, so they keep repeating the same mistakes. Sometimes what they want is for the coach to protect what appears to be their uncrackable self-esteem. In their early lives, most of these clients learnt that 'weakness' was reprehensible and that the slightest expression of it will mean that their emotions overwhelm them. They want us to understand them at the same time as they fear being understood.

Here is how I worked with the forensic scientist I described at the start of this chapter. I'll call her Marci, not her real name. In our first three sessions, she had sketched out the stresses of her work life, had described how she saw her meagre social life, claiming that work was so all-embracing that it left no time or need for friends. We had discussed her career and the likely damage to it if nothing changed. At our fourth two-hour session, I said:

> I've heard a lot from you about your pleasure in finding evidence that enables criminals to be convicted of crimes they thought they had got away with. I'm in awe of the scientific ability and the persistence you've described. I think of that person as

Brilliant Marci. I've also seen the person I'll call Angry Marci, who gets annoyed, cutting and sarcastic with colleagues who can't keep up and who's been angry with me from time to time.

Marci gave a curt little nod at this, but I saw the glimmer of a smile on her face. I reminded her of the dark, expressionless tone she had used when telling me about her mother's suicide, a tragedy that had happened when she was only 8 years old. Then of the same tone in which she had described the ending of her marriage and, later, the estrangement from her son, her only child. I pointed to a third chair in my coaching room and said, 'I'd like you to go and sit in that other chair now as the person who feels whatever she felt and feels about those events and tell me what it's like for her.'

Slowly, robotically, the client got up and made for the empty chair. She looked like a sleepwalker and avoided eye contact.

'Which part of you is this?'

'It's Scared and Sad Marci.'

Scared and Sad Marci did not have much to say, but she did look at me and she did cry a lot.

And then our real work could begin.

18

Using Psychometrics Wisely

The client is sitting open-mouthed. How could it be that answering a few seemingly bland questions could result in a profile which so closely defines her? She is wriggling, laughing, torn between embarrassment that her weaknesses have been so clearly spelt out and gratification that her strengths have been recognised. That client was me, some decades ago, when a member of my team at the BBC debriefed my results on the Myers Briggs Type Indicator. I had never heard the word *psychometrics* before and had certainly never heard of the MBTI. When it was suggested to me that it might be setting a good example if I were to take some psychometric tests, as this was one of the services that my new department offered, the sceptical former journalist-producer in me was prepared to be politely unimpressed.

Despite my amazement at the accuracy of the profile, there was no moment of instant enlightenment. There was just a steady realisation that this was a whole realm of invaluable knowledge that was there for the taking, as long as I was prepared to devote myself to the slog of learning about it. Like other early adopters in coaching, I did this learning eagerly as it was the nearest we then had to anything like training in how to be a coach. Now the question is different. Coaches spend serious money on their initial training and they wonder whether it is worth investing yet more money in psychometrics and, if so, which of the hundreds of instruments available it might be sensible to choose.

When coaches discuss psychometrics, they often use the word as a synonym for personality questionnaire, but psychometrics is a much broader field than just personality. The word itself means the measurement of the human mind and psychometric instruments can assess aptitude, skill, intelligence and a variety of behavioural characteristics. At its best, it is an impressive science backed by meticulous research. There are tests for verbal and numerical reasoning, strategic thinking, motivation, selling skills, stress, career interests – and dozens of others. But personality is the area that is of most interest to coaches as it is here that questionnaires can add so much value.

At its heart, coaching is about increasing self-awareness so that the client makes better choices. We all have blindspots, aspects of ourselves that others see but we don't, aspects of ourselves that we believe we know but would rather other people didn't, and limited understanding of where we differ from others and why that matters. Bespoke interview feedback (see Chapter 20) is one way of revealing these characteristics, but psychometrics add an extra dimension. In that first introduction to the MBTI, as a naïve subject, it astonished me that there could be people who perceived their world predominantly through detail, data and factual evidence. My own preferences are entirely for the psychological opposites of these characteristics: imagination, intuition, the unique and the bigger picture of possibilities. Ah! So that's why my ideas for the future of my new department struck some of my team as wildly flaky and why I had to stop trying to persuade them as if they were just like me. Personality assessments offer coach and client a short cut to those critically important insights. If both you and the client are already immensely erudite about yourselves then you don't need them, but most of us are not in that happy situation.

In her first session, a client says that she finds it impossible to speak at meetings. 'By the time I've got my thoughts together, the discussion has moved on. When I do speak, it seems that people ignore me. I'm feeling useless, I don't know what to do.' At the second session, the coach and client discuss her results on a suite of psychometric questionnaires. All three show her clear preference for introversion rather than extroversion, though they define this behaviour in different ways. The coach explains that introversion is merely one of two equally valuable ways of expressing energy. Just as extraversion does, it has pluses and minuses. The coach sets out what these are, commenting that it's an extraverted world out there, where introverts have to learn how to operate inside it without losing their valuable ability to bring depth, brevity and good listening skills to any discussion. The coach comments that, like many introverts, the client speaks quietly and briefly. It's not surprising that her voice gets lost in the noisy theatrics of the typical work meeting. The client begins to understand how her behaviour affects other people and to respect her own gifts. Then, with the coach's help, she learns to plan and implement tactics for bringing more presence to the meetings she attends.

This piece of coaching could have happened perfectly well without any help from psychometrics. But the value that the psychometric lens added was more than just another way of understanding how to find the answer to a specific problem. It offered a set of insights into many other characteristics as well as a whole new way of thinking about how to influence others whose preferences are different.

One client whose results showed a strong need for planning and control was the boss of a team of self-styled 'creatives' in the media sector. He had been appointed to bring what he called 'common sense and rigour to chaos'. He was puzzled and annoyed by the skilled sabotage that his efforts were producing. There was indeed some undesirable 'chaos' and his disciplined approach was needed, but first he had to understand that trying to impose milestones, targets and monetary rewards, all of these his own preferences, would strike this team as laughably inappropriate. We looked instead at what would be likely to motivate and influence such a group and where their psychometric profiles would most probably differ radically from his. Like many people meeting these ideas for the first time, he struggled to grasp the implications. He said, 'This is like suddenly trying to become multilingual when you've been a monoglot all your life', but becoming 'multilingual' was what he needed to do in order to connect with his team.

Psychometrics are invaluable for clients with career issues, for instance people who are at risk of overusing a strength. A client in a senior role in a consultancy prided himself on his ability to make people laugh and on his skill as a presenter where he could entrance an audience with well-told stories. The firm merged with a foreign company and the culture changed. What had been overtly friendly and informal became cooler and more serious. The client was outraged when he was subjected to a disciplinary process. This only made sense to him when we debriefed his results on the Hogan 'Dark Side' survey. Here he understood, though with some resistance, that what to him were harmless pranks could be interpreted as mischievousness for its own sake, and that his boldness with groups looked to the new owners like arrogance and attention-seeking.

Where career coaching is concerned, most of the classic personality assessments can add depth. So, for instance, the 16PF or the OPQ can suggest in which kinds of work environment you will flourish and which will be energy-sapping. Edgar Schein's Career Anchors identifies which core motivator is most likely to have been the thread which has been running throughout your career and must be present in any new role. Having this information can prevent a client wasting time applying for a job that is an obviously poor fit psychologically.

One client had been devastated by the sudden news of his redundancy from a company where he had worked for 20 years. He had a young family and was desperate to find a new job. He was quickly offered a classic managerial role in a competitor company, but it seemed to me that he had always carefully avoided any role which had involved managing the performance of other people. It was useful for him to see that on Career Anchors, out of the eight possible factors, he had ranked 'Managerial Competence' as number seven in importance to him, with 'Technical/Functional Competence' as his number one, the type of role he had played throughout his career. His view later, when well settled in another 'expert' role, was that he had narrowly avoided a decision that would have been disastrously wrong.

Publishers can see psychometrics as a potential money pot. They envy the profits that the longer established questionnaires seem to be earning for their developers and they rush to create a rival. There are hundreds of possibilities clamouring for our attention, all making similar claims about their uniquely wonderful characteristics, so how do you choose? The place to start is with any assessment that has had meaning for you. If it doesn't have value for you, why would it for anyone else?

Ask colleagues how they rate the strengths and weaknesses of any question-naires that they use regularly and then ask if, through them, you can take and get feedback on any that seem as if they could be relevant to your own work. It pays to be scrupulously aware of your own responses throughout this process. Are the items easy to understand? How much time did it take to complete? How is the report written? Be wary of any reports that seem to be full of lofty pronouncements on your personality. No questionnaire, however brilliant, can say 'X is such and such a person'. The vocabulary should be tentative and tact-ful. A good questionnaire has a high level of internal consistency and can cope with seeming contradictions. For instance, there are many people who like to have their own way but who also need the approbation of others. How does the report recognise this? It is a sign of poor quality development when it is clear that two pieces of copy have been carelessly stitched together in a way that makes no sense. The acid test is: *does this seem like me?* I took one assessment pitched as a rival to the MBTI and the report told me that I was 'shy, detail conscious, loved gardening and wildlife and would avoid responsibility'. I was torn between outrage and laughter when I read this.

There is a case for thinking about which assessments employers tend to favour. It may be a condition of getting on to a suppliers' register, for instance, that you are licensed in one of the popular questionnaires, so while it may not be a commercial advantage to be so licensed, it may be a disadvantage if you are not. There is a minority of questionnaires, mostly those with a Jungian per-spective, that work as well with groups as with individuals. If your coaching offer includes team coaching, this is another element to consider.

Money will be a factor, not just the cost of the training to get licensed, but also the cost per administration, mostly now done online. Fees have risen since the days of paper-and-pencil tests and you will need to recoup the costs through your own fee. There are some excellent questionnaires that do not ask for licensing or training. These include the Thomas Kilmann survey which assesses conflict management styles, and Career Anchors. You may want to consider the quality and range of back-up materials that the publisher provides. The MBTI is unbeatable here.

Where training is a condition of licensing, as it is for the MBTI, stay within your areas of competence. The MBTI is much more than *letter + letter + letter + letter = who you are.* Untrained coaches who have tried this have not infrequently been caught out by discovering that the client knew more than they did about the instrument.

With any questionnaire, take the debrief carefully, step by step, and be pre-pared to abandon any preconceived ideas that you may have formed about the client. The client is always the world's leading expert on themselves and may reject any brilliant insights you or the questionnaire report are offering. Ask about the experience of taking the questionnaire, without bridling if the client expresses irritation at the way the items were phrased. Look for confirmation: 'In what ways does this seem like you?' or 'Can you give me an example?'

Look for places where the client rejects the results, inviting them to tell you why this aspect seems like a poor fit. As the session draws to a close, ask about links to the overall agenda you will have established: 'What insight does this seem to offer to the work we'll be doing in later sessions?' Where it works well, this process will give you and the client a workable vocabulary for potentially discussing any issue that crops up along the way.

It can be a mistake to rely on only one questionnaire. You may have a favourite which you find insightful, reliable and acceptable to clients. But no single questionnaire is perfect. They all have weaknesses. My suggestion is to choose a minimum of three, any one from these categories:

> *Jungian Type* – e.g. the MBTI or the Keirsey Temperament Sorter
> *Trait-based questionnaires* – e.g. the OPQ, 16PF, Wave or one of the so-called 'Big Five' questionnaires, e.g. the NEO, which group personality into five factors (Openness, Conscientiousness, Extraversion, Agreeableness and Neuroticism)
> *Values, needs, personal style, relationships* – e.g. the FIRO-B or one of the many questionnaires which assesses emotional intelligence
> *Strengths* – e.g. Values in Action, Realise2, the CliftonStrengths assessment
> *Career focus* – e.g. Career Anchors, the Strong Interest Inventory.

Whichever you choose, initial training is just the beginning. Clients vary in their willingness to take a psychometric assessment; many are secretly or overtly afraid of what it might reveal about them. Others may be inclined to dismiss it as fake science, comparing your admired instrument to a light-hearted magazine quiz. Some reject or trivialise their report, perhaps because they don't like the picture of themselves that it presents. Occasionally, you might see a so-called *flat profile* where the person appears to be entirely a little-bit-of-this-little-bit-of-that and nothing of interest emerges. Keeping going, despite these occasional discouragements, they will add depth to your understanding and will enable you to finesse how you fit psychometrics into the rest of your work.

As with every other type of coaching, this aspect of our practice starts with ourselves. I could never have predicted all those years ago at the BBC that I would become a dedicated student of the MBTI and, later, of the FIRO-B, writing books about both. Although acutely aware of their weaknesses, these questionnaires have offered me enlightenment about human personality. They colour my work with every client. They have given me insights into myself and appreciation for people who are wonderfully different from me. So, I rein myself in when tempted to offer clients yet another neat little psychological model, reminding myself that while these theoretical ideas interest me, they may strike more practically inclined people as useless waffle; or, that with my preference for introversion and objectivity, I can make a first impression of coolness. Even so, enthusiast as I am, I do not use psychometrics with every client. It's always a matter of judging what value they might add and always a matter for negotiation.

19
Giving Feedback – Carefully

For the previous two days, this presenter at a coaching conference has spent many daytime hours in bed wrestling a fever and a severe throat infection, barely able to speak. But duty calls and she remembers the old joke about these commitments – that if you're ill you go by ambulance – so she struggles to the conference and gives her presentation. Thankfully, she reaches the final slide. There is some lukewarm applause. A woman from the audience bustles up, a frowny expression on her face. She says, 'Can I give you some feedback?' Then, without waiting for the reply, declares, 'You need to work on your voice and you lack presence. I thought you'd like to know'. Then melts away.

That presenter was me and that presentation was without doubt one of the worst I have ever given, though fortunately many of the details are blurred by the fact that my fever had returned and that my voice had finally gone. By the time this feedback-giver had finished her brief lecture about my failings, the whole scene had a hallucinatory and vaguely comic quality to me, not least because one of the topics in my presentation was the importance of feedback and how to do it. Flushed and swaying giddily as I was, I remembered my days in TV. Even the most inexperienced director learns from day one that you never, ever, offer an actor or presenter any serious comment immediately after they have finished their performance. However good or bad you think it was, all you do is murmur some luvvie stuff about how it was all wonderful, darling. Even the most apparently cocksure performer is defenceless in those moments. They have always exposed more of themselves than they may realise and their vulnerability has to be respected. The time for 'Notes' is later when everyone has calmed down.

I have to assume that this woman meant her strictures kindly, that she believed she was acting in my best interests and only doing what I had been encouraging everyone in that room to do, but her lack of tact and skill was breathtaking, especially in a coach.

As coaches, we award ourselves the privilege of offering clients feedback. It is potentially one of the most valuable services we bring – but oh how very, very careful we need to be.

Learning how to give feedback and its importance in management means that at least, in principle, many people understand that it matters. Every management development course will include something on the topic. But giving feedback has a bad name and for good reason. 'Can I give you some feedback?' which, note, is a closed question expecting the answer yes, has come to be associated with a warning that you are about to hear something uncomfortable. The question itself is all too often a kind of faux permission to attack the other person.

For a time, there was a belief that the more you gave people feedback, including positive comments, the better the relationship you would create and the more performance would improve. This is not the case. Feedback is a currency whose value declines the more you use it. Because it is so demanding to do well, what is described by the giver as *feedback* is often actually *criticism* and inexpertly delivered. Linguistic confusion in the English language makes all this worse when we use *feedback*, *criticism* and *appreciation* as if they are synonyms, which they are not. Nor is the type of feedback involved in coaching the same as the process used in training those professionals and technicians where there are strictly right/wrong ways, for instance of giving an injection or of driving a fork-lift truck.

Feedback only works if it is given sparingly, skilfully and if the recipient likes and respects the feedback-giver. If it comes from a despised boss, it will most probably be dismissed even if it contains praise. When we hear comments about ourselves that we find threatening to our self-image, we will find reasons to reject them. Critical feedback, ineptly given, largely results in the recipient getting better at hiding their flaws rather than learning from it. This may explain why staff appraisals seem to have little or no impact on performance and sometimes make it worse.

As children, being socialised means that we receive a barrage of mostly unthoughtfully offered comment on our behaviour every single day. Our parents may overpraise us as 'bright' or 'good looking'. They may criticise, carp and rebuke, telling us that we ARE some unpleasant quality – for instance, 'You are rude' rather than 'I didn't like it when you did x because it seemed rude and embarrassed me'. In all the hurly-burly of parenting, it is easy to elide the poor behaviour with the person. Being at school invariably brings more chastisement or vague praise. Part of the lure of growing up is our naïve belief that we will avoid ever being subjected to this process again, only to find that it is repeated in the workplace. Nonetheless, the majority of us protect ourselves by believing that we perform at the 80th percentile, something that is statistically impossible but explains why, when a poor performer is eventually told that their work is below standard, the news is so often received with astonishment and disbelief.

At some level, we all understand this. It is why, in almost every human society, there are implicit rules for ordinary social engagement which are designed to save face all round by avoiding direct comment on the behaviour of another adult. There are some cultures where nobody ever says what they mean. This especially applies when the relationship is one that we value. Giving feedback breaks these rules, in coaching as everywhere else. That is why it needs to be done with exquisite care and skill.

It starts with a relationship between coach and client of warmth and trust. This is easy to say, but in some executive coaching engagements, the coach can find themselves sliding into a proxy managerial role, asked to sort out performance problems which have defeated the organisation. The coach prioritises their duty to the organisation over the quality of the relationship with the client. Once that happens, it is inevitable that the coach begins to assume, however politely, a finger-wagging stance, 'giving feedback' as a last chance to get the message across to the client. The most likely result is that the client rejects either the message or the coach or sometimes both.

The risk is that the very act of offering feedback disrupts the power balance, evoking a parent–child dynamic which infantilises the client. The only way feedback can work in coaching is if coach and client are in it together, side by side, where the coach's sole motive is to create some benefit for the client. It's possible to state this frankly without seeming sycophantic or cloying. An extremely overweight client begged me to tell her how fat I thought she was and how much it mattered. She said, 'I think I'm deluding myself; I see myself in a kind of distorting mirror where I'm 40 pounds lighter than I actually am.' I suggested that I took a photo of her on her phone and that we looked at it together. She cringed when she saw it, saying, 'I've avoided photographs for ten years.' My reply was, 'When I look at this picture, I do see someone probably 40 pounds heavier than is right for her and it would be wonderful to see that slimmer and healthier person emerge. It's got to be your choice but I'm here for you.'

The time must be right; not too soon and not too late. Agitation is the enemy of feedback. Giver and receiver need to be able to concentrate, listen and speak without distraction from turbulent emotions. If it's too long after the event, it will seem irrelevant or cowardly: *why didn't you mention this before?* As the giver, you have to be convinced that whatever it is can be acted on by the receiver, so it's pointless to give people feedback about characteristics that they cannot change.

Feedback works best when it concentrates on strengths rather than deficits. A client had asked me to coach her on her chairing skills and had bravely commissioned a colleague to make a discreet video of a sample meeting. When we viewed it together, we ignored the weaker areas and the discussion was entirely about how to get even more leverage from the expert way she had handled participation, tactfully shutting down over-contributors, encouraging shyer people to speak – and looking in detail at exactly how she had done it.

Feedback is sometimes delivered as if the feedback-giver has some private hotline to objectivity and 'truth', but our judgement is always distorted by our own experience, values and needs. Anything we say to a client has to be tempered by the confident but humble way it is offered. It's just an opinion. We may be wrong, hence the value of that phrase, 'I'm wondering…'.

'I've observed x and y while we've been talking and I'm wondering how this links to the issue you raised earlier on today.' This is then followed quickly by, 'This is how it seems to me, but what's your own view?'

The best feedback is based on observation and fact. It's descriptive, not evaluative, and begins with a phrase like 'I noticed' or 'I sensed'. You might say, 'I noticed just now that you were using a lot of complicated words when you were describing [whatever]'. The client is more likely to hear this than 'You were using jargon.'

That is why it matters to avoid making all-purpose generalisations and to talk instead about the impact on you: 'I was following your argument fine until you got to the technical explanations and then you lost me; I got confused with all the detail.' That way, you are owning your own opinion without posturing as speaking for everyone else.

You do need to have permission to enter the realm of such personal observation. Real permission is not the same as the perfunctory permission that so often precedes harsh comment. Real permission is granted when the client has already raised a perplexing question with you and sees you as someone who may have clues to the answer. Taking care is just as important here. Some years ago, I became interested in the whole question of colour and style in dress. A friend and I booked ourselves in with a woman who ran sessions where your 'colour season' (which colours suit your eyes, skin and hair) and body shape could be frankly scrutinised along with suggestions about how to make more flattering choices. You only go to these consultants if you know there is something amiss with how you are dressing, or else find the whole business of choosing clothes a mystifying chore and want guidance. The consultant opened her door, having never met either of us before. She looked us up and down coolly. I got off lightly but my friend was greeted with, 'Well, the shorts are OK but the shirt looks as though it's come from the scruffier kind of charity shop.' Fortunately, my friend was able to laugh – and agree. Later, I trained to do this work myself and even now it makes me shudder to think of that sarcastic candour, especially since most of the 'diagnosis' is based on nothing more than an acute eye for colour and an extremely imprecise system of classification. Scientific it is not. Everything is a best guess, no more. This was brought home to me when I discovered during my own training that the consultant's overbearing prescriptions in my own case were comprehensively wrong.

This is why it is as well to be phlegmatic about the possibility of your feedback being rejected. You may run a job interview role play with the detailed feedback that the client has pleaded for. Then you find that in the actual interview the client reports defaulting to their previous tactics and is dejected by their failure to have been offered the job. What is the likely reason? Choose any of these: you gave the feedback more clumsily than you had thought; the content of your feedback was off-kilter, it was bad advice; the client did not rate the content of your feedback, or rated it but could not apply it; the client thought it all mattered a lot less than you did; or the client forgot everything they claimed to have learnt at the session in the stress of the event. Any of these is possible.

Every coaching session brings opportunities for feedback. The risk rises with the potential for improvement. The simplest and least risky is some mild and neutral comment about changes in the client's demeanour: 'I noticed that when you were talking about your current job, your voice dropped and you sank down in your chair, compared with how you seem now when talking about applying for this new job. I'm wondering if you experienced that yourself?' When we are in the client role, we are mostly unaware of these changes and it can be invaluable to have them brought to our attention and their significance discussed.

At the next level, you are seeing the client's behaviour with you as evidence of how they are with the important people in their lives. True, they will be showing you their best side so what you will get is muted, but these are usually vital clues to problems that they have brought to the session. A senior executive has been told that he is 'domineering' and 'bombastic' but cannot recognise the opinion that others have of him. On the contrary, he says he feels 'powerless' and is 'hurt' by the accusations. This is a heavily bearded man with a towering helmet of dark hair. He is unusually tall, sturdily built and has a rumbling bass voice. His sheer physical presence means that he is always likely to be conspicuous but he has firm views and expresses them articulately. He asks me for my opinion. I say, 'It's easy for others to attribute motivation to us on slender evidence. But yes, I'm aware when you come in, for instance, that you are about a foot taller than I am so I have to physically look up to talk to you. So sometimes I feel I have to literally stand up to you. When you speak, I notice that your voice has a magnificently vibrant ring and that I need to make an effort to match it, and sometimes I find it hard to get into the conversation. I'm wondering if people who are more junior than you might feel a bit overwhelmed. What do you think?' This man could do nothing about his physical attributes but he could change his behaviour. For instance, he could make sure that, whenever possible, he was sitting down when talking to more junior colleagues; he could learn how to moderate his voice; and, most importantly of all, he could learn to listen and to make his motivation a great deal clearer by stating it. You may be thinking, *surely someone will have said this to him before?* The answer is: probably not. People had constantly commented on and joked about his height and voice but no one had ever straightforwardly, kindly and with concern, suggested what impact he was having on others, let alone discussed what he might do to change and why it mattered.

Ascending the ladder of risk are those occasions when the client has not truly asked for nor yet granted permission to give feedback but where you feel you have a duty to offer it. This is despite the discomfort it may cause both parties because what needs to be discussed is in the intensely private arena of personal appearance, accent and demeanour. This may well happen during a career coaching programme where a client is stumped by their failure to get past a succession of job interviews.

I was observing a trainee coach working with a woman who was hoping that at last she might be successful after many rejections. The coach pointed out that the client had shrouded herself in what was, in effect, an unflattering beige tent, had avoided eye contact and had brought a strong smell of stale deodorant into the room with her. The coach had preceded this with a heart-felt, gentle statement: 'I can see how upset you are by these repeated rejections and, as you know, when we are meeting people for the first time, these initial impressions are all important. If this goes wrong, it's very difficult for anything to go right. I wonder if I could share my first impressions of you?' The coach smiled, held the client's gaze, paused and waited patiently for the reply. The client's eyes widened and I saw her brace herself, but she nodded her assent, and listened to the feedback, biting her lip. She then joined at first timidly and then vigorously in the discussion about remedies. That client got the next job for which she was shortlisted.

At the apex of risk, and the area with the greatest potential for change, you will be looking for clues about the client's thinking patterns, assumptions and beliefs. All these have profound effects on behaviour. A self-funding client came to me with frustration about his failure to advance to the highest level in the legal profession. This man had won multiple academic prizes, he was a talented linguist who spoke five languages and was the author of a well-regarded book in his field. His question was how to overcome the prejudice that he was convinced lay behind the blockages in his career. He vehemently rejected any idea that I should talk to his boss or ask for structured feedback from colleagues. As he described the background, I was astonished to hear him use the words *jealous* and *jealousy* about 10 times within 10 minutes. Colleagues were *jealous* of his intellectual brilliance. They were *jealous* of his achievements, especially so since, unlike them, he had come from a humble background; they were *jealous* of his linguistic abilities, elegant house, beautiful wife and talented children. So already I had two further sources of data. He was externalising his frustrations and it did not seem to have occurred to him that his own behaviour could be part of the problem. He was consumed by the assumption that the jealousy of colleagues was the cause of his repeated rejections. It also occurred to me, on the basis that 'if you spot it, you got it', that what we criticise in others is often the very thing we know is, or are afraid could be, true of us. In this case, his own possible propensity to jealousy could be forming a toxic barrier to getting on with his peers and seniors. Despite the extraordinary level of boastful confidence that this client seemed to be projecting, my own guess was that this was a fragile ego and that I needed to proceed with great care. At this point, I confined myself to commenting neutrally on his frequent use of the j-word and to asking how he saw it himself. There was a long silence, then, 'I don't know. It's never occurred to me that there was anything strange in it.' From this, we moved to a discussion of how such a firmly held belief was formed, how true it was likely to be, how useful it was to hold on to it and what the implications were for his career and life. Then we went into some of the more painful territory about his eagerness to put all the responsibility for his failures on to others.

You will repeatedly hear such beliefs. They are rarely stated directly and you will need to listen carefully to see the pattern implied through how clients describe their problems. You will notice beliefs such as these: that people are either totally good or totally awful; that if bad things can happen then they will; that the client is helpless because other people have all the power; that all corporate entities are greedy; that it's not fair; that other people's needs should always come first; that conflict must be avoided at all costs – and many others. What all these beliefs have in common is their all-or-nothing nature. They will be garlanded with copious use of 'everyone', 'always', 'must', 'should' and 'ought'. They may be getting in the way of what the client says they want, while the client takes for granted that they are 'true'. Our part is to notice the belief and to name it in the spirit of honest feedback, expressing interest and curiosity. It's not our role to interpret, condemn, mock, nor to seem to wish to change it. Out of this apparently simple process much positive development may flow.

As for me, I concluded that, despite the gauche nature of the comments I was given that day, I did have a long-standing difficulty with my voice and that it needed investigation. A medical consultation ruled out any malign structural problem so I bought myself some enjoyable help from the distinguished Australian speech therapist, Dr Ron Morris. Perhaps this goes to show that even the most clumsily offered feedback may sometimes have positive effects.

20

Collecting Bespoke Feedback for Clients

The point of collecting feedback for clients is that it is a rapid way of increasing their self-awareness, one of the core aims of any coaching programme. '360-degree feedback' has become a popular way of asking colleagues for opinions. You rate yourself and these ratings can be compared with how your boss, peers and direct reports feel about you. The simplest way to do this is with a questionnaire delivered via the internet. But such questionnaires, despite flaunting their appearance of scientific objectivity, cannot guarantee that respondents are using the rating scales to mean the same thing. The items themselves are often ambiguously phrased, or, in an attempt to reduce ambiguity, become too wordy. The longer the questionnaire, and many are far too long, the more likely they are to ask questions about areas such as 'Strategic Thinking' or 'Appetite for Learning'. These are vague, floaty concepts that respondents are likely to find baffling. Reports are bulked out with multiple pages containing different ways of viewing the same bar charts, plus many blank pages for 'notes'. The narrative comments of respondents, the only aspect that has real value, are often pitilessly short sentences, badly spelt and punctuated, seemingly dashed off by people who were not encouraged to add the specifics which would make their feedback more understandable. Sometimes I suspect that respondents are simply exhausted by the effort of filling in such long questionnaires, so by the time they get to the narrative section they just want to get it all over with.

There are some questionnaires that are well designed but they are in the minority and disillusion with them may be part of the trend towards a more bespoke approach. Here, you personally interview the key people around the client. There are powerful advantages to doing it this way. You can probe for examples that get beneath generalities, whether dismissive or flattering. You will develop a reliable instinct for the spiteful person who is looking to pay back some real or imagined insult, though you might note that these people usually believe that they are being tremendously subtle. It is possible to compare one 'constituency' with another, so, for example, you will be alert to evidence that the client may be spending more time and effort on managing their seniors or peers than they do on their direct reports – or vice versa. You will find that in every batch of interviewees there are one or two people whose feedback is outstandingly thoughtful. Where people are at first reluctant, and some people are, perhaps because they doubt the confidentiality of the process, you will probably be able to reassure them. When you interview 10 of the client's colleagues, it is possible that you will have spent more than four hours gathering information on their behalf. Interviewees are far more likely to be candid with a third party than they ever are face to face with the person themselves. To my mind, this has to be in a different league from the hastily filled in items that characterise the average online 360-degree questionnaire.

The client chooses their feedback-givers and emails them all for consent, introducing you and saying what to expect, including reassurance that there is no need to prepare, plus sending you all their contact details. You then go ahead. I recommend doing the interviews by phone because it is unlikely that you would be able to see the respondents, all busy people, in one place in one day, and people often reschedule at the last moment. I suggest handwriting rather than recording their comments, because if you record them you will feel obliged to play them back or even to have them transcribed, a time-consuming expense that I find is unnecessary. Respondents tend to speak slowly and reflectively, giving plenty of time to scribble down what they say.

Most people will already have been reassured by the briefing email that the client has sent. Open the interview by stressing the confidentiality rules again and asking if your interviewee has any questions they would like to ask about the process. It helps to ask every respondent the same first question on each topic and then to probe for examples, discouraging comment that tries to tell you about what 'everyone' thinks. What 'everyone' thinks is likely to be unreliable gossip. The only comment that matters is the impact on the interviewee of your client's behaviour.

The usual topics will be these: leadership style; setting direction; communication in writing and in person, including chairing meetings and contributing to meetings; influencing style; handling conflict; delegation; giving feedback; problem-solving; and managing stress. In the last 5 minutes, you summarise what you have heard and end the interview with a final question: 'If you could give X one piece of advice, what would it be?' Most interviews will take 20–30 minutes.

You write the report up carefully. My own practice is to give it to the client at the session devoted to the debrief rather than sending it in advance. Most clients will say that it is the best quality feedback they have ever had. They will tell you that they have heard many of the points before, but the feedback was fragmentary, muted by politeness, or sometimes by their own inability to hear comments that have felt hostile. Having had opinions moderated through you will make it much easier to accept, including the many strengths that it is likely to emphasise.

When you carry out this process at the beginning of a coaching programme, it can give you and the client a reliable foundation for everything that follows. This does not mean that the client instantly decides to change in the light of some of the more critical comments. They may well choose not to, but at least they now know something of how they strike others and they can elect how much attention they pay it. For your part, you have incomparably valuable data that goes beyond the client's own story or the personal data that you gather from the impression they are making on you in the coaching room.

That's the theory and, when it works, it is one of the pillars of a successful coaching programme. In practice, there is much that can go wrong.

First, you have to offer it to the client. I have never yet encountered a client who has already been the subject of a bespoke process. (If they have, then ask them if they are willing to share the results with you.) Most people will be understandably wary. What are they going to hear? What if they discover that no one likes them? What if people like but don't respect them? What if they neither like nor respect them? Most people will guess that they may get a few jolts which will puncture their self-image to at least some extent. My own way of answering these questions is to say that other people hold views of us whether we know them or not, that most clients get a gratifying amount of affirmation and that feedback is not an instruction to change. But I am well aware, when offering these soothing observations, that I am asking the client to trust me with a delicate task and that sometimes they will say *no, thanks*.

Your own ability to listen is critical to success. You need to be able to set aside everything you already believe you know about the client. You need to consider what you know of the organisation's culture. When you are aware that high levels of distrust are endemic, that there is a rigid hierarchy or a reluctance to grip performance problems, then it may be better to hold back. I learnt this the hard way when I offered the process to a British client working in an organisation where most of his direct reports were political refugees from authoritarian regimes. Many of the people he nominated would not return my calls or emails, despite his reassurances that it was confidential and developmental, and nothing to do with assessment. Those I did interview gave suspiciously brief, bland and cautious comments. My client was disappointed with the scrappy quality of the data I cobbled together for him but said, 'I heard on the office grapevine that people thought you were a government spy. They felt it couldn't possibly be confidential and that either they or I, or both, would be punished as a result of what they said.'

Even when the interviewees are willing, there may be a case for hesitating. Sometimes, despite your care about whether to take on a client in the first place (Chapter 1), you discover that the client has major performance problems; or you realise that he or she is grossly unpopular. It is far better to refuse this type of assignment in the first place, but some organisations will hide the real story from you in their desperation to solve a problem which has so far defeated them. The typical scenario here is that the client holds a highly paid place in the senior ranks of the organisation with unique skills and experience which it believes are critical to its future. The trouble is that the client's conduct has become insufferable – but it has been suffered – and now no one knows what to do. They believe, probably without telling you explicitly, that it is your job to collect and then give the client the bad news in the hope that this will jolt them into acceptable behaviour.

It is possible as a coach to believe strongly in the power of 'truth' and in your own magical ability to give unpleasant messages skilfully. Even when it dawns on you that this disconcerting puzzle is what faces you, you may decide to carry on. I have done this myself and have worked several times with experienced coaches who have deluded themselves in the same way. It is so obvious when you put it like this that the work will be a failure. Underneath the blatant rudeness and anger of the client, there will be a terrified and vulnerable person most probably with an early history of trauma and abuse (Chapter 13), but you are unlikely to see this when you attempt the debrief. You will be sneeringly told that the method is 'amateurish' or 'unscientific', despite having already told the client that this is qualitative and not quantitative data. You will hear that you did not interview people properly, that you misinterpreted, or that, like so many others in the client's life, your aim is to persecute them. Another coach, in somewhat similar circumstances, had a client who was initially outraged on reading her report but who then agreed that she would continue the coaching on condition, as she put it, 'that you address your many shortcomings as a coach'. Not surprisingly, the coach declined this offer and ended the engagement.

360-degree feedback could potentially have complex confidentiality issues innocently embedded into it. When I am interviewing the client's feedback-givers, I explain that I am working on the principle of non-attributable confidentiality, meaning that I will use quotes but that it will not be possible for the client to guess who said what. But what if the client does so guess and takes revenge on someone who has allegedly said something disobliging? Their guess may or may not be accurate but the respondent could come back to you indignantly, saying that you failed to protect them. One of my supervisees had recorded all his 360 interviews and had shown me his report, much moderated from the harsher messages of the early drafts. Even so, the client was enraged at its negative tone. He threatened both the coach and the feedback-givers with legal action for defamation, saying that he would demand the release of the recordings. My supervisee told the client that he destroyed all recordings immediately after he had played them, so, alas, they would not be available. He then made sure that this invented-on-the-spot policy became true, but this could have been a troubling development all round.

A further danger is that a client may receive a 360 report which devastates them, because it literally contains only negatives. They may feel destroyed by it. One coach carried on with the interviewing, despite realising what profound trouble the client was in. Only a month later, she had to cope with the tragic news of the client's suicide. There was no way of knowing whether her report had anything to do with his decision to end his life, but it was enough to drive a conscientious coach out of the profession. If this cascade of negative messages were to happen as you get into the interviews, by far the best tactic would be to call a halt, telling yourself that this is a time when confidentiality cannot prevail. You would consult the client's sponsor, agreeing an appropriate course of action which should always include generous levels of support for the client, even if the verdict is that they should leave their job. In these circumstances, do not disclose any but the minimum of further information nor get drawn into a discussion about the client's future. That is a matter for his or her boss. Prevention is the key to avoiding such a disastrous assignment, making sure that you are thoroughly briefed in advance, refusing to continue if it is obvious that the client's performance is known to be so poor that their job is at risk.

These situations are exceptions. You will already know a fair bit about the client and could well have arrived at over-firm opinions about them. To preserve as much objectivity and freshness as possible, it is wise to share the interviewing with a trained colleague, telling them only what basic facts they absolutely must know about the client at the outset of the interviewing. Then you will need at least two hours to discuss your findings, but don't start this until you are ready to write the report. It is invaluable to have a second pair of eyes on your draft, someone who can challenge anything that they feel was not supported by their own interviews.

Unlike the questionnaire form of this feedback, you cannot hide behind the seeming objectivity of bar charts; you have to write the report yourself. The main danger at this point is forgetting that you are a reporter, not God. It's not the place to add little sermonettes on leadership nor to include your own speculations on the client's underlying motivations, since this is something that no one can ever know. Many coaches need training and guidance here. There is a difference between loftily saying, as many first-timer writers do:

'You struggle with giving away responsibility and delegating to others'

and the much safer version:

'Several people described noticing that delegation can be a struggle for you in some circumstances.'

Make plentiful use of words like *some, a few, many, possibly*. My own rule of thumb is that if only one person makes a specific point, it does not get into the report. A pompous tone can creep in: be careful, it's just a snapshot; you have only spoken to a small number of people so garland any of your points with hesitations. Say 'this may suggest that...' rather than 'this is how it is'. A perfect consensus is unlikely as the same behaviour may strike different people in different ways. If opinions vary wildly then say so, as it is all useful for the client to know.

Remove any quirky forms of speech which could identify individuals, but give direct quotes whenever you can because they add veracity. It helps if you can make a scrupulous balance of positives to negatives, but aim to write the report in a way you know the individual client will be able to hear. This does not mean bowdlerising people's comments. The data belongs to the client not to you, while bearing in mind some of the caveats I mention above. Mostly you will be undertaking this work for outstanding performers and it is patronising to assume that they will not be able to cope with any of the less flattering comments; they don't need rescuing. When you are new to this kind of report writing, it is sensible to allow at least a day for drafting and then to set it aside for a short time before editing again. Nine pages of well-spaced text is a workable limit. Anything longer is likely to lose impact in a welter of repetition.

Never underestimate the anxiety that clients may feel before reading your report, or their puzzlement at some of what it conveys. Set aside a whole coaching session to go through it with the client without rushing, paragraph by paragraph, explaining any uncertainties and asking how well it fits with their own perceptions. Suggest this even when the client initially resists. It is the best chance you will ever have to explore the ambiguities as well as the more straightforward messages. How the client responds will most probably be all of a piece with the feedback you have collected on them. If your report describes a principled, steady person, you will get a principled, steady response. If the report describes someone who takes out their frustration on others, then you might expect a few explosions seemingly directed at you. Some people cry, some are silent and it is difficult to know what they are feeling. If so, ask. Some people – typically the perfectionists who expect far too much of themselves and others – can only see the negatives, in which case you will remind them of the many positives.

Discuss how the client will thank their feedback givers and how they will share the messages of the report. I have known people call a meeting where they have distributed unadulterated copies and watched while their colleagues read it, wide- eyed. Others have kept it strictly to themselves. Encourage the client to give their respondents at least some clues about the impact of the exercise. At your next session, ask what reflections the client has.

'I sniffled with self-pity all the way down your street', said one client, 'because I realised that some people had seen through my carefully constructed façade. Then I realised that it was better to know than not to know what they felt about me. Then I read it all again and realised how much they all admired and needed me. Then I decided it was OK to be me. Then I determined that I would grip some of my weaker areas through the coaching. Then I realised what a privilege it was to have this opportunity.'

21

Understanding That Change Isn't as Easy as It May Look

The coaching probably started with six 2-hour sessions. A number of issues were satisfactorily addressed, the coach and the client connected – they like each other. It's a cordial, productive relationship and the client asked for – and has been granted – more. The coach has had a three-way discussion with the boss and has conducted an in-depth feedback exercise, much of this revealing the extensiveness of the client's strengths. The feedback has pointed up some deficits: despite knowing the theory, the client simply can't delegate, or hugs information to themselves, or appears to have favourites, or mumbles when giving a presentation, or has a short temper, or has a reputation for bullying when under stress. What the organisation has tolerated or pretended not to notice in a more junior role now cannot be tolerated or ignored. A well-rewarded coach working with a highly paid executive will feel that the stakes are high: the client's career as well as their own reputation may be on the line. At this point, doubts may creep in. The client's blindspots have been revealed and the coaching seemed to be going well but advancement is now slow. What on earth is happening? Why isn't the client changing?

One coach put it to me like this in a supervision session:

I delivered the 360 feedback. He liked the positives and he did reluctantly acknowledge that the negatives were accurate. He agreed that he did do that behaviour with women though he justified it as *banter* or *harmless flirting*. He seemed to think that as another man I would find it understandable. When we had a 'mid-term review' with his boss, she again emphasised how highly they all thought of him but expressed polite disappointment with his progress, saying that although he had now stopped all that unwanted touching of women colleagues (this had been described as *groping* in his feedback), he was still making what she called *sexist jokes*.

In our supervision session, the coach visibly sagged in his chair as he said to me, 'I don't know what's going on – why can't he see that this matters?'

Human change is complex but there are a number of principles that it is helpful to remember. They combine biological, psychological and social factors as well as the nature of the relationship with the coach. All are involved. When some desired change seems mysteriously stuck, it is usually because one or more of these vital elements has been neglected.

There needs to be an overall goal and it should be possible for the client to articulate it clearly. Saying it out loud to another person makes it real, rather than being a vague idea that has been hovering mistily in the back of the client's mind. A goal is always more powerful when it is phrased in the positive. 'Get slim and fit' is many times more alluring than the dismal sound of 'lose weight'. It's not enough for the client to say they want to be a more effective leader or a more prosperous entrepreneur, or to have a better job. What would a more effective leader be doing? How would they know they were a more prosperous entrepreneur? What does it mean to have a better job? It doesn't work to have a goal that is about pleasing someone else, so an attempt to work shorter hours to stop your partner pressing you to come home earlier is not going to be sustainable.

At the same time, part of what we must do as coaches is to respectfully interrogate the practicality of the goal. The questions here are: *How realistic is this? How does it fit with your personal values? What would it cost in time, effort and money to achieve it? How far do you have the skills it needs?* I was asked to coach a 23-year-old who had decided that he wanted to be an actor. His parents, who were paying my bill, were dubious – and so was I. This young man had done nothing to suggest that acting had always intrigued him; he had never been in so much as a school play. But he could have been the exception and I had to assume that he was. Meanwhile, I suggested a mission to find out more about what life as an actor would involve, including giving him some contacts of my own, people who knew this world well. He returned much chastened four weeks later to tell me that, after only three of these conversations, he had realised that it was not for him.

Once you have the goal, the quest is to explore what has kept the client stuck. Where people don't know about the differences between the limbic system of the brain and the pre-frontal cortex, or the separate functions of the left and right brain and how they are connected, then it is helpful to explain, pointing out that resistance to change has biological as well as psychological origins. Logic tells the client that the present state is disadvantageous, but emotion, easily the most powerful part of the human brain, tells a different story. Usually, this is about fear or about short-term reward. A client may acknowledge the dreariness of staying in a job he hates, but at least the job is familiar, whereas a future without that familiarity may seem petrifying. Smokers may dislike everything about smoking and yet be afraid that without the prop of nicotine they would be unable to cope. The coach's questions here are: *What would it be like to have a life without [whatever it is]? What are you afraid might happen to you? Let's imagine you're doing it – how would you be coping?* Note here the assumption, buried in your question, that the client will be coping.

For every yes there is a no and for every no there is a yes, meaning that even when we take a path we know to be the right one, there is something that we have to give up. I coached a talented software developer off and on for a two-year period where she had utter clarity about her goal of getting a specific type of job with a famous Silicon Valley employer in the USA. After a tortuous selection process, she was offered the ideal job. But then what? Just before leaving London for San Francisco, she found herself inexplicably weeping every day, while simultaneously having no doubts about the choice being the right one: 'I realised I would never see certain people from my old job again', she said, 'and that I would miss the changeable British weather, maddening though it is, and English accents ... and ... and'. There were innumerable *and ... ands*, all things that she would mourn. Normalise this sadness with clients. Reassure them it is to be expected and will pass.

Sometimes what the client needs to give up is the perverse incentive for continuing as they are. The question here is, *What's the payoff for staying stuck?* A client is frustrated by their inability to get through a job interview successfully, but has avoided up until now seeking the coaching that might help. The payoff here might be secretly thinking, *If I don't try then I can't fail* or *It's the fault of all those bad interviewers that they don't see how good a fit I am with the job*. Sometimes the payoff is about fear of success: ensuring you fail means that you never have to find out if you were up to that job after all. Bringing these thoughts into conscious awareness can help us confront the negative fantasies that they involve.

One of the apparent mysteries of change is how often we will say what we want but then repeatedly sabotage ourselves. You can see this clearly in people with the disordered eating patterns that involve over-eating. They know they are obese. They hate being obese. They feel shame and guilt about their weight. They may be experts in every kind of diet where they have lost weight and then put it all back on again. They are fully aware that shedding pounds means eating less and exercising more. They know about the health risks, yet they stay fat. The same will apply less dramatically in clients who know they should take more exercise but fail to do it, or with people who understand the principles of delegation but cannot bring themselves to let go of control.

Part of the answer here is to spend enough time looking at the client's early life (Chapters 11 and 12) for explanations, but part of it lies, too, in neuropsychology. The human brain prefers the status quo even when the status quo is uncomfortable. The brain prefers short-term reward over longer-term gain. I will explain this to clients by describing how neural pathways have strengthened the habits of decades, along with a degree of 'conditioning' where immediate rewards, even if this is just releasing anxiety, will reinforce the behaviour. The good news is that we can form new habits and create new neural pathways by identifying the triggers that have created the old behaviour. This is where a coach can help. *What situations set off the behaviour you want to change? What typically goes through your mind? What might you do instead? How might you reinforce the new habit?*

A paradox of change is that nothing can happen without the pain of an uncomfortable present. The discomfort gives energy for change and needs to be greater than the reward of staying stuck. If little is at stake, then why bother? It is worth raising this explicitly with clients by letting them fully express their misery with whatever the current situation is. Then ask the killer question, *What happens if you do nothing?* Stay impartial when asking this question. If you seem over-invested in the change then the client will kick back and you will become like everyone else in their lives whom they will probably quite rightly see as 'nagging' or 'having an agenda'. You do not have an agenda and your influence rests in your combination of warmth and neutrality.

Another powerful question needs to be asked at this point: *What's at stake here?* For a two-year period a few years ago, I offered weight-loss coaching and recruited clients, all of them in highly paid professional jobs, who wanted to change the way they approached food and eating. Most of these people were seriously overweight. When I asked then what was at stake, their answers included phrases such as, 'Living to see my children grow up', 'Regaining my self-respect' or 'Being able to have an intimate relationship without awful self-consciousness intruding'. Many of them commented that just articulating these sobering statements was in itself an additional motivator.

This work showed me that there is often a role for information, depending on the issue. I found that despite what seemed to be a plethora of easily available advice on nutrition in weight loss, many of my clients had not heard it in any detail. For instance, few, if any, knew more than some simple information about excessive consumption of carbohydrates, how insulin resistance develops, or that sugar and carbohydrates, not saturated fat, are the likely source of heart disease. When you acquire expertise in one type of coaching, you will probably find that you acquire specialist knowledge which it will pay to pass on to clients. Request permission to offer it, asking what the client already knows so that you don't embarrass yourself by patronising them with explanations that they don't need.

It's easy to get lost in all the difficulties of change so there needs to be plenty of time to discuss what longer-term benefits the change would deliver. One client was terrified of speaking in public, including in large meetings. She began her explanation of the benefits it would bring her to lose her fears by saying, 'I wouldn't be throwing up before any event where I have to speak'. Later on in the discussion, she had identified some far more powerful benefits: self-respect, the ability to influence colleagues effectively on topics that mattered to her, and increasing her chances of promotion to a more senior role. We reminded ourselves of these benefits at every session. By doing this, you are conveying your belief that the client can change. Sometimes you might be the only person in the client's life who holds that a positive result is possible.

One client who had faced the misery of long-term unemployment told me, when we reviewed our work, that its main value to him had been my certainty that he was employable and would get a job: 'You never wavered, unlike all those gloomy people who kept telling me that I was too old or that there was no market for people with my background.'

It is worth spending a generous amount of time on how the client sees the barriers to change. Most of us are experts on why needed change can't happen – just yet. Our favourite reasons tend to externalise the problem: other people, an unsupportive family, never being able to shake off the psychological legacy of a deprived childhood, the government, our social status, lack of seniority, the nastiness of the organisation and its bosses ... we will shrug and say that these are beyond our control and true enough, they are. A coach must always ask how clients are contributing to the problem themselves. The real barriers are often the self-imposed ones of long-held assumptions and beliefs.

A finance director brought me the question of how to manage the relationship with his boss. We discussed what was going wrong. In his view, the answer was that this boss was 'a jumped up little Hitler with minimal emotional intelligence'. I reminded him, with a smile, of how strange it seemed that so many of his former bosses had conformed to this pattern of little Hitlers. He had left three previous jobs because the boss relationship had broken down. We looked back yet again to his early childhood where his father had left the family, married again and had two more children whom he seemed to favour over the children from his first marriage. That 5-year-old boy felt abandoned, angry, powerless – and the grown man assumed that male authority figures would always let you down. This client freely described himself as having been wary, surly and uncommunicative with the current boss, putting the relationship on a perilous footing from the start. I well remember this client's face after we had this discussion. He started laughing. 'How dare you! Are you suggesting that all male bosses are not my father?' Nothing immediately dramatic happened after this, but slowly, very slowly, the client tried out different behaviours and slowly, very slowly, things got better. When the client moved on, it was not because of the poor relationship with his boss.

It is true that the small changes around specific events, usually described as *transactional*, can happen quickly and this can be a pleasing result in the early stages of a coaching engagement. *Transformational* change, which involves changing beliefs as well as wholesale patterns of behaviour, takes much longer. In the traditional pattern of therapy, the client and the therapist meet once a week for a 50-minute 'hour' over an extended period, sometimes more than a year. Alcoholics Anonymous groups meet every week, as do many weight-loss groups. Members get frequent support along with acceptance and challenge. This is mostly not the pattern in coaching. As in the example I describe earlier in this chapter, where the client appeared to have problematic behaviour with women, the coach and client met once a month for 90 minutes and had little contact between the six sessions. Yet everyone – the coach, the client and the sponsor, and possibly the client's team too – expected that this relatively small amount of coaching could miraculously solve all his problems.

Everything we know about how to make change stick suggests that this is the wrong model. The bigger the change, and the more it matters, the longer it takes and the more gradual it is. It is evolutionary, not revolutionary and almost never happens in giant leaps. For this reason, I tend to negotiate longer rather than shorter coaching programmes. I offer clients the chance to use our sessions to design a series of pilot projects – small steps to be seen as experiments. This allows for the inevitable relapses and failures. The idea is to monitor their own and other people's reactions and to assess what seems different, ideally what seems better. I ask the client to keep in frequent touch with me by text or email, reporting back on immediate results.

This is very light-touch accountability because accountability matters too. As coaches, we can offer an informal but vital part in monitoring progress. This can easily turn sour if either side begins to think of it as being like the role a probation officer, manager or teacher would play. Ask the client whether they would welcome regular checks on how they are doing and, if so, how they would like it to happen. Answers to this question over the years have suggested that moderation is what people want: 'Just nod, don't do any of that awful *good boy* praising that I remember from my Mum'; 'Look interested but don't show too much interest'; 'Discussing what worked is probably going to be more useful than discussing what didn't'; 'Don't call it *homework* and don't tell me off if I don't do it!'

Acknowledging that change happens slowly will give you another way of looking at the process. There are many dozens of excellent theoretical models of change. The one I call on most often identifies six distinct phases. It was developed by James Prochaska and Carlo Di Clementi in the late 1970s and is sometimes called the *Transtheoretical Model of Change*. It originally looked at how smokers manage the process of quitting. The six phases are: Pre-Contemplation, Contemplation, Preparation, Action, Maintenance and Termination. The model suggests that there is a natural rhythm to change and that it is normal for there to be a lengthy process of thinking and rumination before we take action. It is easy as a coach to believe that because a client tells you they want something to change they are already at the Action phase, whereas this may be a long way off in their minds. You can waste a lot of coaching time by missing opportunities to coach the client through whichever phase they are in. You might want to share the model directly with a client, asking them where they believe they are in making the change they say they want.

Social backing is essential, so ask clients who and what can be an additional support. When we keep a goal secret, people will expect to see our usual behaviour. Decades of research into what works when you want to stop smoking demonstrate how valuable it is for the smoker to tell as many people as possible that they are stopping and to enlist others as helpers. Changing your social circle or some of the relationships within it may be a necessary part of the picture. When a smoker is surrounded by friends and colleagues who are still smoking, it will be much harder to stop. Depending on how frank a client has been with you about their personal life, explore which close family and friends are likely to be supportive. It may be necessary to prepare them for finding that some of their close family, despite what they say, would prefer the client to stay exactly as they are. One client who had severe problems with self-esteem gradually became more confident during a year-long coaching programme. However, her husband began some dismaying behaviour, seeming to belittle her newfound poise. Her conclusion was that he had relished the feeling of moral superiority it had given him to be 'the self-assured one' in the relationship, and resented the way she had changed. The marriage survived his scorn, but things were rocky for a while.

In summary, this is what speeds change along: a relationship of mutual trust and respect; a clearly stated, achievable goal with its benefits spelt out; a candid look at self-imposed barriers, including links to the client's early life; small steps which allow for some failure; vibrant social support; emphasising the expectation of success; accountability and plenty of time – which should include frequent contact, even if this is only by email or text. As ever, all of this applies as much to us as coaches as it does to clients – which is why we often need our own coach as well as a supervisor.

22

Working with Loss

It is inevitable that we will work with many clients who are struggling with loss. Since it will surely come our way, the question is, what is it appropriate to do?

It could be that the issue bringing the client to you in the first place is one where loss is inextricably involved. This will be true for any of us whose remit is executive coaching and it will be especially true if your offer includes career coaching. People are fired, made redundant, their companies merge or get acquired, and even if they still have a job, it may have changed out of all recognition. The client may have held on to their post when so many pleasant colleagues have not, creating feelings of guilt as well as anxiety about whether they are likely to be next. Equally often, the coaching programme may start out with familiar issues about life decisions or leadership style but then be derailed by an emotional emergency: the client gets bad news about their own or a loved one's health, or someone dear to them dies. Any jolt to stability can create crushing feelings of loss: divorce, the death of a parent or partner, suddenly losing financial security, a miscarriage, the ending of a friendship, the death of a beloved pet or moving reluctantly into retirement.

Any major social and economic change will involve loss: war, recession, migration, natural disaster. The Covid pandemic upended so much that was predictable. When friends, parents, colleagues or partners died, it was impossible to mark their passing with a traditional funeral. There were sudden job losses for millions of people worldwide as well as exposing all of us to risk from an invisible enemy. Easy social contact with friends and family was replaced by the awareness that other people could be agents of infection. Familiar treats like cinema, theatre and restaurant meals disappeared. While some people enjoyed lockdown because of the relief it gave from social pressure, for many it created bewilderment and anger. These feelings need to be named for what they are: grief.

One sweeping change so often triggers an unstoppable cascade of further unwelcome upheaval. Loss of a job may mean a change of city and a house move, then a personal relationship may be put under strain, separation may follow and with it financial difficulties and health problems.

What all these events have in common is that the change has been imposed, there are high levels of ambiguity and the emotional impact can be overwhelming. I was working with a marketing director who had given 25 years of loyal service to his company when he found himself caught up in a public scandal where the entire executive team was obliged to resign. He was furious with the colleagues who had created this disaster, disbelieving at first that he would lose his job. He had tried unsuccessfully to negotiate his survival on the grounds that his own hands were clean. He had then collapsed into numbness when at last he understood that he would have to leave.

The more unexpected the crisis, the more power it has to destabilise. After being reluctantly single for many years, a woman client found a loving partner and they had spent three contented years together. Coming back from a transatlantic trip where she had given a successful conference presentation, she discovered her partner's body in their apartment where it had lain for many hours after he had had a fatal stroke. She bravely turned up for her scheduled coaching session only four days later. Telling me this horrible news, she wailed with despair, berating herself for not having been there, wrongly believing that if she had, she would have been able to save his life, something that she had already been assured would have been impossible.

In these circumstances, it's no good thinking to yourself, *I'm not a bereavement counsellor*. The client is right there in front of you.

It pays to be prepared, starting with familiarising yourself with the psychology of grief and loss. Most coaches and many clients are already conversant with the ideas of Dr Elisabeth Kübler-Ross. Kübler-Ross was a psychiatrist who had had a difficult childhood and who remained interested in traumatic experience throughout her career. Her model, often described as The Kübler-Ross Change Curve, grew out of her experience with terminally ill patients and proposed five stages, starting with denial, then moving through anger, bargaining, depression and acceptance. Her colleague and co-writer, David Kessler has subsequently added a sixth stage: meaning. This looks at how to find meaning in loss. Kübler-Ross herself never meant to convey a rigid or once-and-for-all approach, and research has failed to support the idea that there are set 'stages' or types of grief response which apply universally or that 'must' be gone through. Nonetheless, the accessibility of this model has made it serviceable in coaching because it gives names and structure to perplexing emotions. I find, for instance, that clients might diagnose themselves as 'stuck at anger' or 'in denial'. The model is less enlightening if clients believe that it is a map and that somehow they should be moving quickly to 'acceptance'. It is equally unhelpful for clients whose response to grief and loss doesn't fit any of the stages and emotions that Kübler-Ross described.

You may notice that clients describe regret or guilt about some of their actions. But it seems that the actions we did not take have more power to destabilise us: 'I wish I'd spoken up, but I didn't'; 'I wish I'd been able to be there when my father died'. Encourage clients to accept that these omissions cannot be changed now and that they happened for what seemed like good reasons at the time. One client told me of his regret that he and his late wife had never had a frank conversation about the way the demands of his job had damaged their marriage. Instead, they had fallen into a pattern of resentful bickering. He wrote her a 'letter' saying what he would like to have said during her life, printed it, carried it around with him for many months and told me how much it had helped him. His comment was, 'In the end, it felt as if we had had that conversation. It eased me a lot.'

'Closure' is another popular idea. The reality of bereavement and loss is that there is no closure because the feelings of loss can reignite at any point – they never truly go away, though the intensity and frequency of the pain virtually always lessen. One client who had been the main carer for her dying husband over a two-year period said, 'It's ten years since he died and I still think of him every day. I've remarried, I have a wonderful little boy and I'm happy but the slightest thing can set off a spike of grief and I think it always will. But now I can absorb it in a way that was impossible at first.' Reconciliation is a more workable idea than closure. When you reconcile yourself to loss, you gradually accept that it has happened, you can experience joy in your life again without guilt or remorse, and you can remember the positives about the dead person or the lost job. Clients who struggle with the idea of closure can feel guilty about the way they are still experiencing intense feelings of loss. 'I can't manage my grief', one client said, a full year after her beloved mother had died suddenly. 'Eruptions of crying can overwhelm me.' My question to her was, 'If you could magically prescribe something for yourself that would reduce your grief to a more manageable level, what would be happening?' Her comment to me later was that this question implied hope for the future without attempting to minimise the reality of the present.

You may want to de-mythologise other common ideas, for instance that if you don't cry you are not sorry about the loss, or that there is some 'normal' timetable for recovery, or that being seen to 'move on' means that you have forgotten all about the loss. None of this is true. I worked with a client in his 60s whose adored wife had died after two years of gruelling chemotherapy. He was distraught at her loss but quickly began internet dating, telling me that life without someone to love was intolerable for him. A year after her death, he met the right person, someone whose marriage had ended in a publically humiliating divorce. The Twitter trolls busied themselves with poisonous comments, but so did a number of disapproving 'friends'. These people seemed to believe that it was their duty to upbraid him because his new relationship showed 'disrespect' to his late wife. As he said to me, 'It's actually a tribute to her. When we realised she was dying, she urged me to remarry.'

Grief is far from a purely emotional process. Our immune systems can be weakened by emotional overload. It is normal to experience fatigue, insomnia, raised blood pressure, respiratory and gastric infections, nausea and headaches.

Clients may want to discuss their physical health with you, including how to get medical advice if this seems to be what they need.

When a client brings you their grief, they are not asking you to make it go away nor to help them feel better. Mostly what they want is listening and acceptance. This can be hard to do as the urge to offer suggestions and nostrums can be so powerful. Seeming to do 'nothing' but listen can create anxiety in the listener. Despite this, the best response is paying close attention, nodding and making brief comments such as 'that sounds distressing, I'm so sorry', or 'I can see how upsetting this is', or 'I can't begin to imagine the depth of this loss for you'. The most helpful attitude is to see yourself as witness to the loss. If grief and loss are not witnessed, the pain goes inside; it burrows deep and reappears as physical or mental illness. It is rarely beneficial to describe your own or other clients' stories, as this might appear to be setting up a competition about whose experience was the most tragic, or, even worse, inviting the client to offer comfort to you. Your own loss is always the one that is the most intense. To double-check, you may want to ask, saying something like, 'I'm ready to listen to this for as long as you like. I'm wondering what would be helpful to you in this session.'

Sometimes what clients describe is difficult to hear, especially if it triggers the memory of something similar for you. It is often impossible to prepare for the way a client's issue can set off something unexpectedly upsetting for a coach. One of the coaches I supervise told me about a client who became tearful as she described her terrifying recent experience of being robbed at knifepoint. Something similar had happened only a few weeks earlier to the coach. She said:

> It was instant tears for me too. I had to tell the client why. Funnily enough, we each stopped crying almost straight away, just gazing at each other. I suggested we took a pause. I opened the French doors, and without speaking a word we both stepped out into the garden and gave each other a hug. I asked if she was OK to go on and she said yes and then asked me if I was OK to go on and I said yes. So we did, and it was.

These incidents are rare and I remind myself that in the normal run of coaching, I cannot be effective if I allow myself to be overwhelmed by a client's story. I can certainly show that I am moved by what they say but my aim is to be calm, accepting – and unshockable. This will include those unusual occasions when the client appears strangely blank about what they are telling you. For instance, one client, who had welcomed her pregnancy then had a scan which showed that the baby had severe abnormalities and could not survive birth, told me that she had gone through the termination stolidly, including the experience of giving birth at 21 weeks, saying, 'I felt and feel disappointment but nothing else and I don't want people swooning all over me and telling me they "feel sorry for your loss"'. I had to take that as my cue to stay as unruffled as she appeared to be – and not to probe.

The common theme here is loss of control and the feeling of helplessness that it creates. This applies whether the predicament is losing a job, losing a substantial amount of money, making a forced house move or dealing with a death. Recovery is always associated with regaining a sense of agency in your life. When a client does ask what practical steps they might take, though I note that this is rare, there are some suggestions you might offer, all of them about putting the client, even if only marginally, back in charge.

One practical tactic is to construct a short script designed to manage the unwanted enquiries, advice and clichés of colleagues or friends, acknowledging that, hard as it seems, the person experiencing the loss has to be the one who takes the lead in managing other people's responses. Clients have repeatedly told me in these circumstances that other people's well-meant interventions are mostly exhausting, tiresome and intrusive or else that their studied avoidance is hurtful. The client may be surrounded by those who find other people's distress unbearable. They mean well but they want you to 'get over it' so that they do not have to watch you suffer. They may want to tell you how you should feel or that they already know how you feel. They may want to pass on their hints and tips. If it's a health emergency, they will know of someone who was totally cured after taking a special pill or by following a diet of beetroot juice. Stopping them politely but firmly through a script that has been rehearsed with you can work well.

It can help to confide in a journal as there is ample research to show that the act of writing down harrowing experiences can soothe some of their sting. Writing the story of a loved person's illness, death and the aftermath for the survivor can help: it gives a narrative arc to the loss – a beginning, a middle and an end. Writing a letter that you never send can also work, as can a memorial page on a Facebook account (with privacy controls to keep trolls away). Running a marathon or creating some other way of fundraising to support a suitable charity has eased the pain for many people; you feel you are doing something that might offer relief to others in similar circumstances.

Where the loss involves organisational change, people's instincts can be to withdraw. They want to hide. I have seen many clients benefit from getting involved rather than retiring hurt. They seek out information rather than avoiding it, offer to be on working parties or to be a mentor to more junior people. Where people have lost their jobs, a career coaching or outplacement programme is a healthy and natural way to recover that vital sense of agency. Expect the first session to be dominated by anger – 'what ifs' and 'if onlys'. After that, the process of reviewing options, looking at strengths, constructing a new CV/résumé and learning how to search for a job can all contribute to feeling that, once again, the client is managing their career.

Sometimes people want revenge as their way of regaining control. This is understandable when they have suffered because of the mistakes of another person. One client found that most of his pension savings were locked up in the trading account of a fund owner, previously the darling of the financial press as a stock picker, now a dying enterprise, where the owner had shamelessly awarded himself millions in compensation, even when his fund was obviously failing. The client was engulfed by anger. He wanted to join others picketing the fund owner's home and told me eagerly that he had planned exactly how he would parcel up some dog faeces to send to the man he described as 'the world's biggest shit, so he may as well get some'. I thought this was possibly an idle threat but treated it in exactly the same way as I would any other decision that a client brought to a session. Inside I was longing to say, Don't do it! It will achieve nothing! You could get caught and punished. But I simply asked the client to assess the pluses and minuses, including the risks. In the event, this client opted to join a class action and, as far as I know, never sent the nasty parcel. The same will apply to clients who want to sue their organisation for wrongful dismissal or for seeming to turn a blind eye to sexual harassment. Sometimes this is the courageous option and the right thing to do, and it is always the client's decision, but, in so many cases, taking the issue to court results in long-term unhealthy preoccupation with the alleged 'injustice' and may still not go the client's way. A measured appraisal of the options may result in a better settlement for the client without all the disadvantages of a court case.

Every now and then, there will be a client who cannot adjust to their loss. I think here of a woman who could not accept that she had lost her job because of poor performance and insisted that the real cause was racism. A tribunal had rejected her claim and she had been unemployed ever since. It was not my role to judge whether or not this was fair, but four years on she was still consumed by anger and we had to agree that she was not ready to start the journey to a renewed career.

Where bereavement is concerned, I have never worked directly with a client suffering from complicated grief, sometimes described as traumatic grief. This is where the bereaved person cannot accept the finality of their loss, especially if a violent death has been involved. However, I have worked with family members where they have become perplexed and exasperated by the behaviour associated with complicated grief. One client described her mother as being 'utterly committed to her six years of mourning'. The client's much younger brother had died in a motorbike accident at 20 years old. Her mother dressed in black, went to the grave every day, where she 'conversed' with her dead son, and kept his room exactly as it had been, saying that he was 'still with us' because she 'saw' him in the street. She talked about him to anyone who would listen. Complicated grief is treatable but only if the person is ready to accept help. In this case, my role was to avoid getting involved in discussions about the technicalities of her mother's mental health, and rather to listen carefully and then to coach the client around managing the relationship.

Grief is a normal reaction to loss. It's not an illness. You can't ever make assumptions about how the client will feel because the range of emotions is so wide. Most people recover without needing counselling or therapy. On the rare occasions when they can't seem to recover, your coaching will be about how to find and benefit from help, as it will in any other situation where the client's responses seem to be out of proportion to the original event.

However maturely you feel you have coped or are coping with similar losses in your own life, you can't do this work and expect to be unaffected by it. If you feel deadened, then you may have reached burnout (page 156) and need to get help fast. While I was writing this section, I had an email from a long-standing and much-liked client telling me that he had been diagnosed with lung cancer. I was immediately pierced with profound sadness, remembering his many jokes about how he would give up smoking 'one day'. Simultaneously, I was suffused with worry about the two dearly loved smokers in my own life. This jumble of responses is natural. The task is to notice them and manage them. Our personal worries have to be dealt with elsewhere and in a different way. When we are in the coaching role, it's the client's needs that matter.

23
Coaching through Crisis

As the Covid-19 pandemic tightened its grip in 2020, we saw the extremes of human behaviour. First, there was the panic buying and hoarding, the tales of selfishness and reckless risk-taking. Then a different picture emerged, one of sacrifice and generosity. The military metaphor became so commonplace that people paid no attention to it. What made it different was that in this 'war', we 'civilians' were involved, not just the 'troops', because we were all at risk. It was far worse for clinical staff in hospitals and GP practices, those working in supermarkets and pharmacies, the teachers who turned up as volunteers to care for children whose parents were deemed to be in essential jobs, the delivery drivers and many others. We were aware of what it took from them to do their jobs so that some simulacrum of ordinary life might continue.

The pandemic reminded me, and colleagues, of how serviceable and appropriate coaching can be in a crisis and its long-lasting aftermath, whether a pandemic of the future or being available for people caught up in major accidents and natural disasters of any sort.

Thousands of coaches, counsellors and therapists came forward during this time to volunteer their services and many were disappointed to find that their offer was never taken up. In some schemes, the volunteers outnumbered the clients many times over. There is a warning buried inside this phenomenon. It was not true that 'everyone' was suffering. We should beware of making a crisis out of a crisis. Some businesses did well: the owner of a chain of restaurants who had gloomily forecast to me that his business would go under, found that he made his biggest profit ever. He centralised his kitchens and within a week had turned the company into a slick online and delivery operation.

Even at the height of the pandemic, I heard from friends who vowed that they were content in their isolation. Client sessions were as likely to focus on a topic that had nothing to do with the Covid virus as they were on its immediate impact. Some clients confided that they felt more fulfilled and animated than at any earlier point in their career. As one said to me, 'I'm having "a good war", I know I'm doing excellent work and I know how vital it is.' Others described feeling less stressed than they had for many years. They no longer had the long commute to work. They no longer had to worry about being harshly judged on their appearance, performance or social skills; isolation was a relief.

In supervision, many coaches worried about their own competence: *Is coaching what those frontline people need? If so, am I up to it?* I noticed that many of these coaches assumed at first that something special was needed in the way of coaching technique. This was not the case – just the attitudes, beliefs, frameworks and skills that they were using every day. The difference was that it was much, much harder to hold on to them. The same criteria apply to whether what the client needs is therapy not coaching. The essential discriminator here is that the client needs therapy when their reactions seem more intense, more engulfing and last longer than the situation seems to justify. I never found that this was true in the work I did with clients during that time.

What did make it more stretching was the context and in what was at stake. I found that I needed to remember how this extraordinary experience of isolation and physical distancing was likely to ignite long-buried trauma from childhood for some people (Chapter 13). If you were in isolation at home, regardless of whether you were living alone, it could well recreate the feelings of abandonment and helplessness which engulfed you as a child. The constant media messages about danger must, for many people, have reminded them at some level of how unsafe they had felt as children with parents who did not provide enough care. I worked with many clients during this time where we had already established that their attachment style was anxious (Chapter 12) and where rescuing was a constant temptation for them. These clients were at risk of believing that their organisation was asking them to rescue, sometimes literally. The responsibility could feel crushing, unreasonably demanding compared with what was achievable. All this applied to coaches as much as to clients.

One intensive care consultant brought me his anguish, in the earliest stages of the pandemic, at the lack of adequate personal protective equipment available in his ward, then the painful decisions about which patients should have priority. A palliative care nurse expressed her sorrow that the family of a dying patient could not be at their bedside. A funeral director could not contain his frustration that the helpful rituals of his profession could not apply. 'I've become heartless and super-efficient', he said. 'It's just about dealing with the bodies, no time for the living – and I hate myself.'

Others had complex personal decisions to make. A director of nursing saw it as her clear duty to get back into uniform and to take her place in the rotas, but this would mean that she had to live apart from her husband, 15 years her senior and in fragile health. To ensure his wellbeing, she would have to persuade their daughter to move temporarily into their home. A young entrepreneur, facing the shutdown of his business for an unknown length of time, agonised about which of his loyal staff he could retain on furlough and which would have to leave, knowing that the leavers would be unlikely to find other jobs quickly.

When I described these dilemmas to one fellow coach, she looked horrified. 'But how could you advise them on making those decisions?' she cried. My reply was that there was no way I could ever offer advice on such problems, but nor is there on 99% of the more ordinary questions that clients bring.

Covid-19 made it clear that to work with people in any kind of crisis, personal or professional, you, the coach, have to be as grounded as possible. You cannot do this work if you are overwhelmed with anxiety yourself. It is not for everyone. Questions to ask yourself here are: *Have I got my own anxiety under control? If I have any tendencies to rescue, can I accept that rescuing is not what clients need? Can I hang on to my belief that everyone is resilient, even when they appear not to be?* This matters because if the answer to any of these questions is 'no', then the phenomenon known as *parallel processing* will kick in.

This is how it happens. The client is expressing confusion and distress. They don't know what to do; they feel out of control. Their dilemma reminds you of something similar in your own life. Or empathy becomes sympathy, you can't stay unattached, you have identified with your client and you feel as helpless as they do. Panic sets in. Coaching skills desert you. At its worst, I have known coaches who describe breaking down at this point, or else who become wooden and tongue-tied – they literally cannot speak. Their inner dialogue is that they have become incompetent, the client's problem is too big for them and a better coach would know what to do.

Awareness is the key: notice that it is happening, take a breath, step back mentally, remind yourself that your value to the client starts with being able to listen without getting involved, and then to maintain your belief in the client's ability to solve their own problems. You cannot do it for them.

We now have a hundred years of research and thinking into what happens to people in organisations during periods of profound change, and much of this is immediately applicable to coaching during a national and international crisis. The work of the writer William Bridges is especially relevant here. Bridges talks about three phases of change: Beginnings, Endings, and between them, a Neutral Zone. He describes the confusion we feel when we are living through change. We are uncertain what has ended and even less so of what has begun. The psychological adjustment takes much longer than the formal beginnings or endings. It's no longer clear who has the power, which rules matter or what will stay the same. The new can never be the same as the old – things don't just go back to how they were before. Old assumptions, some of which it has taken decades to create, can be jettisoned in moments. Bridges' description of the Neutral Zone uncannily describes how so many people felt during the Covid-19 pandemic: bewildered, buffeted but strangely peaceful and aware that it was a time for creativity and learning. The key to surviving and thriving is to regain at least some sense of control by getting involved in what is happening rather than being a helpless bystander. This was at the heart of my own practice during this challenging time and was my aim with every client.

There was usually no time for the normal kind of introductory session. The client wanted to address their immediate concerns. Few of these clients will have had coaching before, so you need to have a swift discussion about what coaching can and can't do, perhaps asking them what their own expectations are. Just as you would in any coaching conversation, you will draw out goals, distinguishing between the immediate and the longer term. A client might tell you that the whole situation is making them question whether they want to continue with their current career, but it is likely that there will be more pressing issues in the foreground. Suggest that you deal with these first, returning to the bigger questions later.

All the usual coaching conventions apply. Clients will benefit from the time and space to explore their feelings, to review what is happening. They will appreciate being heard with empathy and acceptance by someone who is not immediately involved. They will benefit from some simple goal-setting and from being asked incisive questions. They are not looking for advice. When we are experiencing crisis, we need to express how we feel and all my sessions began with some unloading from the client. I found it worked well to give some structure to this part of the session by asking four questions in this order:

- What is your immediate concern?
- What is it that angers you most (because there was always anger)?
- What are you most worried about?
- What are your assumptions here?

The final two questions are the most revealing. People's answers included, 'Being unable to cope', 'Getting sick, infecting my family' and 'Making a terrible mistake because I'm so tired'.

While some of these answers could be well justified by the extremity of what these clients faced, many were catastrophising, that is, believing that the worst possible outcome was not imaginary but likely and imminent. Here, I would ask clients to give me answers to three questions, each with its follow-up of 'and what would you do?'

- What's the worst that could happen?
- What's the best that could happen?
- What's the most likely thing to happen?

When we catastrophise, the most powerful question is, 'Let's imagine that does happen. What would you do?' There is relief in facing the worst and saying it out loud. Most people can reply in ways that show they believe in their ability to cope. One ICU nurse dreaded making a specific serious mistake. She said that if she did make this mistake, she would report herself immediately and would do whatever she could to rectify it. Having this part of the conversation reminded her that she had every right to ask for some training in how to use the equipment that was involved. The underlying principle here is that 'failure' is not 'the end'. If you did fail or if you have failed, there is always something you can do.

Some clients were struggling with anxiety which had got out of control. A highly paid director of strategy had to stand down from her job, watching her firm's financial resources draining away during the lockdown. We knew each other well as I had worked with her through three job transitions, each time seeing her anxiety spiral as she worried about paying her mortgage, imagining herself unemployed for long periods and, this time, convinced that at 52 she would never work again. Another client wanted ideas about how to help his wife. She had experienced chronic health anxiety all her life and this was her worst nightmare come true; it seemed that what had previously been an irrational dread of 'germs' was now fully justified. Survivor guilt was common: why have I survived when others have suffered so terribly or have actually died?

The first question for clients like this is to check what they know about the function of the amygdala in the human brain. If they are unfamiliar with it, then it is worth a brief explanation which will show them that there is a biological as well as a psychological dimension to anxiety, but that the brain can be relatively easily fooled into calming down. When I experienced chronic anxiety myself after a bereavement, I found a therapist who taught me a number of what she called 'anxiety first aid' techniques and I have passed these on to many clients since.

One is what is known as 7/11 breathing. You breathe in through your nose to a slow count of seven and then blow the breath gently out through your mouth to a slow count of 11. Repeating this a dozen times produces immediate calm. The other approach is 54321: notice five things you can see, four things you can hear, three things you can touch, two things you can smell and one is a long breath out – then repeat. Both these techniques sabotage the anxiety and the process of ruminating by interrupting them through focusing on something else. Visualisations and progressive muscle relaxation will be valuable. I demonstrated and then did some of these exercises along with clients many times during this period. It helped us both to steady down during the sessions themselves.

In situations of immense stress, we lose our sense of proportion. Some of the people I coached at this time reported feeling flattened by pessimism or anger, sometimes both. I found that two questions were especially effective here. The first draws on the well-known idea of the 'circle of concern', the elements we cannot influence or change, and the 'circle of influence', the elements that we can influence. It is usually drawn as one circle (influence) nestling inside the other (concern). There is no point in putting energy into the circle of concern, in this case government policy, the unpredictability of the virus itself, the behaviour of presidents in other countries, or the conspiracy theorists who are always lurking on Twitter. The question here is: *What is within your own circle of influence?* One emergency medicine doctor raged about what he described as 'chaos' in how patients were being treated. He was aiming his anger at the hospital manager in charge of his department. The answer to the question about what was within his control was that he had sound ideas about improving triage systems and a regular forum in which these ideas could be expressed. He rehearsed them with me, took them to the meeting and got them accepted immediately.

The second powerful question suggests testing ideas by looking for evidence. When so many people are panicking and when there is a dearth of reliable information, the vacuum is filled by rumour. Fake news thrives and can reproduce itself at lightning speed, thanks to social media. When my strategy director client was giving full vent to her fears, I asked, 'What is the evidence that you are unemployable?' The answer was that there was none. She was regularly receiving calls from head-hunters, a reliable sign that she had a good reputation in her sector. I suggested to this client, as I did to all the others, that she might limit her exposure to news media, given how little of it was based on fact and how much on the often ill-informed speculation of journalists, people whose stock in trade is gossip.

At such times, it is all too normal to be trapped in problem-based thinking. It goes like this: something horrible has happened; whose fault is it? It's probably mine: it's awful; there's no help available; I feel helpless; I feel panic. Then the cycle begins all over again. When clients describe the intensity of the problem, you will hear them in the grip of this pattern. Show them how it works, perhaps drawing it on paper for them. Then show them the alternative: resourceful thinking. It goes like this: OK, there is a problem. What contributed to helping it happen (a systemic perspective)? What might be possible here? What other options are there for solutions? Who else could help? What are my choices? What might my first steps be?

I found that clients typically brought three other types of problem, often overlapping. The first is *moral injury*. The term was developed to describe American military personnel returning from the Vietnam War. The diagnosis of PTSD did not fit and treatment for PTSD did not work for them. Their question was whether they could still see themselves as moral beings when they had been repeatedly told to carry out acts, such as killing civilians, which went against their own moral code. People such as healthcare professionals may also experience moral injury. A young doctor instructed to ignore an elderly patient lying on a trolley, or to refuse a ventilator to a child with Downs Syndrome, is contravening everything their training has prepared them to do, which is to put the welfare of individual patients at the heart of their practice. Cynicism, panic, helplessness, depression, sleeplessness or physical collapse may result. This is very different from burnout or rustout because the cause is not a broken individual but a broken system. Where clients are not familiar with this concept, it may be helpful to explain it to them as part of our duty to normalise what they are feeling.

The second type of problem concerns personal resilience: *Can I see my way through this? Do I have enough resourcefulness?* The third area that such clients bring is a familiar moral dilemma about prioritising: *Whose needs in my personal and professional lives come first? Should I protect my family by saying that I will look for low-risk work or is it incumbent upon me to sacrifice myself? Which patient should have my attention? Who should get these scarce resources?*

Despite their obvious urgency, these problems are classic dilemmas. You can deal with them as you would any other dilemma that clients bring. First, you ask clients to identify the dilemma, realising that they rarely want to make the decision there and then. What they are looking for is clarity. You agree the wording of the dilemma with the client, then ask the usual coaching questions about who and what else might be involved, which part of it the client owns and what they have already tried in the way of resolving it. Then you might identify the possible choices, looking at the upsides and downsides of each, including practicality, cost and fit with the client's values, acknowledging that there is probably no perfect solution, maybe only a least-bad option. It is unlikely that you will have any ideas that the client has not already considered, but if this seems to be the case, then toss them in for the same level of scrutiny.

When we are in the middle of a crisis, nuanced analysis may desert us, increasing our sense of helplessness. We fall prey to all-or-nothing reasoning. We overthink the problem because we are afraid of experiencing emotion. We may exaggerate the scope of our duties and the terrible results if it all went wrong. The most valuable question to ask here is, 'What's the immediate problem to be solved?' followed by 'What are the first steps you might take towards a solution?' Realism which accepts limitations rather than looking for a perfect answer can be the key to feeling more at peace. I heard several clients who were parents voicing worries which implied that unless they home-schooled their children as expertly as a professional teacher would, their child would be permanently damaged. I heard conscientious public servants who really did have awesome responsibilities, inflate these to grandiose proportions with matching catastrophic consequences, were they to do less than heroic work. In these circumstances, our language becomes clotted with generalisations like *always, everyone, no one, can't, mustn't, have to, never*. Challenge these: are they true? A senior manager in the NHS running operating theatres at the height of the pandemic swore to me that 'No one cares about teamwork any more!'

'Is that actually true? Absolutely no one?'

There was a long pause. 'Well, no, there are some people who still do, but we're the minority.'

Our conversation was then about how this minority might work together to demonstrate and re-establish the teamwork that was so clearly necessary.

During the Covid-19 pandemic, there was a yawning ambiguity about when it would end. People asked for certainty where there was none. I heard many people – clients, friends and people in the public eye – complaining that they felt 'imprisoned'. One client objected to this language. As part of his determination to turn the experience into a learning project, he familiarised himself with the memoirs of people who actually had been imprisoned, either as a punishment for a crime or because they had been kidnapped and held hostage. His conclusion was that the secret to inner peace was never to focus on when it would end, for instance with calendars where you cross off days. Nor should you fantasise about what you would do when it did end. His motto was *Vivo Propter Diem*, a Latin tag meaning Live for the Day. He took great pleasure, as he said, in 'showing off' his motto, despite never having learnt a word of Latin at school. When similar ideas came up with clients, they and I discussed how to make them a reality.

The challenge of coaching through a crisis like Covid-19 and its continuing aftermaths was that we were and are potentially as much affected by moods of pessimism, panic and helplessness as any of the clients we coach. How we respond will depend on our general emotional stability and circumstances. Even so, we were and are likely to be fearful for ourselves and our families, and concerned about the devastating longer-term impacts on the economy, politics and international relationships. All of this had to be set aside if we were to be effective. I found that it helped to remind myself of the incomplete nature of the information that was available and to remind myself that, as my client said, living for the day was never more important. Before I began every one of the coaching calls I was involved in at this time, I took 10 minutes to sit quietly, grounding myself and emptying my mind as far as possible of distractions.

As ever, the value to the client was not in the technicalities of what we do. The feedback I and other coaches had at this time was that the benefit of our coaching was our offer of a place where fear could be expressed and contained by someone who would listen without judgement or offering platitudinous advice. A coach I was supervising reported proudly that one client had said, 'I began to feel that optimism was possible again.' Another coach said that her client's gratitude for the coaching was, 'I trusted you with the craziness in my head.' That was praise indeed.

24

Working on Life Purpose

When clients say that they are troubled by a lack of purpose and meaning in their lives, I am eager to engage with them. This is despite knowing that there is no harder question that they bring and that, as far as I have been able to see, there are no quick answers to the issue of how a coach might help.

In the early years of the last century, most people in the UK lived only to their 50s; your expectations were probably modest, you were grateful for what you had. The idea of worrying about 'life purpose' would probably have seemed ludicrous. In the 21st century, the 100-year life is a reality and old ideas about predictable challenges at set life stages don't make much sense, nor do old ideas about 'retirement'. I have friends whose post-paid-work life is already longer than the period when they were employees. The concept of retirement has been upended when so many people continue with portfolio careers combining salaried work with volunteering and an extensive range of leisure activities. It no longer makes sense to apply the patronising label 'pensioner' to everyone over 60 when this can now include two whole generations, with wide variations in health and wellbeing.

In society at large, there are more people than ever before who are prosperous. At the same time, health and income inequalities have increased. Nearly half of any 18-year-old cohort in the 'global north' has access to higher education. 'Millennials' and 'Gen Z' are far less likely to be subservient to authority. Young people no longer expect 'starter jobs' as a right; they may do a few years in the gig economy instead. A freelance career can begin at any time, not just in late middle age, and the idea of staying in one organisation for life seems unthinkable. Redundancies, re-training or making abrupt changes in direction are common.

The decline of religion has played a part in explaining why this issue can seem pressing. Religious belief shapes your values and usually includes ideas about an afterlife. Living virtuously according to the principles of your faith may have been enough for many people in the past, but Western societies have become steadily more secular. If we are without religious beliefs, our mortality defines us and there is nothing more to life than living it now, making the most of our transience. As a result, we can be pursued by the sense that we have unlived our lives, haunted by the tragedy of gifts that have lain fallow.

I notice patterns in who raises the question of life purpose. These clients are unlikely to be under 40. The predominant feeling in your late 20s and 30s may be that there is little time for worry about issues like 'purpose'; you are too preoccupied with finding a partner, establishing a home, building your career, arranging childcare or hanging on to enough work to pay the bills. Later, in your 40s, 50s and 60s – or older – you may feel that you are facing what the great American writer and psychotherapist, Irvin Yalom, calls 'an existential crisis': *What meaning does my life have?* Certain kinds of client seem especially vulnerable here. Often, there is nothing amiss with the profession or job in itself: for those who are suited to it, there may be ample sense of purpose and satisfaction. But people who enter professions like medicine, accountancy or the law may do so as a result of family pressure. Some of them realise as early as their initial training that it is the wrong choice, but they stick with it out of loyalty to their parents, sometimes hoping that the dissatisfaction will go away once they are fully qualified. If this doesn't happen, they become robotic, slogging through their work, feeling crushing guilt that they cannot enjoy it. I worked with a gifted doctor, popular with her patients but not with her peers. She had a reputation for squabbling over rotas and picking fights with what she described as 'silly bureaucratic rules'. For years, she had held a secret ambition to be a children's art therapist. She slowly made this transition, starting with opting to work part time as a doctor and then with making the much bigger decision to retrain and to leave medicine. At this point, her comment was, 'I made trouble because I was so angry and unhappy.'

There are jobs which have no higher purpose, however kindly you look at them. These include the tick-box roles designed to satisfy some regulatory entity, or those jobs that enable things that should not be enabled, manage people who don't need managing, protect, lie, schmooze, make money for owners who already have too much ... the list is endless. People who do these jobs can feel a sudden and visceral self-disgust when it dawns on them that what they do is pointless and possibly a breach of moral principles which they have set aside or somehow forgotten.

You may work with clients who describe disillusion with the reality of organisational life where the stated values of the organisation are at odds with their daily experience. One well-paid director told me that, after years of loyal service, as soon as she reached the highest levels in her international charity, she realised that she could not tolerate the overt sexism and bullying that she saw all around her. She found herself asking, 'Have I wasted my life by being in this organisation?' These people may be suffering from *moral injury* (page 136), a useful phrase to describe feeling obliged to behave in ways which are contrary to your own principles.

Sometimes there is a crash in confidence as people realise that they do not have the talent and chutzpah to make it to the very top: this can be common in 'creative' sectors like music, dance, acting, publishing, TV and film, where the apex narrows sharply at the top. I felt some of this myself when I slowly came to terms with the high-level mediocrity of most television production and acknowledged that I was part of it. I was never going to win the Palme D'Or at Cannes or a BAFTA for Best Documentary. Television production had become tedious. Once I had acknowledged this out loud, it was just a matter of time before I left.

Occasionally, you will work with people who have lost their identity. They have melded with the organisation, it has become an idealised parent figure and the role has become who they are. I worked with a police officer who described what 'The Job' had represented for him: comforting jargon, easy companionship, reliable hierarchy and routine. Policing had given him intense inner satisfaction – it was obvious what it contributed to the common good. Reaching retirement age had hacked this away and he felt adrift, wondering what could give him the same sense of meaning in the new phase of his life.

Enquire into these feelings. Ask how long-standing and how intense they are. Is it, *I can't stand this organisation* or *I can't stand this job*? How would it be to do a similar job in a different organisation or a different job in the same organisation? Ask the client to do a life scan: what else is going on that could have a bearing – health, partner, children, parents, money, housing? The focus of this phase of the quest is into the present: What is at the heart of the client's dissatisfaction? What is missing?

It is tempting to wade straight into the life purpose question, but, before you do, it is worth looking at the more everyday, yet equally important, dissatisfactions in the client's life. Putting more energy into improvements there will often pay off. One client in a senior marketing role was clear that he no longer wanted to devote his life to what he called 'making money for foreign shareholders'. He confessed himself tormented by what to do instead that would have more meaning. He wanted to find the answer at speed. We did eventually identify what this might be, but not before we had talked through how he might reconnect with his estranged adult children and grandchildren.

Sometimes there is a good deal that can be done to improve enjoyment in the current role while the client takes stock of what the alternatives are. It was in this spirit that a client revamped her team, reducing her stress by halving the number of her direct reports. She did it by promoting a promising junior and giving him responsibility for a newly created project. Meanwhile, she jogged on with her private plan to become a self-employed consultant, investigating what people already established in her potential market were doing, making contacts and drafting her first business plan. Another client realised that before he did anything else, he needed therapy to tackle painful issues concerning his long-dead mother.

All these clients demonstrate what I have found to be a reliable principle: that the process of finding new or renewed life purpose does not work on a smooth arc where you consider your options, make a plan and then work through it in neat steps. What happens instead is that dissatisfaction comes and goes in bursts. There are pilot projects, tentative explorations, failures and modest successes. A sudden moment of epiphany is unlikely, though in retrospect the transitions can seem startling. In his early 50s, my brother-in-law left a successful career in education to go through ordination and became a full-time minister in his church. A client who had been a family doctor became first a local and then a national politician. A strategy consultant became a garden designer, while a senior physiotherapist became a tour guide to places of religious significance in Eastern Europe.

Many of these clients negotiated part-time work to create space for their initial experiments. The freed-up time allowed reading and thinking; they used it to take courses, to volunteer and to create new networks. Warn clients that this rarely takes less than 18 months, sometimes longer. Encourage the idea that when you are seeking a major change of direction, it is not helpful to mix with the same old crowd. Enlightenment comes from people who will challenge you with new ideas, introducing you to others who will do the same. Where people have neglected their networking skills, it may be worth spending some time on what genuine networking is and how to do it. This is not the self-promoting fake bonhomie that clients often assume it means, but a generous willingness to facilitate introductions as often as you benefit from the same process yourself. Alert clients to the idea of *finding your tribe*: those people who share your enthusiasms and skills. When you are in their company, you feel at ease, at home.

Where people are puzzled by their own feelings of discontent, you might want to explore whether they are familiar with the differences between extrinsic and intrinsic motivation. Clients who are troubled by the lack of meaning in their lives have sometimes sought reward in extrinsic motivators: money, impressive titles, prizes. One Olympic athlete was frightened by her confusion after winning a gold medal, realising that she would be too old to take part in the next Olympic cycle. Training routines imposed by others had dominated a life devoted to pleasing her coaches or to avoiding their rebukes, feeling, as she said, 'like an athlete android'. She told me, 'I lost all sense of who I was. From the moment I stood on that podium, I realised I didn't want to do any of it any more but the thought of the blank space it would leave was so alarming.'

Intrinsic motivation is more powerful. It comes from the pleasure of developing yourself to meet a challenge that is self-set. One woman client had been a much-honoured academic and public servant. She shrugged away her awards as cynical gestures that were politically motivated. In reviewing her current life, she said she had become 'a committee drudge, mostly spending time on stuff that would never matter, committees that reported to other committees in a never-ending cycle of trivia'. She became CEO for an organisation devoted to a cause dear to her heart, spending at least a day a fortnight working direct with this organisation's clientele.

The answer to finding satisfying life purpose is often about serving others and not yourself. This may involve volunteering, raising money for good causes or doing paid work which has a direct connection to improving life for other people. Alternatively, it may be finding satisfaction through calling on skills which have been muffled by years of doing a job which needed something different. This was true for a client who had inherited a successful business from his father and had felt oppressed by his assumed filial duty to keep it going. The business supplied luxury goods to some of the world's wealthiest people and, although there was satisfaction for him in maintaining the quality of the product, he found his role joyless. The first part of our work was exploring his unhappiness. The second was in working out how to sell the company with minimal disruption to his staff and family. The final part was about how he could set up a cookery school, devoting himself to his one true love: Italian food.

There are no special techniques for working with clients on this topic. Psychometrics can be helpful (Chapter 18). They let the client see themselves clearly and self-awareness is essential in making any major decision. Any strengths-based approach may work: a card-sort, a psychometric such as Realise2 or just a discussion. You might try well-known exercises such as drafting your own obituary or writing 'a postcard from the future'.

An exercise where the client identifies what is happening when they are 'in flow' can be illuminating. Here you explain the idea of 'flow' or 'peak moments': feeling self-confident, knowing you are using all your gifts, a tangible aim, an intense sense of pride and achievement. You ask the client to identify three or four such moments from different phases of their life and then discuss the themes that emerge. The results are often astonishing. This was true for a client who was chief operations officer for a packaging company. His 'peak moments' were nothing whatsoever to do with packaging or managing people, the essence of his job. They involved solitary activities: walking outdoors or being in his garden shed where he had set up a photographic studio. The exercise encapsulated exactly how he had become trapped: he was good at his job but disliked it. He had confused the knowledge that he excelled in his work as a COO with a duty to go on doing it.

This client illustrates another principle: that it is not about money. Giving up his job involved financial sacrifice, not just for him but also for his family. Their income was halved and they moved to a cheaper house, though it was in a picturesque part of Cornwall. His wife became his business partner. They committed to a life of low-carbon footprint, renewable energy and community involvement. It is common for such clients to wonder in retrospect why it took so long to make the change.

There are some exercises in this quest that are fun to do. For instance, I did this one with a client whose question was, 'I need to make a radical change in my life, but what would bring me joy?' He wrote the question in massive letters on a large piece of paper and we put it on the floor, imagining a large circle divided into segments. As we walked around it, I asked him to answer the question from different perspectives. These included: 'What's your favourite film? What message would this film give you?', 'What's your favourite book?' and 'Which leader from history do you most admire?' I chose these perspectives on the basis of what I already knew about his interests. We were both helpless with laughter as his answers emerged. The classic film *Casablanca* said, 'Being neutral is for wimps and love must come first'; Richmal Crompton's children's book *Just William* told him to trust that humour would always trump seriousness; and 'Winston Churchill' ordered him thus: 'Get off your arse and make that change!'

It may seem as if this question of life purpose is the exclusive province of the affluent and confident, but that is not my experience. I have had many similar conversations with the women I meet at the charity where I am a volunteer job interview coach. Our clients have often been unemployed for long periods. Many have been seriously destabilised by life events they could not have controlled. A 52-year-old single woman of African heritage had been a refugee as a child, had scrambled through poverty and a fragmented education to get a law degree and pass her Bar exams, only to find that she had to give it up to care for a dying mother and a disabled child. As her route back into employment, she was willingly competing for a junior legal job way below her capabilities. When I asked about her ambitions, she was cool and realistic: 'I'll stay two years getting my confidence back and my legal knowledge up to date. Then I'm going to be a barrister again, looking for a Chambers specialising in human rights. That's my calling. I want to give other people the help I never had.' I was sure that she would get the humble job. She did, and I was absolutely certain that she would be successful in her longer-term plan too.

Clients may be curious about your own journey as the chances are that you will have passed through all the stages I describe in this chapter: vague dissatisfaction turning into intolerable frustration, experiment, retraining, discouragement, encouragement, determination, making new networks, increasing your clarity about why you wanted to become a coach and why you love what you do. When clients ask, this is one time when your own story might be worth telling.

25

Putting Away the Toolbox

In training and supervising many hundreds of new coaches, I notice how many are preoccupied by anxiety about whether they have a big enough 'toolbox'. At coaching conferences where, as a rule, beginners predominate, I guarantee that you will find that the workshops which offer new wonder-techniques are the ones that fill up first. I'm quite sure that when I was a beginner coach I was just the same. A new technique? A new psychometric? Bring it on!

Listening recently to the recordings of two brand new coaches, each with a lot of natural aptitude, I found that both had deployed a complex technique in the first meeting with their client. It would not be unusual to find that a newly trained coach was using several such techniques in every session. I define a tool as anything that needs a diagram, a form, a piece of equipment, a change of seating, or a lengthy theoretical explanation.

How does it feel as a client to have a plethora of tools and techniques practised on you in your session? I sometimes inherit clients after what they will describe as 'failed' coaching assignments. When I discreetly enquire into what has gone wrong, the client will invariably tell me that the coach seemed to be obsessed with 'techniques'. Don't ever fool yourself that clients will not notice: they do. For instance, there was the coach who always imposed 10 minutes of mindfulness on his client, the one who loved visualisations, another who insisted on 'anchoring', and yet another who reduced every problem to a particular 'pyramid' of needs. There is nothing wrong with such techniques. It is wonderful to be familiar with them and to know how to use them, but not if every session comes to be about which technique you can use. Preoccupation with a technique can easily mean that you misread what the client wants, or fail to explore the meaning that is lurking below the surface of what they are saying.

What does it do for a coach to use these tools? The answer is that you don't quite trust the power of questioning alone. You feel you always have to have something up your sleeve in case some awful silence were to descend. It boosts fragile confidence. It gives you some control. It's why so many coaches feel a lot more confident about the first than the second session because in the first there is an essential set of rituals to be gone through: the what-is-coaching conversation, contracting, early life, or looking at appraisal feedback and action plans from a course. But then what?

There is an even bigger challenge than being wary about tools and techniques. This is to avoid being carried away by fads which come with their own built-in tools. Crazes come and go in coaching as elsewhere and they are always much in evidence at coaching conferences. The give-away is the magnitude of the claims made for whatever the current fad is: there is always some usefulness in what they describe, but rarely justification for the amazing results that the presenter promises are guaranteed to work with every client, whatever their problem. When describing their conference sessions or workshops, the ideas might be presented like this:

> This session will bring you the profound insights of Theory Z consciousness to support holistic fluidity in your leadership coaching. You will work with bodily constellations and ontological awareness, generational spirituality and collective intelligence, reaching far back into morphic resonance.

Or maybe like this – mix and match any words:

> Your coaching will achieve holistic awareness through spiritual consciousness, morphic resonance, along with constellations work with leaders and bodily intelligence. You will be introduced to Theory Z which combines age-old wisdom with generational fluidity.

The presenter starts their session dramatically, suggesting that as coaches we may ask too many questions of our clients – we're too much in our heads and we need to get into our gut, though they don't quite explain how. They may forbid facial expression: only expressionless will do. They may say that every coach should restrict themselves to only three questions of their clients, which should be repeated endlessly, for instance:

- What is the question?
- What is the question about the question?
- If you knew what the question about the question was, what question might you ask?

If I imagine asking some of my chief executive clients only these questions, I have a vivid picture of them believing that I had gone quietly crazy and finding a way to end the session as swiftly as possible. When the presenter does a coaching demo, their volunteer client usually avers that they have achieved a massive breakthrough with whatever their problem was. When I saw one such demo a few years ago, it reminded me strongly of seeing a 'cold reading' session that I once watched at a spiritualist church. Here, like all mediums, the very skilled operator at the front started with generalities: 'I'm seeing an older gentleman who might be called John – anyone here lost someone of that name recently?', and working it from there with the sadly desperate and vulnerable person who came forward.

I wonder how many people are like several friends and colleagues who come away from these conference sessions, either privately marvelling at how so many people can be so credulous, or else feeling like a friend who said, 'I trudge home wondering – why can't I make this work in the coaching I do?'. What a powerful story 'The Emperor's New Clothes' is. Don't be afraid to be that little child who calls it like it is.

Be sceptical about fads. Close the toolbox. Spend the first 5 minutes of any session reconnecting, encouraging the client to unburden, telling you what has happened since you last met. Spend the next 5 minutes getting clear what their goals are for the session. Then ask coaching questions. Listen carefully to the answers, being especially alert to the language the client is using. Trust the coaching process. And see what happens.

At the same time that you vow to close the toolbox, it may help to do a stock-taking exercise from time to time. Every so often, there is a place for one of these techniques, but to be able to choose you need to be sure that you are well informed about what the range of possibilities is. Swap ideas with other coaches, buy one of the books that offers a collection, give them a try every now and again, and keep an open mind about when and how they might be useful.

One client who was an ardent fan of coaching once entertained me over a drink with his account of the foibles, including my own, of the many coaches he had worked with over a long career. His worst experience was, he said, with a coach who had, according to him, tried to make him what he called a 'convert' to Psychosynthesis, a respected school of therapy which has branched out into coaching. His account of how well-meant enthusiasm can get the better of us made me alternately laugh and cringe with its accuracy. Sometimes, we coaches can get too fixed on one set of theoretical ideas. The source can be the organisation where we had our first exposure to coaching ideas, most commonly a school of therapy or an approach to change, which has adapted to embrace coaching. Examples are Neurolinguistic Programming, Transactional Analysis, Jungian therapy or Non-Violent Communication, but there are many others. The same can happen to coaches who train in psychometrics that may seem to some to offer universal explanations of human behaviour, for instance the Myers Briggs Type Indicator or the Enneagram. Some proponents of these ideas see them as offering a universal wisdom that unites 'everything', using the language of spirituality and faith to draw in adherents.

Each of these sets of ideas has strengths but they all also have weaknesses. It is unlikely that any single approach will offer a way of working with every client. The challenge is to broaden your theoretical base, however much you like the ideas of your chosen school. Coaching draws from science, psychology, sociology, medicine, sport, education, adult development, neurology, leadership, organisation and management theory, among others. It's beneficial to dip into at least some of these so that you broaden your thinking. Most clients are profoundly uninterested in which theories underpin what we do. They will be suspicious of anything that looks like a one-track approach and are likely to resist attempts to be enrolled as disciples.

When you review a coaching programme with a client, it is instructive to ask them what made for the biggest impact. You may be surprised to find that they rarely mention your magnificent coaching skills, for instance complimenting you on your incisive questions or the tremendously useful role play you did with them to prepare for a job interview. It's not that they don't value these things because they do, but they take them for granted.

What they will mention instead is any signs that you have gone above and beyond what they expected in terms of the human relationship. I have collected countless examples of these small touches, all of which have far more power than the effort it took the coaches to give them. For instance, there was the coach who made a diary note to text a client on the day her son was having a heart operation, wishing the family well. Then there were the many coaches who followed up sessions with encouraging messages about how to get through the especially stressful meeting that they had discussed in their session, or who arranged to talk in the evening or very early morning when a client had had bad news about the future of their job. Another coach sent a set of tiny baby clothes as a gift for the client whose wife had given birth to an extremely premature baby. His comment was, 'So many people avoided us because they thought the baby would die. Very few people sent gifts but you did and I will always value that.'

One of my own clients said that what stood out for him was offering him sunscreen lotion, a shady panama hat and a spare pair of sunglasses on a glaringly hot day. We were sitting, at his request, on my balcony for his session. I had then encouraged him to leave with this protective gear as he was facing a long journey home in the sun. These small touches are different from taking clients out, sending Christmas hampers or arranging parties for groups of clients to meet each other, all of which can be seen clearly for what they are: attempts to buy loyalty and gratitude. There is nothing wrong with that – they are standard marketing techniques, but it's not the same as making a gift out of genuine liking and respect. Sometimes what clients describe is intangible. A client had lived through an intensely demanding year where he had lost his job at the same time as he had been diagnosed with a serious illness. His comment was, 'You somehow conveyed through all of it that I was employable and that I would recover my health; you never said any of that explicitly, but you never wavered in the feeling you radiated that this was what you believed. And if you believed it, then I could too.'

26

Understanding the Challenges of Becoming a Coach

Coaching can look easy when you watch it done by an experienced, skilled professional. It can look as if this was the only discussion it was possible to have. It is seamless and elegant. It seems fluent: the client and coach share the talking, and yet when you think about it more carefully, you understand that it was nothing like the usual sort of conversation between friends or colleagues. I have known beginner coaches feel utter despair when they slowly realise the gap between their own faltering first steps and this masterful performance.

One problem with coaching is that not only does it look effortless when you see it done well, but also that so many people believe they are already doing it without ever having had a single day of training. I have trained many hundreds of line managers in how to use coaching at work and they virtually always have an unwelcome surprise in the first few hours of the workshop when they realise that what they have been calling coaching is nothing like the definition and approach that we offer. Like many people who believe they are doing coaching but are not, what they have in practice been doing is advice-giving, though very kindly. At one glamorous party, I met a number of people recently retired from well-paid jobs, several of them claiming that they were 'doing a bit of coaching'. When I asked one of them where he had trained, he winked cheerfully, saying, 'School of Life!'

When you don't know what coaching is, in the sense that professional coaches now use it, it can be hard to grasp the differences between what you have assumed and what you now need to learn. You thought it was about passing on your wisdom and experience. But now you find that assumption turned on its head. It is the other person's wisdom that matters. The challenge is how to work with the client so that they access it. This is why, whatever the tools and techniques that are taught on the event, any good coaching course will start by exposing participants to the *coaching mindset*. The fundamental principle of the coaching mindset is that all of us can think for ourselves and that, when we do, we are far more likely to act on what we think than when we are told what to do and think by others. This apparently simple principle is profoundly challenging to almost everyone who embarks upon coach training. Surely, participants are inclined to say, people often actually ask for advice, they know I am more expert, they are looking to me for help – or they are so upset that they beg me to make suggestions.

In an everyday conversation, people are often queueing to speak, distracted by their own concerns, only half-listening, disagreeing with opinions they dislike or never questioning a friend for fear of disrupting the friendship, or hoping to have the last word. An alternative is where the listener is so over-whelmed by the distress the other person expresses that they are reduced to making vaguely supportive noises or offering clichés such as 'plenty more fish in the sea' or 'time will heal'.

I see four stages of learning how to coach.

Stage 1: Absolute Beginner. There has to be a lot of unlearning. First, you need to unlearn the habit of advice-giving, including all those advice-in-disguise questions that come from your own agenda and that begin, 'Have you thought of ...?' 'Wouldn't it be a good idea if you ...?' You need to understand that telling your own story is mostly not at all helpful, even when it appears to be saying, 'Look, I'm just like you!' Then you need to understand why and how advice-giving creates defensiveness as well as conveying the belief that the other person cannot solve the problem for themselves. This is why the typical response to advice is 'yes ... BUT'. Energy goes into keeping the other person at bay, sometimes behind a mask of pretending to pay polite attention to their ideas and suggestions.

Beginner coaches can feel panic when they start to understand how much there is to notice. Panic can lead to an over-investment in wanting to understand all the facts that the other person has not named and that, suddenly, it appears vital to know. How many? How often? How much? What is the background? Who reports to whom? This is an especial trap for certain kinds of professional, such as lawyers and doctors, who have been trained to extract the details that are rarely so important in coaching. Facts are inert. Coaching problems are usually rooted in emotion, not facts.

At this stage, it is helpful to rely on frameworks such as GROW or OSCAR, which give you a ready-made shape for the conversation. The danger is becoming overwhelmed by how much there is to learn and some people give up at this point because they are aware that their questions might be clunky; keeping themselves out of it feels awkward.

Stage 2: Apprenticeship. You have internalised coaching principles and your confidence grows. You have customised the questions that you learnt during your training and everything feels more natural, but many of us still have to learn how poor our listening skills are: we tend only to hear ideas we already agree with. Instead, we learn to look out for which words are being subtly emphasised or repeated and which are being used to describe the emotion that the client is experiencing and, sometimes, which words are being avoided altogether. We need to listen with our eyes as well as our ears: how does the other person look? What small signs are there of a surge of energy, of wilting attention or of anxiety?

Sometimes it seems as if the session has gone down some inexplicable path that makes no sense. The client's problem is complex and seems intractable. You have been working together for an hour and the client is no nearer to finding answers. The client seems to be looking to you. You've asked your best questions. Maybe when they leave the session, they will say they are feeling worse than they did when they came in. This is when anxiety can become intolerable and the urge to give advice or to deploy some 'tool' can overwhelm you. This is why at the Apprenticeship phase many coaches find themselves giving ill-advised little lectures on human psychology, or describing their favourite circle-and-arrow diagram to the client, regardless of whether the client has asked for it or is likely to find it relevant.

Stage 3: Learner Psychologist. You have realised that coaching is complex because people are complex. If you have not already done so, you discover the rich world of human psychology. You may start with an accessible approach such as Transactional Analysis or discover Gestalt. You may be drawn to what can be learnt from the world of psychotherapy or you may start with getting licensed to use some psychometric instruments – it all helps. The danger here is of seeing everything through the lens of one particular school of thought, so suddenly every relationship issue that a client brings you seems 'co-dependent' or 'parent–child'. It's just like the old joke about giving a person a hammer for them to discover that everything needs hammering. There is a risk of feeling overwhelmed by how much there is to learn – and there is literally an infinite amount.

Stage 4: Mastery. This will always feel unreachable, but there are reliable signs that you are at a different stage of learning. You find yourself working comfortably with a much wider range of clients. While you now see that there are few neat solutions, you can tolerate the ambiguity that this involves. You can take a systemic approach, looking at the wider issues of family, organisation and community that will be affecting the client. You can draw from an eclectic mix of theory and practice from a wide range of sources. You are confident enough to bid for and get coaching programmes that extend over a year or more, instead of over just a few sessions. You can work flexibly with these clients. You use 'tools and techniques' sparingly. You develop your own unique style where you may have an animated and conversational approach in which you appear to be contributing a lot to the discussion, or your style may be to make minimal interventions. There is no one right way. You become less concerned about whether the session has recognisable goals. There are risks here too, the biggest of which is complacency, closely followed by 'rustout' (see page 156).

There may be an especially big leap between stages 2 and 3. People who come to coaching from professions where psychological know-how has never been part of their development may struggle to find their way. Some are fearful, clinging to outmoded ideas about the boundaries between what they think of as the safely objective territory of executive coaching and what they dread might be the messy human emotion which they would like to believe is the job of a therapist.

I sometimes work as a supervisor with coaches who have been trained in what they tend to call *performance coaching*. One such coach was formerly a senior partner in an actuarial firm. Her typical clients were other actuaries, accountants or lawyers and she specialised in people who wanted to make the leap to partner or senior partner in their firms. She accurately described her approach as being more like mentoring than coaching as it included advice-giving. She had resisted any idea that it might be necessary to explore the hints it seemed to me that her clients were repeatedly giving her about the emotional difficulties that were poking up through the apparently bland surface of the issues they brought to her sessions. This resolute ignoring seemed to work until the day one of her clients raised the direct and unavoidable question of how to support his father in his terminal illness. The coach's beloved father was also terminally ill. She and I spent two whole supervision sessions on the confusion, panic and sorrow she had felt during and after this session. She admitted her absolute lack of any mental preparation or psychological frameworks to have managed it or to have done an adequate job for the client. Instead, she had found herself stumbling into giving the client platitudinous advice. She said sadly, 'Even at the time, I knew this was a mistake.'

The most important part of learning to be a coach is to accept that it is the client's job to find the solution. The coach's job is to ask the right questions. This is often much easier said than done, but resistance and puzzlement are your friends. They will point to where the real problem lies. A scientist client insisted that we spend the whole session discussing whether or not to accept the offer of a new job. It looked obvious to me that the new job was better. It seemed to be the solution to the many complaints he had expressed about his current role: more opportunity to extend his research interests, more money, better working conditions. We took a good 30 minutes going through the pros and cons until I suggested that we look instead at what it was that made the decision so hard for him. This took us to a different place: his fear that he would be isolated or incompetent in a leadership role and might find the stress unbearable.

Training as a coach can be an exhilarating process. A good course invites you to work on yourself and on raising your own self-awareness while you are learning how to do the same for others. You are encouraged to take the risk of being vulnerable and you get a lot of support. You bond with the other course members. When you practise your skills, you want to help each other. This almost always means that there is a significant degree of well-meant playing along when you are in the client role, of seeming to find answers to problems or of bringing issues which are not that important or which have already been resolved. That is why it can be dismaying when you leave the course and start working with 'real' clients. These people don't know those hidden rules about being helpful. They may be inexperienced as clients and come expecting advice or have been storing up multiple upsetting problems for many years. It all comes gushing out in the first session. Or they may be there reluctantly because someone else thinks it will be good for them. It's a far cry from the softly embracing bubble of the training course.

Coaching is unregulated and it fails many of the tests of what constitutes a genuine profession, for instance a long full-time or part-time equivalent training period at degree and postgraduate level, statutory controls, an extended apprenticeship phase and the rigorous supervision that protects standards, with the possibility of being struck off a licensing register if you misbehave. Anyone can call themselves a coach because the word itself is not protected. If you belong to one of the professional coaching associations, there are no real consequences if a complaint from a client is upheld. By contrast, becoming a psychotherapist can take anything from four years upwards, and accreditation for one of the main national bodies usually involves 450 hours of supervised practice after initial training. Even the most rigorous coach training programmes come nowhere near meeting such standards.

This makes it essential to choose the best coaching programme you can find, noting that a high price is not necessarily associated with quality. Look for realism in how the course is described, check that the tutors are practising, experienced coaches themselves and that there is a generous ratio of tutors to participants, as this increases the chance of getting the targeted feedback which is the best way of improving your skill and confidence. A thriving alumni community with an extensive events programme is another good sign. Look for accreditation in a national or international scheme which includes feedback on recorded sessions and that insists on familiarity with the underpinning theory.

Coaching has often been described as a 'revolving door' profession, meaning that people exit as quickly as they entered. Sometimes this is because of financial pressure: they struggle to make a five-figure turnover let along the six figures they had hoped for. Some coaches see it as a hobby so they never make the investment in business development that all new enterprises need. Growing a coaching practice depends almost entirely on personal recommendation so if you don't do good work you will not get new clients. This can feel like an impossible conundrum: How can you get good enough quickly enough to build a reputation? The answer is to recruit practice clients who get their coaching free or at a minimal price, to press them for feedback as their part of the deal, to record some of your sessions and then to invite a tough but merciful supervisor to listen to them with you. That way, rapid improvement is possible.

It is neither quick nor easy to learn how to coach. After the unlearning phase, your confidence surges as you realise the true power of coaching, followed quickly by severe feelings of incompetence as you understand that human change is more complicated than you had ever believed. More training will help, and regular supervision is essential. But to climb out of what can be a dark place, you have to get back on the horse and keep going. There is no substitute for building your coaching hours. When you clock up 500 hours, you can begin to relax. When you get to 1,000, it will feel different again. When you reach 3,000, you will understand how much you had no way of grasping when you were a beginner.

27

Continuing to Learn, Staying Connected

In most of the clinical professions and in many others where potentially life-changing advice for others is involved, you have to show that you have completed a minimum number of hours of continuing professional development (CPD) every year, presenting certificates of attendance as proof. Nor can this be from any provider – they have to be approved and the number of CPD hours stated. The rapidity of scientific advance and of social transformation makes this essential. It would be hard to impose anything as rigorous on coaches and the speed of change in coaching is glacial by comparison, but the underlying need is the same. When you work alone, or even if you work as an associate or principal of a bigger practice, it is so easy to get stuck in ways of thinking and behaving that are out of date.

Be alert to signs and symptoms that something is amiss. One such sign is a conviction that you already know what a client is going to say before they have said it. You are sure that their particular problem is just one variant of what you have heard so many times before from other clients. What is more, you already know what you are going to say to them and how the rest of the discussion will take shape. When you apparently 'know' this, it drains all interest from the client and prevents you realising that every client is unique. No matter how much their problem appears to resemble those you have met many times before, what this client needs is going to be different. Irritation will follow: how dare the client use up your time and energy this way? Next, you begin to feel detached – it's just a job, it doesn't matter what's at stake for the client. From this, it is a short step to feeling incompetent and helpless: perhaps you are a terrible coach, other coaches are better. This is 'burnout', the classic spiral which starts with exhaustion, goes on to cynicism and ends with depression.

Rustout is different. It is characterised by apathy, boredom and finally by a deadly loss of confidence. The symptoms are a sense of weariness as you get ready for a coaching session, surreptitiously watching the clock during it and a profound lack of energy when it is over. In the people I supervise who describe this pattern, although the specific triggers will vary, the real causes are that they are under-challenged by the work and lack any evidence that it is effective. Too much of it is the same. Virtually always, these coaches have settled for the apparently 'easy' route of being a modestly paid associate with one company that specialises in a particular kind of coaching. Examples are women returning to work after maternity leave, debriefing questionnaire feedback before or after management development courses and coaching young graduates as part of their entry into the world of work. These types of engagement are characterised by their brevity – often at most three or four hours. The clients themselves can be puzzled by why they are being offered coaching at all. There is no chance to develop a productive relationship with any individual; the work feels wholly transactional. It lacks meaning and impact.

Rustout is exhausting. Routine work can look at first like a low-stress way of earning a living as a coach, but it can all too soon turn into a flatlining blur of monotony and frustration. People who believe they have rusted out have sometimes taken the courageous step of doing their basic training all over again. This revives their confidence and reminds them that the heart of coaching is clients who come as genuine volunteers and who have enough space to explore their issues thoroughly. After some years in practice, you may experience mild versions of rustout at any point. If so, and assuming you want to stay working as a coach, it's time to take action.

If you still have the course manual from your initial training, take a look at it. How many of the skills and approaches you learnt on that course are you now using? Possibly some will feel unfamiliar from lack of use because skills decay after a surprisingly short time if they are not reinforced. What level of confidence would you feel about taking on a client in a totally unfamiliar sector and where the presenting issues were apparently new to you? If the answers are that your confidence is low, then it may be time to connect with the coaching world in a different way.

It can start with broadening the number of other coaches in your professional circle. Joining a coaching association is the easiest way to meet other coaches and the modest fee is chargeable against tax. There will be a menu of short workshops, normally run by other members and at minimal cost; there will be an annual conference and perhaps it will have keynote speakers from all over the world. These conferences are not cheap by the time you have factored in the opportunity cost of attending, accommodation, travel and the conference fee itself, but they offer a benchmark for your own practice. Are you already familiar with many of the ideas? Have you made contacts that you were unlikely to have made elsewhere?

When you go to such conferences, there is no point in dreading unfamiliar social contact so much that you become the person who sags around the walls of the coffee room. Many other people will be feeling shyness and reserve. See yourself as an honorary host, introduce yourself to strangers and then introduce them to others. As you get to know whichever association you join, there is everything to be said for offering to run a workshop yourself – yet another way of meeting people who would be unlikely to come your way in the normal course of events.

Coaching associations can become stale. They are largely run by volunteers and there is sometimes a lack of professionalism. The honorary officers can get too dependent on the sense of importance that their roles bring and can cling on long after they should have retired gracefully. It may be the case that your particular association attracts mainly beginners to its conferences and you find yourself wondering what value it is delivering. I felt this myself at one international conference and was about to leave when I spotted one last workshop that looked intriguing. As a result of attending that workshop, I met its presenters, Karen Whittleworth and Andrew Gilbert. They had developed the OSCAR framework, a rival to and, in my opinion, a considerable improvement on the well-known GROW model espoused by John Whitmore. Two years later, we published our book *Manager as Coach*, which has enjoyed lively sales to managers who want to learn how to bring coaching into their daily work. At the same conference some years earlier, the highlight for me had been meeting Dr Leni Wildflower, a distinguished American coach and writer who introduced herself after coming to one of my workshops. We have been close friends ever since and she has generously paved the way for me to meet many other American coaches and thinkers.

The company that delivered your training will offer alumni events and these, too, are an effective way of meeting other coaches and learning about developments in the coaching world. There may be workshops where you can practise new skills, 'fishbowls' where you can watch an accomplished coach at work with a client, or 'conversations' where a well-known coach is interviewed about their work. Often, these events are subsidised or run at cost to keep them affordable. If you found your training rigorous and enjoyable, it is an excellent idea to ask whether you could join the training faculty, initially as a 'graduate assistant', probably unpaid, a useful person to act as 'runner', to make up a pair or trio in the practice exercises, and maybe as an assessor for any kind of end-of-course activity that involves formal feedback. There is nothing like seeing other coaches make all-too-visible mistakes for realising how often you make them yourself, as well as for realising what a long way you have come since you were a beginner.

Keeping active on LinkedIn, Twitter and Facebook is another way to learn about ideas that challenge your existing thinking, and to do the same for others. When you follow interesting people, organisations and publications, especially on Twitter, you will find a constant stream of online articles, podcasts, blogs and videos that will be worth reading, passing on to your clients and sharing with others. One of my own favourites is the *Harvard Business Review*, tweeting as @Harvardbiz.

A former colleague generously hosted a late afternoon coaching book group for a number of years, blagging a free room from the club where she was a member. We met every month and took turns to suggest a book, not necessarily one with the word coaching in its title. At the meetings, it often happened that the book had not been read by many people, but the discussion was still lively and some long-lasting friendships were formed as a result. It was another effective way of refreshing our ideas.

The coaching world is relatively small and you may feel that you have temporarily used up all the novelty and stimulus that it can offer, in which case it may be an idea to see what the psychotherapy community can offer because it is so much bigger. I subscribe to the newsletters of a number of therapy training providers and regularly attend workshops and lectures on topics which have relevance to coaching.

There is no limit to the possibilities. It may seem like a stretch to make the link to coaching but some of the best CPD I have done recently was attending a series of lectures at the Royal Academy in London on fakes in the art world, and a short course on women film directors at one of my local cinemas. Both these events have given me much occasion for pondering. The art course made me think more carefully about the differences between the many clients who describe feeling like impostors and the real thing: the genuine faker. The course on women in film was directly relevant to understanding how and why so many women clients feel that popular concepts such as 'Leaning In', Black Lives Matter and #MeToo are only a small part of an extremely complex social structure where many of the traditional barriers to career progression remain firmly in place.

Opportunities for learning are intimately connected to keeping your network in good order. 'Networking' can suggest pointless meetings with people you don't particularly like and who don't particularly like you. I see it differently – as a prime opportunity to give as well as to take. A vibrant network is one of the best ways to ensure that you get constant refreshment in ideas and people and that you in turn can do the same for others. Ideally, your network will include people who can do all of this for you: challenge, listen, offer new ideas, comfort you when upset, celebrate success, give honest feedback, remind you of your strengths, introduce you to new people, and provide some fun. As well as this personal connection, you need a reliable network of professional contacts which could include psychotherapists, medical professionals, financial advisors, lawyers, other coaches with specialisms such as voice, business development and image. You will frequently want to make referrals. Again, this is a two-way process and these people could equally well make referrals to you.

There needs to be a genuine purpose behind making contact. When people who are complete strangers send me an email asking for a meeting, the only purpose being to do something they call 'reaching out', I see no reason to say yes. On the other hand, if they say they need help with a PhD thesis or with trying out a new theory, I am happy to help if I believe that I can. Fear of rejection lies behind the excuses we make to ourselves about why we dislike networking, but what's the worst that can happen? Answer: someone you need never see again is rude or dismissive. So what?

28

Remembering That You Are Vulnerable Too

A while back, I found myself routinely giving four 2-hour coaching sessions a day, four or five days a week. It was relentless. As fast as one client left, the next was sitting in the waiting room. Sometimes I ran a whole session with an uncomfortably full bladder or fidgeting from hunger because I had made no time for looking after my most basic physical needs. At weekends, I drafted reports and did all the 'adminstrivia' associated with my professional role, along with organising the shopping, cooking and cleaning for my family. I was constantly yawning, perpetually tired. With clients, I hope my behaviour was impeccable and that I did work that was good enough, though possibly I was fooling myself, but at home I was irritable, feeling sorry for myself and resentful. Although none of us in the family or in his close circle was willing to acknowledge it, the health of Alan, my husband of many years, was deteriorating rapidly. He was still working, a crucial and active partner in our coaching and consultancy business, but he had become even more immobilised, heavily dependent around the clock on a team of carers, paid and unpaid. I was one of these carers. Most nights I was awake at least twice to turn him or to bring him a pee bottle. No wonder I was exhausted.

I could only see how foolish it was after Alan had died and I slowly began to realise that there was absolutely no need to have worked at that pace and that in any case it is unsustainable – human biology simply will not tolerate it for long.

I look back on that time with horror. Where was my supervision? I was telling myself that I was 'between supervisors' and would find a new one 'when I've got time'. Instead, I was jumping on any colleague who looked as if they had a few moments to spare and hastily blathering on about some issue that was troubling me and hoping they could gabble a reply just as fast. Quite separately from supervision, I urgently needed a coach, someone who could offer me a refuge from the emotional turmoil of Alan's approaching death, allow me to express my anguish and help me see how self-defeating so much of my behaviour was. Instead, I retreated into the 'Be Strong' mode I had learnt in childhood from a household where feelings were suppressed as secrets, making it harder and harder for anyone to offer me the help which would have made such a difference.

To do coaching well, you have to bring your whole self to it. You can't be distracted or working on auto-pilot, half-listening while you silently worry about who is meeting the children from school or whether anyone has emptied the dishwasher. When you work like this, it is most unlikely that you will be able to do your best coaching. Yes, we may work in a comfortable coaching room with flowers, a pleasant atmosphere and a peaceful setting, but more often than not we are working alone. It would be rare for there to be colleagues to share silly gossip as you make that welcome cup of coffee, or to have another coach who could offer some minutes of listening after a session that has felt uncomfortable or puzzling. It is common to feel isolated and sometimes to feel lonely. It can be effortful to make time for conferences, group sessions, workshops and all the other occasions when we meet others whose interests and values are the same.

One result can be that we impoverish our personal life. This is a well-known hazard of any job involving 'emotional labour', such as medicine, nursing, social work, the priesthood or psychotherapy, a phenomenon well described as 'compassion fatigue'. We put ourselves at other people's service. We make it clear that they can express distress, joy, anxiety, while we remain a steady presence, ideally offering a role model of how to manage life's challenges. After a day of such work, we can be drained; it can feel as if there is nothing left for ourselves and our closest loved ones. And what if they, too, begin to make demands on us, rightly expecting that they are entitled to tell us their woes and triumphs? 'I've been listening all day!' one of my supervisees said to me, someone who at the time was overdoing her coaching commitments: 'I'm listened-out, I just can't do it again in the evenings, I don't want to talk to anyone or anyone to talk to me.'

Cutting off the very contact that we need because we have already had too much of it during the day can lead to other problems. It cannot be chance that so many professionals such as doctors, who spend all day listening to other people's problems, are at serious risk of developing an addiction to alcohol or drugs. Reaching for the 'reward' of that evening glass of wine can quickly become embedded as a habitual crutch, creating more problems than it solves. The effort of containing the distress that the job creates can literally be overwhelming: doctors have a suicide rate which is more than twice the norm for the general population.

I recently attended a large event for therapists and coaches. The topic was emotionally taxing. I was startled to realise that I was the only person in the two back rows who was not continually nail-biting, hair-sucking, hair-twirling, face-stroking, scalp-scratching or, in one case, skin-picking that left the inside of the picker's right thumb red-raw and bleeding. To carry out these self-soothing and self-harming activities so compulsively and openly suggested high levels of unmanaged personal stress.

It can happen that we become too involved in certain clients, especially those who seem to answer some need in us. This might include the one who overtly admires us at a time when admiration and intimacy are in short supply, or the one who writes too frequently with needy emails and is potentially at risk of becoming dependent on us, or we on them. It is possible to be over-invested in the relationship with such clients. They could start mattering more than our domestic relationships. These could be parched, withering from lack of attention, and then it might all become a downward spiral. These personal relationships are unrewarding and we neglect them even more, so they deteriorate yet again. There is greater risk of this happening if you specialise in coaching where pain and emotional intensity are built in, for instance with people who have just been made redundant, with mediation work or with any kind of personal coaching such as parenting or weight loss.

During the period I described at the start of this chapter, I did at least have the sense to keep some physical activity going by building in an early morning swim at a local pool several times a week, and I cycled 4 miles a day to and from work. Today, I have a fitness tracker that I have programmed to make bossy reminders to get up and do at least 250 steps every hour and to do 5 miles of walking a day. Physical activity, hard enough to have you slightly out of breath, releases adrenaline and helps discharge tension from a job where it is all too easy to sit in a chair all day. Wellbeing involves mind and soul as well as body. It is essential to find good workshops to jolt us out of any complacency we may be feeling about the quality of our practice: most professional coaching associations offer a range of options here at low cost. If you live in a big city, as I do, there is no excuse for not seeking out other events that will stretch your mind as well as offering much-needed fun, whether this is indulging your love of film (my personal favourite), listening to great music live or going to a series of high-flown lectures on philosophy. The spiritual area is more difficult for those of us with none of the religious faith that obliges the review and confession of our misdeeds, some mechanism for forgiveness and renewal as well as the chance to slow down, surrendering to the comforting rituals of communal worship. We may have to make do with mindfulness, or my own choice, walking for several hours among the trees of Kew Gardens in West London – in my own prejudiced view, the best botanical garden in the world.

Coaches sometimes ask if there is some magical ideal working pattern and my answer is that there is not. At the point where you are still building your practice, it can seem as if it would be delightful to have the problem of too many clients, but if your market is big enough, you do good work and keep at it, it is inevitable that this will become your problem too. How you manage it will depend partly on whether clients come to you or you go to them, and, if so, what kind of travel is involved. Zoom or phone coaching reduces the stress of travel but has its own disadvantages, often feeling more intense than a session which is face to face. You will need to decide what length of session feels right for you. One colleague claims that she is such a full-on presence that an hour of her is more than enough, though she does offer a 2-hour introductory session. Whatever the length of the actual session, you need minimally 15 minutes of preparation to read your notes, get the room ready and yourself into the right frame of mind. After it, I find there is at least 30–40 minutes of follow-up: picking up the cups and glasses, making notes, sending links to articles or emailing about the next session. For me, this means that I aim for two 2-hour sessions a day in a 3-day week of actual client contact. I work more or less exclusively from home, I am rigorous about keeping evenings and weekends free and I take minimally six weeks of holiday a year. I find this is practicable, but everyone is different in what they need to earn as well as what they can tolerate and enjoy where work is concerned.

Coaches who come into the profession with the idea of making a lot of money can find the description of this working pattern dismaying. I had one supervisee who told me that his aim was to make a very large six-figure income every year for three years and then to go off on a round-the-world trip of sybaritic luxury. I privately doubted that this would happen and it did not. The wish to make money as the prime motivator does not sit well with doing good coaching. Coaching is not an easy way to make a lot of money, though there are some coaches who do.

It's worth thinking about whether to employ some PA help. It would be rare to find a coach who has a taste for what to me are the tedious tasks of invoicing, tracking debtors, paying suppliers, bookkeeping, filing sales tax returns and negotiating diary dates. If I were to do these things myself, I would approach them with dread and procrastinate endlessly, most probably making simple mistakes which it would then involve many hours of apologetic emailing to unpick. Almost from the outset of my career as a coach, I have employed a wonderful part-time PA who excels at these tasks, managing them in a fraction of the time and with 100% more efficiency than would be possible for me. This frees me up to do what I enjoy: the actual coaching.

Many coaches realise the need to develop self-protective routines. They learn meditation, join a support group, or make scheduled time for play and for enjoyable exercise or a hands-on hobby such as gardening, textile crafts, ceramics or painting. They download helpful apps, they watch their alcohol intake and monitor their mental health. Some go on regular retreats where a week away from the world once a year is part of what keeps them serene.

Don't stint on self-care – not just, to quote the shampoo ad, because you're worth it, but also because by looking after yourself, you look after your clients too.

29

Getting a Supervisor

Oh dear, there is so much virtue-signalling in the coaching world where supervision is concerned, when conference organisers, publishers of magazines about coaching and the great panjandrums of the professional coaching associations frequently speak or write as if it were taken as read that every coach has a supervisor. I remember being a distant eavesdropper on a conversation between committee members of such an organisation, where one contributor seriously proposed an hour of supervision for every 8 hours of coaching as an essential standard.

In practice, I'm perfectly sure that supervision is a thinly supported activity, taken with that level of conscientiousness only by a minuscule minority of experienced and well-paid coaches. My impression is that, in practice, most coaches see it as an optional extra and pay for it sparingly. I say that this is my impression, because, at the moment, all the data comes from self-selecting samples where the amount of supervision they report is likely to be unrepresentative of what the majority of coaches do. I do not know of any reliable data from a large randomised sample that would tell us how frequently coaches do actually have supervision, who they are in terms of experience or what they pay after their initial training period is over.

Some of the confusion about supervision comes from its early role in psychoanalysis, the first formal type of therapeutic conversation. To train as an analyst, you had to have your own analyst, still true of people undertaking this training today. So, the 'training analyst' had a dual role – a cross between a trainer and a therapist. Today, where the supervisor has a formal training role, they have a responsibility to measure your performance against the standards of the professional body. There is a faint echo of this in those coach training courses where, after you have completed the face-to-face part of the programme, you are assigned a supervisor who will listen to a small number of your recorded coaching sessions, offering you detailed feedback. The role includes assessing whether you have reached the required standard over an agreed period of time. This may account for those over-weening claims often made for supervision as a quality control measure.

The European Mentoring and Coaching Council (EMCC) has usefully defined supervision, putting the emphasis on reflection and learning:

> Supervision is the interaction that occurs when a mentor or coach brings their coaching or mentoring work experiences to a supervisor in order to be supported and to engage in reflective dialogue and collaborative learning for the development and benefit of the mentor or coach, their clients and their organisations.

There is a strong case for supervision in coaching. We do our work alone. Our coaching is rarely observed, recorded or transcribed, so we can lose all sense of objectivity. It's just us in that room with the client. If the client books more coaching, then we can probably assume that they find our work valuable but this may not mean that it is as good as it could be. If the client does not re-book or, as is often the case, disappears without giving a reason, even for coaching that has been paid for in advance, then who knows what is going on? When a coaching session includes a distressed client who breaks down, have we 'caused' this? If so, how do we manage it? When the client is under pressure from their organisation to change their behaviour in some way and yet does not appear to be making progress, many coaches will worry about their own reputation with the organisation sponsor: should they, the coach, be applying more pressure and, if so, how? When a client reveals a traumatising secret from their childhood, something they have never previously disclosed to a soul, what is the coach's responsibility – is it to refer the client immediately for psychotherapy or is it just to listen quietly?

It is unlikely that you will have any everyday way of discussing these issues. Confidentiality will prevent you talking about them with friends and probably with partners too, but, even without these boundaries, it is unlikely that people who are not coaches will understand the subtlety of the issues, let alone be able to make any sensible comment on them. One of my supervisees told me despairingly of how a pressing unease drove her to confide in her husband, telling him that one of her clients seemed to be talking about suicide: 'My husband just stared at me', she said, 'and told me to order the client not to do it; it was selfish and unthinkable, she should just pull herself together.'

I used to believe that it was only the most experienced coaches who would encounter a client who spoke of taking their life or who suddenly developed serious mental health problems. This was based on my then-prejudiced view that a beginner coach was unlikely to be able to create the level of trust that would encourage a client to reveal such raw feelings. I was wrong. Creating immediate rapport is something that many beginner coaches can do effortlessly, so it may easily happen that, in your first few weeks as a newly-trained coach, you hear a highly upset client disclose something that creates an immediate dilemma. Is it an emergency? What is your responsibility? Should you tell someone and, if so, who? How do you manage your own feelings of anxiety and concern?

A few years ago, a client emailed me following her session. It was midway through her second coaching programme. The email was three incoherent pages, describing a series of bizarre and hideous recent events that she said had subjected her to torture, kidnapping and sexual attacks, all in public places. It seemed most unlikely that any of them could have taken place. I could see, without benefit of any expert advice, that this woman was very ill and in the grip of a psychotic breakdown. How extremely grateful I was to know that I had expert help on hand. I got on the phone immediately to my supervisor, herself a former GP, and then to two people, one of them a current client and one a former client – both consultant psychiatrists – for practical advice. Nothing in this client's behaviour or in her previous sessions had alerted me to the possibility of such an episode, although I found out later that she had a history of severe mental health difficulties, all of which she had resolutely concealed.

These challenges are unwelcome but they are not uncommon. Even more common are ethical dilemmas involving confidentiality. For instance, it would be normal for coaches to protect the names of their clients. The only exceptions are those where the client has talked openly about their relationship with you. But what do you do if two clients, previously safely separated by being in different divisions of the organisation, are moved into the same team and cannot bear each other? Do you intervene to stop them complaining about the allegedly insufferable behaviour of the other person? If so, what do you say?

Supervision will probably have different roles to play at different stages of your coaching career. It will always be vital as a place to take the kinds of immediate problem I have described here: someone who understands the complexities, can give you a nuanced view, offers support and helps you decide what to do. On a more mundane level, it is the place to discuss those coaching encounters where you have a nagging feeling that something went wrong, without being able to say what it was. The supervisor may not know either, but will probably be able to offer you a different perspective on what happened.

Later on, it's a good idea to look for a more experienced coach who might suggest working with you on the agenda that you bring, but offering a mixture of mentoring and non-directive comment. Later on again, you will probably look for another experienced coach where you might do co-supervision which could involve robust peer-to-peer discussion and debate.

When you are looking for a supervisor, it is sensible to ask what their operating principles are, for instance whether they will offer coaching on personal or business issues as well as on purely coaching topics. Some supervisors come from a psychodynamic or psychotherapeutic background and if you are unprepared, you might be taken aback to find them asking about your own attachment experience and looking at every case you bring from a Freudian, Transactional Analysis or Jungian perspective. This may include a level of interpretation and directive comment that you could find uncomfortable, or just exactly what you need. Other supervisors have their own quirks and interests: ask what they are before agreeing to work together.

Qualifications in supervision are emerging but standards are variable and I know of at least one organisation offering to train you as a supervisor when you have only just completed a basic training. When this is the case, it is unlikely that such an inexperienced coach-supervisor can offer much value to a supervisee as you are still likely to be at the stage of not knowing what you don't know, the most dangerous kind of ignorance. My own rule of thumb is that it takes at least three years of successful practice and around 2,000 hours of coaching to be at the stage where you could supervise another coach with any confidence. Supervisors should still be highly active in coaching themselves, otherwise they may begin to acquire a somewhat grandiose idea of how easy it is to coach well, so ask about this. Ask, as well, whether the potential supervisor encourages contact between sessions and, if so, on what basis, for instance by email at no additional cost or by phone, but with a phone call that is longer than 30 minutes being chargeable.

Mostly, you will only find out what it's like working with a supervisor when you actually do it. Don't be afraid to end the relationship if you feel it's not delivering value. I have worked with a number of different supervisors at different stages and with different types of need throughout my coaching career. Most have been wonderful but there have been exceptions. I felt humiliated by the man whose aim appeared to be to trump every one of my client issues by informing me of how much better he would have handled the same situation, even though all he knew about the client was what I was telling him. It's not the supervisor's role to second-guess what was going on for the client – the emphasis is on what was going on for the coach, the person you have in the room. Nor did I get on well with the supervisor who was eager to use me as a guinea pig for a particularly elaborate 'model' of supervision, insisting on plodding painfully through its various stages, regardless of whether they seemed pertinent to what I had brought to the session.

Becoming the client is valuable in itself; it reminds us of how selective any client is in what they bring to discuss, and of how what they bring is tempered by how far they are willing to make themselves vulnerable. Supervision cannot work unless you are prepared to discuss all those areas of failure, doubt, incompetence, uncertainty and lack of confidence which every coach feels at some point, along with being a place where you can celebrate triumphs and successes. When for whatever reason you cannot do this, then either you have the wrong supervisor or you need to reassess your own attitudes and behaviour – or both.

A long-lasting supervision relationship has a different flavour from those that are pragmatic and time-limited. I typically work for several years with the majority of my supervisees and we know each other well, making it much easier to identify those evolving themes that will appear in any coach's work: the clients we like and find it easy to work with, the clients we can admit that we dislike, find annoying or fear; the themes we welcome, the themes we avoid – and what all this says about us.

Just as it is in coaching, the decision to work together is a two-way choice. As a supervisor, I am choosing my supervisee as much as they are choosing me. I look for people who are prepared to make a regular commitment and who understand why they need it. I shy away from people who openly tell me that they are doing it reluctantly and only because their professional membership body or employer insists that they have some supervision. Experience has shown me that these coaches never truly engage with the process and may book as little as they think their membership rules will tolerate. A 90-minute session once every seven weeks feels like the ideal and is what I look for myself.

It is good practice, with clients' permission, to record the occasional session, to listen to it yourself and then to bring extracts to your supervisor for comment and discussion. Many beginner coaches tell themselves that they will find a supervisor when they have an established practice and can afford it. If you are serious about a career as a coach, that is to say, you see it as a business that, like any business, will take time to build, then this could be an unwise economy. Supervision is an investment in you and your business.

Value to coaching clients is hard to quantify and is always at least one large step removed from anything the supervisor can offer. Essentially, supervision is for your benefit as a coach. Use it, learn from it, lean on it and be thankful that you have it.

Conclusion

My coaching career has been longer by far than the time I have spent in any other role. The pure privilege and enjoyment of working in a profession which gives so much obvious sense of purpose and satisfaction are what has kept me in it. It's true that there have been failures, mistakes and the occasional bracing dose of harsh feedback from clients. These failures have been upsetting but then I remind myself that few other jobs give so much direct feedback even when it's uncomfortable, or so many opportunities for learning and personal development.

As coaches, we hear and hold secrets that have sometimes never been divulged before. When this happens, I realise I am one of a small number of people privileged to see fellow humans without their disguises or masks. Sometimes what I hear is distressing and awakens half-buried pain from my own past. Sometimes it is exhilarating and I marvel at the suppleness of the human spirit. Many times, the sessions are punctuated by shared smiling and laughter. As coaches, we witness people's courage as they struggle with dilemmas and weighty responsibilities that we are probably glad not to have to face ourselves. We see people grow steadily in wisdom and confidence and it is only right that we give ourselves at least some of the credit for creating the psychological space where this can happen. Listening to people talk through what can often be heart-rending problems, some of them people in considerable trouble directly caused by their own misjudgements, has made me a much more compassionate person, aware of how flawed we all inevitably are.

Coaching is hard to beat as a crucible for our own development. To do any of this work for clients, we have to work on ourselves in the same way. There is an old proverb which says, 'What we teach is what we most want to learn' and that is as true of coaching as it is of any of its sister disciplines. I learn from clients all the time. This might be something as simple as the client who looked beadily at my laptop and informed me that I was risking serious back problems if I did not buy a cheap 'riser' from Amazon, sending me the link as soon as he got back to his office. Or it might be the psychiatrist client who stayed behind to give me a concentrated half-hour tutorial on how to understand a particular mental health problem, later ordering me a substantial book on the subject as a gift. Mostly, it is the opportunity to learn so much more about human psychology – what destabilises or motivates us and what makes for a good life.

John Launer, a distinguished British doctor and writer, has devoted a lifetime to thinking and writing about what makes for excellence in medical practice. Sometimes there is a straight cause and effect and he quotes his own case: a man in his 60s presenting with clear symptoms of ischaemic heart disease. But every doctor meets many patients where symptoms have no obvious explanation. Dr Launer emphasises the value of listening and of how it matters to abandon the idea of 'getting to the bottom of things' when so often there is no 'bottom' and there are no 'things'. The role here is to live with uncertainty, to understand the problem through the other person's eyes, and to offer unrelenting positivity. Healing can happen when you convey that the patient can recover or adjust without needing a professional to sort it out. Dr Launer compares traditional medical practice with the hard labour of digging a hole, whereas stitching a large tapestry involves delicacy and collaboration. In coaching, our aim is to work with the client to stitch the tapestry when, as a result of our joint efforts, something beautiful may emerge which astonishes us both.

Coaching thinks of itself as a new profession but in truth it is not. There is nothing that we do whose component parts have not been done before. We inherit a long tradition of healers, listeners, teachers and thinkers. This tradition embraces the Greek physicians, philosophers from every era and continent, religious leaders like Christ and the Buddha, the great psychoanalysts of the early 20th century and the blossoming after them of therapeutic research and practice, now stretching back many decades. I am proud to be part of this line.

As I am in the final stages of writing this book, we are in the grip of the Covid pandemic where so much that we took for granted has been overturned. I began this book counselling realism about what to expect from coaching. But I end it with words of encouragement and hope, despite writing them at a difficult time when the coronavirus is disrupting so much that we prize. The world will adapt, as will we all individually. I am already working in different ways, using my coaching skills for people and in settings that I could never have imagined a few months ago. It is an article of faith to every coach that human beings are resilient. Coaching in this new world will be needed as never before, testing our clients' resilience and our own.

Further Reading

Chapters 1–6: Boundaries

Many books on coaching give some nod to the ethical and practical issues involved in setting boundaries: I give a selection here where all these books have more than one section on the subject. It may also be worth entering these topics into your browser for an up-to-date view, as many people blog on the subject.

Amis, K. (2017) *Boundaries, Power and Ethical Responsibility in Counselling and Psychotherapy*. London: Sage Publications.

Dean, K. and Humphrey, S. (2019) *Coaching Stories. Flowing and falling of being a coach*. London: Routledge.

Morgan, K. (2019) *The Coach's Survival Guide*. London: Open University Press/McGraw-Hill Education.

Rogers, J. (2017) *Building a Coaching Business: Ten steps to success*. 2nd edition. London: Open University Press/McGraw-Hill Education.

Chapters 7–10: Authenticity, listening and judgement

I list some classic books here which offer insights and definitions into what genuine listening means. For elegant eavesdropping into how it works in practice, it is hard to beat Irvin Yalom's many books on the subject and also Stephen Grosz's stories in *The Examined Life*.

Egan, G. (1998) *The Skilled Helper*. New York: Brooks Cole.

Grosz, S. (2013) *The Examined Life*. London: Chatto and Windus.

Kline, N. (1999) *Time to Think*. London: Ward Lock.

Rogers, C.R. (1951) *Client Centered Therapy: Its current practice, implications and theory*. Boston, MA: Houghton Mifflin.

Yalom, I.D. (2002) *The Gift of Therapy*. London: Judy Piatkus Publishing.

Yalom, I.D. (2017) *Becoming Myself: A psychiatrist's memoir*. London: Piatkus, Little, Brown.

Chapters 11–17: The past, attachment, trauma and its consequences in client behaviour

Bessel van der Kolk's book *The Body Keeps the Score* is essential reading for coaches who want to understand how early life shapes us as adults. It has several chapters on different approaches to eliciting autobiography. David Drake's book is a powerful plea for understanding the power of the stories we tell ourselves and how changing them may lead to greater self-understanding. Entering *attachment theory, John Bowlby and Mary Ainsworth* into your browser will take you to a number of accessible descriptions of the essential ideas. Amir Levine and Rachel Heller's book is a popular treatment in the self-help genre.

Training is important in this area. Entering *training on trauma* to your browser may throw up a number of events which have trauma as their theme, some of them offered to therapists and counsellors. Julia Vaughan Smith and I run a website where we post blogs and information about our own masterclasses. www.coachingandtrauma.com. Julia's book on coaching and trauma specifically addresses trauma and coaching including clear guidance on boundaries with therapy.

How not to be a perfectionist has been a popular topic for self-help books, most of them giving similar advice. The best introductory treatment of the psychological dimensions of perfectionism that I have found is the Wikipedia entry. This gives a neat summary of the many links with recognised mental health problems and a long list of references. Robert Leahy's book *The Worry Cure* has relevance to several of the topics in these chapters and is a wonderful source of good ideas.

Bowlby, J. (1979) *The Making and Breaking of Affectional Bonds*. London: Tavistock Publications.

Bretherton, I. (1992) The origins of attachment theory: John Bowlby and Mary Ainsworth. *Developmental Psychology*, 28: 759–75.

Broughton, V. (2017) *Becoming Your True Self*. Steyning, UK: Green Balloon Publishing.

Drake, D.B. (2018) *Narrative Coaching: The definitive guide to bringing new stories to life*. 2nd edition. Petaluma, CA: CNC Press.

Emerald, D. (2016) *The Power of TED: The empowerment dynamic*. Polaris Publishing.

Goleman, D. and Boyatzis, R. (2013) *Primal Leadership: Unleashing the power of emotional intelligence*. Boston, MA: Harvard Business School Publishing.

Leahy, R. (2005) *The Worry Cure*. London: Piatkus Books.

Levine, A. and Heller, R.S. (2019) *Attached: Are you Anxious, Avoidant or Secure? How the science of adult attachment can help you find – and keep – love*. London: Bluebird/ Pan Macmillan.

Lewin, K. (1948) *Resolving Social Conflicts: Selected papers on group dynamics* (ed. G. Lewin). New York: Harper & Row.

Mathews, A. (2007) *Restoring My Soul: A workbook for finding and living the authentic self*. Bloomington, IN: IUniverse.

Mintzberg, H., Ahlstrand, B. and Lampel, J. (2005) *Strategy Bites Back: It is a lot more and a lot less than you ever imagined*. Harlow: Pearson Education.

Ruppert, F. (2014) *Trauma, Fear and Love*. Steyning, UK: Green Balloon Press.

Sandler, C. (2011) *Executive Coaching: A psychodynamic approach*. Maidenhead: Open University Press.

Van der Kolk, B. (2015) *The Body Keeps the Score: Mind, brain and body in the transformation of trauma*. London: Penguin Books.

Vaughan Smith, J. (2019) *Coaching and Trauma: From surviving to thriving*. London: Open University Press/McGraw-Hill Education.

Weinhold, N.C. and Weinhold, J.B. (2013) *How to Break Free of the Drama Triangle and Victim Consciousness*. Asheville, NC: CICRCL Press.

Chapters 18–20: Psychometrics and feedback

Entering the names of the leading psychometric instruments, including those
mentioned in Chapter 18, into your browser will take you to the publishers'
websites. Most will have sample reports and will give you an idea of their
cost, style, substance as well as how to get training and licensing.

Passmore, J. (2012) *Psychometrics in Coaching: Using psychological and psychometric tools for development*. London: Kogan Page.
Pfeffer, J. and Sutton, R.I. (2006) *Hard Facts, Dangerous Half Truths and Total Nonsense: Profiting from evidence based management*. Cambridge, MA: Harvard Business Press.
Rogers, J. (2017) *Coaching with Personality Type: What works*. London: Open University Press/McGraw-Hill Education.
Schein, E. (2006) *Career Anchors: Self assessment*. New York: Pfeiffer.

Chapters 21–23: Change and crisis

There is an extensive literature on change and it can seem overwhelming to
make sense of it. In my book on coaching skills, I summarise (Chapter 8)
many of the main psychological theories and give references. The weighty
research round-up edited by John Norcross includes a detailed treatment
(Chapter 14) on the Prochaska and di Clementi model. There is a plethora
of books on organisational change, including a classic book by John Kotter.

Bridges, W. (1991) *Managing Transitions*. Reading, MA: Addison-Wesley.
Brock, R.N. and Lettini, G. (2012) *Soul Repair: Recovering from moral injury after war*. Boston, MA: Beacon Press.
Kessler, D. (2019) *Finding Meaning: The sixth stage of grief*. New York: Scribner.
Kotter, J.P. (2019) *Leading Change*. Cambridge, MA: Harvard Business Review Press.
Norcross, J.C. (ed.) (2011) *Psychotherapy Relationships that Work: Evidence-based responsiveness*. Oxford: Oxford University Press.
Rogers, J. (2016) *Coaching Skills: The definitive guide to being a coach*. 4th edition. Maidenhead: Open University Pres/McGraw-Hill Education.

Chapter 24: Finding purpose

There is a shortage of books for coaches which address this question directly.
One exception is Herminia Ibarra's book *Working Identity*. The classic book
on why we need a sense of purpose on our lives is Viktor Frankl's short book,
Man's Search for Meaning, based on his imprisonment during the Holocaust.
It is a book I have re-read many times and I own several editions of it.

Frankl, V. (1959) *Man's Search for Meaning*. New York: Pocket Books.
Ibarra, H. (2003) *Working Identity: Unconventional strategies for reinventing your career*. Boston, MA: Harvard Business School Publishing.
Rogers, J. (2019) *Coaching for Careers*. London: Open University Press/McGraw-Hill Education.
Rogers, J. with Whittleworth, K. and Gilbert, A. (2012) *Manager as Coach*. Maindenhead: McGraw-Hill Education.
Yalom, I.D. (1980) *Existential Psychotherapy*. New York: Basic Books.

Chapters 25–29: Conclusion – development and self-care for coaches

Launer, J. (2020) Digging holes and weaving tapestries: two approaches to the clinical encounter. *Postgraduate Medical Journal*, 96 (1135): 307–8.

McMahon, G. and Archer, A. (eds) (2010) *101 Coaching Strategies and Techniques*. London: Routledge.

Paice, L. (2012) *New Coach: Reflections from a learning journey*. Maidenhead: Open University Press.

Passmore, J. (ed.) (2011) *Supervision in Coaching: Supervision, ethics and continuous professional development*. London: Kogan Page.

Thubten, G. (2019) *A Monk's Guide to Happiness: Meditation in the 21st century*. London: Yellow Kit.

Wildflower, L. and Brennan, D. (eds) (2011) *The Handbook of Knowledge-based Coaching: From theory into practice*. San Francisco, CA: Jossey Bass.

Index